BINGE

BINGE TV

*The Rise and Impact
of the Viewing Revolution*

EMIL STEINER

McFarland & Company, Inc., Publishers
Jefferson, North Carolina

This book has undergone peer review.

ISBN (print) 978-1-4766-8407-9
ISBN (ebook) 978-1-4766-4749-4

LIBRARY OF CONGRESS AND BRITISH LIBRARY
CATALOGUING DATA ARE AVAILABLE

Library of Congress Control Number 2022054438

Front cover images © 2023 Shutterstock

Printed in the United States of America

*McFarland & Company, Inc., Publishers
Box 611, Jefferson, North Carolina 28640
www.mcfarlandpub.com*

To Lori, Elsa, and Jonah

Table of Contents

Preface

When I've tried reading this book to my daughter, she's said, "Daddy, just tell me what happens" and "Can you skip to the good part?" On the one hand, I worry that too much screen time is rotting her brain; on the other hand, she's in first grade. But she does have a point. Everyone who can read has felt that frustration at times with certain books and with certain authors, particularly those published by academic presses. When it comes to scholarly writing, the exciting things that authors report—"the good parts"—may be buried beneath painstaking methodology and intimidating theory. That's not to say that methodology and theory are not vital parts of rigorous academic work; they are. However, including them in all their turgid glory can clog the narrative flow and, far worse, alienate the vast majority of potential readers. That's problematic for a number of reasons.

This book started out as a dissertation—possibly the least engaging genre ever invented. Dissertations exist to demonstrate expertise to a small committee of established experts. Or, as my father, a now-retired professor, puts it, "a dissertation is how you earn your union card so that you can teach for a decent wage." In form, they resemble military dining trays—theory in this compartment, methods in that one, findings on the left, Jell-O cup on top. They serve their single-use purpose, but they are seldom appetizing. When dissertations are adapted into books, authors face a dilemma. After spending years building the theory and practicing the methods and writing it all up for an audience of four, you develop a certain attachment to all those fancy words—at least I did. You try to hold on to too many of them because real adaptation is hard. Oftentimes, you can end up with a book that is only useful to a slightly larger committee of established experts with whom you happen to share a narrow patch of your academic field. There are of course many wonderfully adapted dissertations. I aspire for mine to be one of them. But there are also many academics who believe that broadening the readability of their work is a mistake. I am not among them.

1

I believe scholarly writing should be accessible to people other than scholars, especially when it deals with the culture, technology, or media that most people use. Binge-watching involves all three. Moreover, part of the appeal of binge-watching is that viewers have greater control over how they experience a story. Since my dissertation was about binge-watching, I've fashioned its adaptation to be approachable in a variety of ways for a variety of readers (though my daughter may still have to wait a few years). Tapping my roots as a journalist, I present the findings of this project through a mostly chronological narrative that relies heavily on quotes from the texts and people who shaped it. I also do what you're traditionally never supposed to do in journalism and in academic writing—I put myself in the story! You probably noticed that.

While this book includes a detailed accounting of the painstaking research necessary to execute such a project, I have removed much of it from the text's main body and used notes to create numerous sub-narrative threads that weave their way through the history of television coming of age. Like the *Choose Your Own Adventure* books from my youth, I have placed links in the text that allow you to decide how deeply you wish to go into the diversity of theories and methodologies that make up this book, allowing a variety of different experiences. I leave it up to you, the reader, to find your story in these pages.

1

Turning on the Idiot Box

Like a lot of American kids growing up in the 1980s, I spent my Saturday mornings watching cartoons. All week I looked forward to the solid 7:00 a.m. to noon block of uninterrupted television shows just for me. And like a lot of American parents in the 1980s, my parents didn't approve of me watching cartoons for five hours straight. They wanted me to play outside or, better yet, read a book. Our house was filled with books. But books were their thing; TV was mine. Back in those days, television was called the idiot box or the boob tube. People who sat in front of it for hours were called couch potatoes. It had always been that way, I was told, and for years it seemed like it always would be.

As I grew up, my love for television grew along with the number of channels and later with the number of pixels on the screen. New technologies began to allow me to watch more of what I wanted, how I wanted. My library of VHS (video home system) tapes began to compete for shelf space with my parents' books. Soon shows I loved—*The Simpsons* and *Seinfeld*—became available on DVDs and on-demand. But even as a young adult in the early 2000s, I always felt guilty doing what I loved. That's because I had been conditioned, like most everyone else, to believe that television was bad for you. Even when it was educational or artistic, it was always a poor substitute for reading and a distraction from "real work."

Then a funny thing started happening around 2012: TV got better. Not only the quality of the shows—the acting and scripts and production values had been improving for years—and not only the To read more about my backstory, jump to Chapter 6. quality and variety of screens and channels, and not only the streaming technology that allowed us to watch whatever, wherever, whenever. I mean, its image got better. Better in the sense of being healthier and more worthwhile. The identity of TV and of the people who watched it seemed to fully and finally transition to something better than the idiot box during the final years of U.S. president Obama's administration (2009–2017). By my estimation, this was when the idiot box died, and it was when couch potatoes like me got rebranded as binge-viewers.

There were multiple factors that contributed to TV's new image, many of which I explore in this book, but central to all of them was a perceived shift in control from broadcaster to viewer. And while that shift had been happening since at least the early 1980s (Lotz, 2014), the techno-cultural phenomenon called binge-watching is what cut the cord and pulled the plug on the idiot box. This book is about how that happened and why. I explore what binge-watching is, who binge-viewers are, and how those ironic terms, which almost no one used before 2012, could disrupt our understanding of the world's most popular mass medium. To do so, I approach the topic from three perspectives—news coverage, corporate marketing, and user experience.

I chronicle the history of television and report binge and marathon TV consumption, as told by journalists (and by a few scholars) from 1948, when it first appeared, to 2011, its last year of obscurity (Chapters 1–2). I then analyze the definitions of binge-watching journalists constructed from 2012, when it became a buzzword, through 2016, when binge-watching became accepted as the new normal of television (Chapter 3).

Switching my focus from TV to viewers, I explore the subversive marketing campaigns of Netflix and other "new" media companies to reimagine couch potatoes as savvy connoisseurs using powerful new technologies and services (which the companies owned) to disrupt the old idiot box culture (Chapter 4). Additionally, I share my interviews with a range of TV viewers to explore how they understood and practiced binge-watching and how they felt about television during that phenomenal period of change (Chapter 5). In the final chapter, I synthesize what I learned from the news, marketing, and users to explain how binge-watching killed the idiot box. I conclude by turning the analysis on myself through a reflexive narrative that explores my role in this project as a binge-viewer studying binge-watching (Chapter 6).

This book explains what binge-watching is, how and why people do it, the role it played in our collective reimagining of television, and how stakeholders wove and exploited that narrative for profit. Originally, my goal had been to answer those questions and analyze how they have affected the fields of media and communication studies. That's still in here, particularly in the second half of this chapter. But, as I adapted this from dissertation to book, I began to see an overarching story that touches every aspect of this project. Television is, and has always been, a struggle for control between creators and consumers. Binge-watching, the practice of gaining control and losing control through a remote control, unleashed, accelerated, and mainstreamed that struggle that had been raging since the first TV set was turned on. Who controls the story? The author? The reader? As you read these words, those boundaries have never been less clear.

Cultural Boogeyman

Television wasn't named the idiot box at birth; its christening didn't come until 1953 (Wolters). During its childhood, 1930–1945, there was actually a great deal of optimism about TV's potential. In 1941, RCA president David Sarnoff predicted that "television drama of high caliber, produced by first-rate artists, will materially raise the level of dramatic taste of the American nation" (p. 148). Some scholars even fantasized about TV's potential to improve education by bringing lessons to remote schools (Kelly, 1955). We would have to wait until the Great Lockdown of 2020 for those fantasies to be put to a mainstream test. As TV became a ubiquitous fixture in American households during the early 1950s, a vigorous debate raged between TV optimists who believed the new medium could improve the society and culture of America's better-educated, post-war middle class and TV cynics who saw the best path to commercial success through mass production, broad appeal models that had worked so well for radio. Spoiler alert:

> Great disappointment came as the medium settled on a set of practices or "rules" that in effect standardized the business of television in the late 1950s. Risk taking became much less common. Cultural choice narrowed largely to whatever (morally mainstream) productions appeared likely to reach the largest number of viewers.... Commercial television gradually stopped caring [Baughman, 2007].

The voices of those mid-century TV optimists seem largely forgotten now, muted by the alarms of 20th-century cathode ray criticism. No technology has been so universally maligned and so universally adopted as the TV set during the second half of the 20th century. Between the intellectual forebodings of social, political, and aesthetic obliteration (Adorno, 2001; Horkheimer & Adorno, 1977) and doctors' dire warnings of the medium's "hypnotic and seductive action on its audience" (Meerloo, 1954, p. 290), the academy often treated TV viewers as passive receivers (Bandura, Ross & Ross, 1963; Carpenter, 1955; Gerbner, 1976; Schleuder, White, & Cameron, 1993) and classified the medium as a low-brow, mind-melting menace (Blazer, 1964, p. 164).

Twentieth-century scholars, critics, commentators, and educators

largely delegitimized TV texts, casting them as culturally beneath literature, inappropriate for curricula, and difficult to study using traditional methods (Coward, 1990). Television's mass adoption was linked
to an apparent surge in anti-intellectualism that some feared would lead
arts and humanities to an untimely death (Hofstadter, 1966; Wagner,
1978). Sound familiar? This perspective contributed to a perception of
the TV audience as a culturally ignorant mass. The non-typographic
nature of the medium was lambasted for allowing viewers to substitute
the hard work of interpretation and analysis for the passive observation
of for-profit performances that uncritically reified consumerism. Neil
Postman (1982) characterized the popularization of television texts over
written texts as the "Las Vegasizing of America," claiming that TV's
very nature is "to transform every aspect of life into a show business
format" (p. 265). And so, less than a decade after its mainstream adoption, TV had become "a scapegoat for a handful of ills—e.g. intellectual
flabbiness and declining morality—that critics believed had befallen the
nation" (Collins, 2012, p. 1).

Government regulators bought into that narrative, charac-
terizing television, in the words of Federal Communications Com-
mission chair Newton Minow (1961), as a
"vast wasteland." Journalists, artists, and
other authorial stakeholders depicted TV
as, at best, a waste of time (Laurent, 1960)
and more likely a threat to American culture and citizens (Mittell, 2000, p. 234). The
primitive yet intimidating technology with

Do you want to learn
more about the Frank-
furt School's foreboding
of aesthetic obliteration?
If so, go to 197 (note 1).[1]

few channels, fuzzy reception, and ceaseless corporate sponsorship
became the vehicle for easily digestible shows, which critics argued
reinforced dominant ideology manifestly in their presentations of
American life and latently in their formulaic constructions of consumption (Horkheimer & Adorno, 1977). If culture was nourish-
ment, TV was fast food. Those shows and the standardized structure
of programming flows (Williams, 1990) shaped a perceived passivity of TV-watching readily associated with that most loathed American sin—sloth (Kisselhoff, 1995). The action's objective embodiment,
a flickering, energy-hungry behemoth annexing post–World War II
family rooms, became an obviously pernicious boogeyman that parents, who had survived the Great Depression, could sensibly unite
against.

Lincoln Diamant (1971) captured the social, psychological, and
ideological alarmism in the introduction to his lengthy analysis of commercials from 1948 to 1958:

Cartoonist Carl Rose's "Television Party" depicts a crowded mid-century American living room after the invasion of neighbors and acquaintances eager to watch. The image appeared on August 1, 1948, in Jack Gould's *New York Times* story "Family Life, 1948 A.T. (After Television)" with the caption "No more is the family's evening tainted with such an archaic pursuit as one person talking to another, once known as conversation."

> There seems no question now that something is very wrong with our society. Materialist infection was always with America; but it is no accident that it started festering in the years immediately after World War II, when television took hold of home after home and—almost without exception, like a narcotic—mind after mind, sliding us nightly into a flickering era of national schizophrenia [p. xi].

Thus by television's adolescence, its reputation became fixed to the "idiot box" narrative (Meyrowitz, 2009; Mittell, 2000; Spigel, 1992)—an industrialized mechanism of mass-produced pablum with the power to manipulate its passive audience into consumerist ideology (Ward & Wackman, 1971) and potentially into violent behavior (Bandura, Ross, & Ross, 1963). This narrative was reinforced in the news coverage for much of the 20th century (Ouellette & Lewis, 2000) to the point where the terms *idiot box, boob tube,* and *couch potato* became fixed in the vernacular of Americans including me (Ammer, 2013). Television's own archetypal American idiots—Archie Bunker, Al Bundy, and Homer Simpson—were often presented, domestic beers in hand, slouching toward the glow of their prized sets. The boundaries of TV's identity became shaded on all sides by the lowest common denominator (Fiske, 1987), its mind-rotting effects accepted as commonsense, its viewers marginalized as anti-intellectual (Fields, 2016). This was TV's mainstream 20th-century identity.

Resisting and Consuming the Masses

Television entered its second age, "TV II," in the 1980s and 1990s through the public adoption of three important technological advancements—VCRs, cable services, and remote controls (Jenner, 2018; Kompare, 2005; Lotz, 2014). Theories about audience consumption also began shifting from ones of mass-produced domination of the patriarchy to ones in which the possibility of agency could be expressed through the choice of identification and through the escapism of the viewer (Stacey, 1994). At the same time, television technologies—remote controls, VCRs, satellite and cable services, and pay-per-view— were pushing the TV industry toward less homogenized interpretations of viewer consumption than during the network era of the previous four decades (Lotz, 2014, p. 9). Programming of the 1980s and 1990s reflected those industrial and cultural shifts. The expanded textual diversity and viewing control, sometimes referred to as TV's second Golden Age (Thompson, 1996), coincided with scholars reinterpreting the consumption of popular culture as resistance and even as transgression (Storey, 2012, p. 140).

To learn more about how a new generation of critics at the Birmingham School began resisting the social hierarchies of culture and taste in the 1960s and 1970s, leading to the academic study of popular culture, go to 197 (note 2).[2]

Even as TV technology pushed toward its multi-channel transition during the 1990s, through cable and satellite penetration, the networks controlling the media remained largely unwilling to treat their viewers as anything but revenue-generating "silent majority" (Ang, 1991, p. 6). As Lotz (2014) states, it wasn't until the technology of the new millennium moved TV into the post-network era that "changes in competitive norms and operation of the industry became too pronounced for many of the old practices to be preserved" (p. 8). This destabilizing of TV's identity followed a shift in the American economy from service to experience (Pine & Gilmore, 1998). Both transitions involved technology and culture, and, as I will explore, coincided with the conception and the conceptualization of binge-watching.

To read more about how these late 20th century TV scholars made the idea of viewer choice a powerful statement go to 198 (note 3).[3]

Binge Technology

Around the time American cultural theorists were beginning to validate popular media, VCRs (videocassette recorders) were beginning to change how television was watched (Levy, 1987). This proto-binge-watching technology lacked the capacity for wireless portability and streaming variety, but VCRs did grant viewers control over their TVs as never before (Gaver, 1991, pp. 79–80). For the first time, viewers could set their own schedule and fast-forward through commercials, thereby weakening the broadcaster's control over the communication circuit (Hall, 1990). I can still remember the tingly joy I felt at pressing the fast-forward button to skip through commercials of my broadcast recording of *It's the Great Pumpkin, Charlie Brown* (1966). Stevens (2021) found that tech-savvy fans were actually proto-binge-watching in the late 1970s (p. 23). That said, a VCR viewer was beholden to the constraints of tape storage and to broadcasters' control over available content (or a distributor's expensive and limited video catalog). Although at the time that technology challenged television's identity (Levy, 1987), a "gulf of exclusion" still remained for viewers in terms of technological mobility and content selection (Norman, 1988, p. 51).

DVDs digitized the content of VHS tapes in the 1990s, expanding commercial-free video libraries for viewers with "never-before-seen" footage, interactive features, and paratextual content (Wolf, 2005). Box sets allowed fans to experience their favorites beyond the screen through tactile aesthetics (Kompare, 2006). The discs' thin design and expanded storage capacities made home video collections more space-efficient. This spatial dynamic, along with viewer migration from VHS to DVD, contributed to a shift in the kind of video content that studios released. While individuals had been recording their favorite TV shows since the 1970s, the shows were seldom released for sale or for rental (Wickstrom, 1986). From a technological perspective, VHS tape storage (internal and external) made old TV shows a cumbersome product to market. NBC's critically acclaimed police drama *Hill Street Blues* averaged around 20 episodes during each of its seven seasons from 1981 to 1987. With a 49-minute runtime per episode, a single season could take upward of 10 SP cassettes equating to about seven feet or more of shelf space when accounting for packaging. From a cultural perspective, few TV shows of the time were considered, at least by mainstream critics, to be good enough to pay to re-watch. If broadcasters reran a show, then viewers could tune in, and fans with VCRs could record it. But the market for purchasing or for renting parcels of the vast wasteland was believed to be too small to justify the costs. From both perspectives, films were the commonsense choice for VHS content. DVDs changed that and created the possibility for binge-watching TV in a manner similar to today. But the technology wasn't without its flaws. While sharpening the resolution of video, DVD players often lacked the ability to record, and their controls, particularly the early generations of players, limited a viewer's ability to move as nimbly through the content as they could with VCRs.

On-demand services and digital video recorders (DVRs) made it possible for viewers to watch a wider variety of content without having to get out of their seats to acquire and to change discs (Tryon, 2013). First released in 1998, TiVo became known as one of the first DVRs to compress and save broadcast content to a set-top drive. By the turn of the millennium, TiVo had established its brand as the technology that enabled viewers to pause live TV and to schedule-record programs that they could watch later without commercials (by fast-forwarding, like a VCR minus the tape). This was reflected in the company's advertising, the most famous of which showed a sports fan pausing the final play of a football game so he could run to church and pray his team makes (or has made) the game-winning field goal. He returns home, presses play, and jumps for joy at the miraculous power TiVo afforded him. Another famous TiVo ad showed a sports fan cheating Death by pausing his sporting event to ask the Grim Reaper for more time. Eventually the Grim Reaper decides to take his TiVo-less neighbor instead.

While Death may have been cheatable, the networks still controlled a viewer's potential content library. To record on TiVo, or on any other DVR, the viewer had to wait for the content to be broadcast (Christine, 2012). On-demand programming services eliminated the necessity to record and to store content, but their choice of content was limited and under the control of multichannel video program distributors (MVPDs) like Comcast. By the 1990s, MVPDs offered free prerecorded shows through video on-demand services along with pay-per-view sports and films (Mullen, 2003). Still, binge-watching remained a niche activity for dedicated superfans (Oxford, 2013).

In the early 2000s, however, the technological capacities and the cultural value of television were improving (Leverette, Ott, & Buckley, 2008). The "better than TV" narrative promoted by HBO, with prestige shows like *The Wire* and *The Sopranos*, increased demand for access to highbrow content while changing the model for content distribution from DVDs toward streaming and on-demand (Reeves et al., 2002; Thompson & Mittell, 2013). This perceived improvement in televised content, particularly serialized dramas, spread across other pay cable channels in the early 2000s, before reaching basic cable and eventually network channels with shows like *Lost* and *Mad Men* (Leverette, Ott, & Buckley, 2008). Television scholars often refer to this as the Third Age or as TV III (Jenner, 2014; Pearson, 2011). News outlets including *Slate*, *The Atlantic*, and the *Washington Post* responded to the new "cultured TV" by assigning specialized media critics to curate discussions around the highbrow shows. As Liz Kelly, who produced "Message in a Bottle," the *Washington Post* online *Lost* discussion platform, explained, "this is way more than TV" (2010).

By 2010, faster broadband Internet, improved digital compression and streaming video services like Netflix, Hulu, and YouTube allowed viewers to watch a variety of content on computers and on mobile devices. Streaming video's portability and infinite potential memory began to push DVDs out of vogue. With the evolution of digital media players (DMPs) from game consoles to sleek, user-friendly plug-ins like Apple TV, Roku, and Amazon Fire, and the proliferation of smart TVs, viewers could stream video to the large screen format of television in sync with their portable devices (Goel, 2013). Netflix's full-season release model, which began with *Lilyhammer* in February 2012, was the final innovative ingredient for binge-watching to become the all-you-can-eat video buffet that starving viewers had craved since before the VCR. I know I had.

The remainder of this chapter is dedicated to some of the more theoretical and methodological considerations that went into developing, executing, and situating this project. It speaks to the struggle of control and legitimacy within television as well as within media and communication studies. It also recounts the challenges of attempting to study binge-watching as an emerging scholar. I believe that this sub-narrative enhances the overall story, which is why I kept it in. But I also understand that such theorizing may be of less interest to you than it is to me. If so, you can jump to Chapter 2 to learn about binge-watching's origin story and how it differs from TV marathons.

The Trouble with Binge-Watching

Television's cultural ascendancy began slowly in the 1980s, but by the 2010s, it had supplanted cinema as the preeminent format for video storytelling (Epstein, 2010). Gone are the alarms over the vast wasteland; today the loudest laments of TV critics seem to be about the challenges of keeping up with the overabundance of high-caliber shows produced by first-rate artists (Pagels, 2012; Wolcott, 2016). So why is the body of binge-watching scholarship still relatively small thus far? The obvious answer is its novelty. While mainstream media has produced thousands of articles about binge-watching since 2012 (see Chapter 3), the methodical academy is somewhat removed from the pressures of the 24-hour news cycle. But I believe there is more to the story.

On its surface, the term binge-watching is linguistically challenging for scholars. It is difficult to define and thus difficult to situate as something that can be studied systematically. This challenge feeds into latent, lingering notions of TV watching as anti-intellectual and justifies marginalization of, or at least trepidation about, the new media behavior. When I tell colleagues that I study binge-watching, the first reaction is almost always a chuckle, and the second is usually a question about how bad it is, followed by admissions about what shows they watch. Of course, binge-watching itself is neither good nor bad, and that ambivalence makes it difficult to negotiate or to take a position on. Its liminal and conflicted identity further complicates its study. On the one hand, it seems like something that has been studied for decades—TV-watching. On the other hand, it seems to be disrupting the culture, economics, and technology typically associated with TV. Binge-watching is often done on laptops, on tablets, on phones, and even on TV tuner-free displays, which look and sound remarkably similar to TV sets, none of which need to receive a broadcast signal. Are we watching TV if there's no TV? As Amanda Lotz (2017) points out, "screen became far less important for most analyses than distribution technology" (loc 206). But is binge-watching a part of new media or old media or social media or all of these? In the absence of criteria or parameters, binge-watching may be too many things at once, so scholars instead focus on tangible or on definable aspects of contemporary television—texts, contexts, and technologies—and overlook the term and its rituals. Furthermore, now that almost every viewer has binge-watched and many binge-watch regularly, a number of scholars have advocated for the theorization of binge-watching subtypes to better explicate the ubiquitous practice (Castro et al., 2021; Pittman & Steiner, 2021).

This new normal is still relatively new. When I started my exploration of binge-watching in 2013, there were almost no scholarly articles that mentioned the term. Without a well-articulated foundation of literature, the terrain for building new research is challenging, particularly for emerging scholars. At a 2015 conference, a senior professor politely told me that numerous studies had been done on the effects of long-term exposure to television. (I assumed he meant cultivation theory [Gerbner, 1976], but he has yet to respond to my email seeking elaboration.)

Such a perspective not only overlooks the changing identity of TV but also marginalizes the role viewer rituals like binge-watching have in the metamorphosis. As the technological understanding of television became unfixed during the 2010s, so too did the understanding of its texts and the professional roles of those producing and consuming it (Andrejevic, 2008; Lotz, 2014; Thompson & Mittell, 2013). The activity of social media, with its "performances and the production of user-generated content" (Banet-Weiser, 2012, p. 64) and self-conscious audience participation (Sender, 2012) justify the narrative of viewer and broadcaster as participants in cultural co-creation. As Perks (2015) observes, "marathoning blurs traditional media demarcations: reader/character, reader/text, reader/programmer, and reader/author" (p. xi). From an industrial perspective, the conception of "audience" as a massive group of participants sharing "media events" (Dayan & Katz, 1992) has shifted to viewers—a diversity of individualized niches with unique members customizing their TV experiences (Lotz, 2014, pp. 4–5). The affordances (capacity and portability) of streaming video technology and the influx of cinematically respected auteurs to the "small screen," under the new profession of "showrunner," have hoisted the perception of TV texts out of the vast wasteland toward a (new) "golden age" of viewer agency, while simultaneously reifying power structures of hegemonic control (Braun, 2015; Wohlsen, 2014). And yet, binge-watching, with its conflicted connotations of pathology and irony, its hybrid identity of culture and technology, and its ubiquitous practice, remains relatively unexplored by media scholars. It is because of that ambiguity and liminality that I find binge-watching fascinating. I believe that its ambivalence and fluid identity reflect the post-industrial experiential economy (Pine & Gilmore, 1998), and this is why this period, 2012–2018, when it raced from fringe practice to new normal, is so important to study.

Situating This Project

Before 2018, many of the scholars studying binge-watching employed quantitative methods to operationalize user behavior and to measure psychological effects, often with tools designed for 20th-century broadcast television technology (Kruger et al., 2015; Pena, 2015; Pittman & Sheehan, 2015; Wheeler, 2015). For these to work, large-scale surveys are administered, and audience responses are controlled and aggregated, thereby treating individual viewers as a homogenized mass of passive TV receivers rather than as unique, active agents of cultural exchange. By building on the literature of 20th-century television studies, these scholars approach binge-watching with an implicit bias that TV-watching may be harmful and addictive and that binging may exacerbate those risks. The studies are not designed, nor perhaps can they be used, to analyze the complexity of meaning loaded in the term.

The research that recognizes shifts from broadcast to streaming tends to focus on the interfaces between humans and new technologies like streaming video and online advertising (Logan, 2013; Schweidel & Moe, 2016), but these studies do not specifically examine binge-watching rituals. Until 2016, little attention was paid to the discursive and to the historical contexts, power structures, and culture of binge-watching outside of industry studies. Some of the articles that do address critical and cultural issues have focused on the texts and on the advertising paratexts associated with shows like *Orange Is the New Black* (Belcher, 2016; DeCarvalho & Cox, 2016; Fernández-Morales, M., & Menéndez-Menéndez, 2016). These important contributions to the binge-watching literature blend textual and narrative analyses of the shows with rhetorical critiques of the television industry and audience engagement. DeCarvalho and Cox (2016) examine Netflix's role in creating identity and parasocial relationships through its advertising, but the examination is focused on the identity of *Orange Is the New Black* fans rather than on constructions of binge-viewer identity through ritual or mediated articulations.

There is a developing body of literature that seeks to assess binge-viewer rituals phenomenologically (Castro et al., 2021; Perks et al., 2021), which I explore more deeply in Chapter 4. Lisa Perks's *Media Marathoning* (2015) was the first scholarly book focused on the actions of binge-viewers and their relationships with the texts. She used mixed methods to explore not just binge-viewers but also binge-reader rituals and the implications of convergent, multimedia content. Importantly, Perks acknowledged the role that the press may play in constructing public attitudes toward "marathoning," though she didn't offer a systematic analysis of that coverage (p. x).

Perks found that the interactivity of "marathoning" contributed to greater feelings of immersion in the stories among "marathoners." This world-building experience afforded by binge-watching appears related to new forms of advertising, such as branded and user-generated content, that blur traditional lines of producer and consumer while simultaneously using paratexts to immerse fans more deeply and interactively than a DVD box set (DeCarvalho & Cox, 2016). One of the more interesting facets of Perks's project is the requirement that her participants "marathon" TV shows and books. Such a move acknowledges the convergence and the intertexuality of contemporary media. It speaks to the lingering cultural bias against those who choose to spend a weekend binge-watching versus those who choose to spend the weekend binge-reading. That bias is reflected in Perks's choice to call the practice "marathoning" and not "binging." Despite the advancements of TV's cultural standing and convergence of media culture and technology (Jenkins, 2006), there remains, in our collective consciousness, a sense of shame about TV enjoyment. That terminal choice—marathon or binge—carries clues about the history and about the changing identity of television.

Executing This Project

In this book, I explore what binge-watching is, how it is practiced, and its relationship with contemporary identities of television and viewers. I examine binge-watching from the perspective that viewers' voices are vital to the action of binge-watching and to the identity of television. I agree with Hall's (1980) assertion that it is impossible to be apolitical when exploring how people interact with media. I

> To learn more about my research orientations and methodological perspectives, turn to 199 (note 4).[4]

follow Fiske's (1989) contention that viewers are not "dupes" and Ang's (1991) position that the "neutral" instruments of television's industrial knowledge are inadequate to gather the descriptions necessary to constitute a viewer's structures of feeling.

While I maintain that viewers are central to understanding the action, the articulations of that action (binge-watching) and the constructions of the actors (binge-viewers) are mediated. Until 2012, the noun *binge* connoted unhealthy behavior—a period of uncontrollable excess. It is still commonly associated with the actions of binge drinking and binge eating—psychological symptoms associated with a pathological loss of control. But, if TV content evolved into a viewer-empowering Platinum Age, as numerous TV critics insist (Bianculli, 2016), then why has a term that connotes pathology and addiction emerged as the name for its quintessential ritual? Clearly, the popularization and the understanding of binging involved articulations from people other than viewers.

Beal and Bohlen (1956) argue that the diffusion of new ideas and new practices typically follows a curve of adoption that begins with a few pioneers then hockey-sticks from early adopters to the mainstream (p. 117). During the "early adoption to early majority phase," when a technology rapidly moves from obscurity to ubiquity, interested adopters rely on authorities in journalism and in industry to gain understanding of the technology (pp. 114–115). Binge-watching involves both technology and culture, and it followed a similar trajectory of adoption from 2012 to 2016. During that time, journalists and media companies produced a great deal of information about it. Their articles and their commercial rhetoric were a negotiation of public understanding of the phenomenon (binge-watching and binge-viewers). That mediated discourse was an "active debate and amendment" (Williams, 1989, p. 4) of how we understood contemporary television in contrast to its vast wasteland history.

The rapid transformation of binge-watching from obscurity to ubiquity stretched the popular understanding of the words *binge* and *TV-watching* with it. The blending of those two words into the portmanteau of binge-watching involved a subversive use of the signifier *binge* to ironically exaggerate the signified *watching*. It is important to note that the noun "TV binge" appeared with some regularity in the 20th-century media, but its connotations and its implications were, like TV technology and culture of that time, less complex.[5] The action of watching TV is also being renegotiated because of the technology and the culture that allows for binges. That this wasn't possible during the network TV era affords the culture and technology of binge-watching a novel and marketable contrast exploited in the media rhetoric of advertising. When new media consumers, like binge-viewers, are constructed through contrasts to older ones, like couch potatoes, the new role gains distinction, and their action, binge-watching, gains a unique understanding even though it may look like TV-watching (Torfing, 1999; Vološinov, 1973). Because the meaning making of binge-watching takes place through our collective memory of traditional TV, it is important to also account for the mediated articulation of those memories.

Mating Action with Articulation

There were people watching the same TV show for hours on end before the word "binge-watching" was ever uttered, but they were not binge-watching until the term became articulated and branded into the zeitgeist. They were no more binge-viewers than people who kept an online journal were "bloggers" prior to Jorn Barger coining the term "weblog" in 1997 (Wortham, 2007) and Evan Williams popularizing the noun and verb "blogger" and "to blog" in 1999 (Coleman & Augustine, 2014, p. 21). Obviously, people had been performing the action of blogging prior to then, but since the term had neither been articulated nor popularized, they weren't actually blogging. An action only achieves identity through its articulation, which, when repeated and professionalized, gives new meaning to similar past actions and actors.

Calvin Schrag (1997) theorizes that identity is found in this relationship between action and articulation—a useful theoretical foundation for this project. The binge-viewer gains identity by binge-watching but also through external articulations of what binge-watching is—how the media depicts it. Mating action and articulation demonstrates how the "who of action lives between autonomy and heteronomy, active and reactive force" (p. 59). Action may be individualized, but it is always also in reaction to previous discourse and actions. Binge-watching is performed by individual viewers, and its understanding is shared in the imaginations of groups. Therefore, to explore binge-watching, I have approached its identity from three fronts: (1) articulation of meaning, (2) construction of actor, and (3) action.

Scholars such as Lotz (2014), Serazio (2015), and Sender (2012) unpack this kind of new media complexity through hybrid qualitative methods and multi-perspectival data collection that attempt to fashion an interpretation that covers the interplay of political economy and culture while addressing the discourse between agents along the communication circuit. This is why I have chosen multiple methods to explore binge-watching. Because it is an action performed by a viewer, it seems most sensible to speak with the "audience." But while a viewer may binge-watch, the behavior's articulation also takes place in the media through journalism and through commercial rhetoric. I analyzed purposefully sampled texts to gather and to interpret data of (1) journalistic coverage of the history and usage of the terms binge-watching and marathon and (2) marketing of media companies who depicted binge-viewers to promote their products and their services. I also conducted in-depth, semi-structured interviews and open-ended conversations to gather descriptions of (1) contemporary TV viewers' rituals and motives and (2) viewers' impressions about television's identity. I then synthesized my findings in the context of contemporary cultural and economic narratives on media consumption. Finally, I wrote

> *If you decide to explore the articulation of meaning, go to Chapter 2.*
>
> *If you decide to explore construction of actors, go to Chapter 4.*
>
> *If you decide to explore the action, go to Chapter 5.*

a reflexive narrative to explicate my own position and motives for studying binge-watching and how those motives influenced this project. Ultimately, I leave it to you, the reader, to choose your path through this project.

2

From Roots to Stem

The Journalistic History
of Binge and Marathon TV

"It's a not-so-pretty name for a highly enjoyable experience"
[Meyer, 2013]

In the internet's dark ages, before social media was a thing, like-minded people would congregate in Usenet newsgroups to read and to post messages about their shared interests. These online repositories of digital discourse were organized by topics in the form of member posts (text only) that fellow members would respond to and comment on, creating threads of users' communications that could be further responded to and commented on throughout time. As with Subreddits or Facebook fan groups, the flow of newsgroup conversation threads varied in direction, in civility, and in logic, depending on their topics and on their participants. With insider jargon Usenetters would pontificate on a show's picayune minutia to flex their bona fides and thereby gain cred as superfans. It was in an *X-Files* Usenet newsgroup (alt.tv.x-files), on December 20, 1998, at 8:53 a.m. Central Standard Time, that a user called GregSerl posted the oldest known written use of the verb "binge watch" (GregSerl, 1998).

The topic—Some HTGSC [How the Grinch Stole Christmas] Thoughts—had been started six days earlier by the user Steve Pagano to pour cold water on some recent fan complaints about the Fox sci-fi show's realism and character development and the nature of the relationship between the protagonists—the FBI agents Mulder and Scully (David Duchovny and Gillian Anderson). Within a few hours, the conversation had degenerated to such tribal in-fighting that GregSerl posted the following summation, which sounds oddly prescient in the wake of recent U.S. presidential elections:

We basically are seeing passion from two diverse groups. Those who love the show so much that they can't believe anyone but a troll could hate it, and those who hate it so much this year they can't believe anyone could possibly love it unless they're medically brain dead. Both groups are wrong about the other. There *are* fans who are very disappointed this year and there *are* fans who are very happy with the way things are going. The problem as I see it is the chasm between the two is at the widest point it's ever been.

Despite this attempt at diplomacy, GregSerl appears to troll the thread on December 17 when he accuses Agent Mulder of pornography addiction. This sets off another angry debate, first on whether Mulder is, in fact, addicted to pornography, and then on the nature of what constitutes porn use and porn addiction. After three days of fervor, GregSerl offers the following summation:

In a way I think it's endearing how Mulder's interest in pornography is being defended. It can be anything *but* addiction. There's also the idea that something isn't an addiction unless it severely compromises a person's work performance or interaction with friends and family. Of course this isn't true. If someone can't be sociable in the morning until they've had a dose of caffeine, then they have some dependency on caffeine, I ought to know, because I sure do. An addiction is usually defined by how much anxiety the idea of being without the addictive substance would cause. Does a sudden cessation of the addictive substance cause physical, emotional or mental withdrawal symptoms?

(1) Does missing a new episode of *The* X-*Files* make you feel anxious or agitated?
(2) Could you skip a new episode of *The* X-*Files*, not even tape it, and not feel anxious?
(3) Do you sometimes think of *The* X-*Files* at work or school?
(4) Have you ever read or written fanfic while at work or school?
(5) Have you ever read or posted to usenet or message boards while at work or school—not being able to wait until you are home?
(6) Do you spend more than an hour a day in pursuit of X-*Files*-related interaction?
(7) Do you subscribe to more than one online service such as AOL, Compuserve or Prodigy *only* because of *The* X-*Files*?
(8) Do you refuse to answer the phone, or even leave it disconnected when a new episode of *The* X-*Files* is airing?
(9) Do you sometimes watch *The* X-*Files* alone if only to keep from being judged by family or friends? Re: "Are you watching that *again*!!!??"
(10) Do you watch the reruns on FOX, FX or local affiliates even though you have every episode on tape?
(11) Do you ever binge watch (marathon)? [bold added for emphasis]
(12) Have you ever drifted away from a friend who lost interest in *The* X-*Files*, or if you remained friends, *The* X-*Files* is something you agree not to discuss in order to maintain a civil interaction?

(13) Can you name the titles of all 100+episodes without the help of an episode guide?

(14) Does the question "Why does Mulder tape an X in his window" cause an irresistible urge to post a flame or joke response?

(15) Do you become angry or upset when Krycek is spelled "Krychek," "Cricheck" or "Wheatcheck"?

(16) If you can't be home when a new episode of *The X-Files* is airing, do you set more than one VCR in the paranoid fear that one might malfunction?

(17) If you're a guy, and you bought *The X-Files* Barbie dolls, did your father drag out the rosary beads and weep?

(18) Have you spent some serious cash on X-*Files-* related merchandise?

(19) Have you ever worn out a VCR or a remote (especially "pause," "frame advance" and "slo-mo" buttons

(20) Did you read all the way down to this last question?

If you answered "yes" to three or more of these questions, you may have a problem. If you answered "yes" to six or more of these questions, you may be an addict. If you answered "yes" to more than half of these questions, then don't worry, you're just a big fan of *The X-Files.*

In that snarky, obscure, mock questionnaire, *The X-Files* Usenet newsgroup member GregSerl not only recorded the first known usage of the verb *binge watch* but articulated a viewer behavior and identity which would redefine television over the next two decades. Without providing a formal definition, GergSerl captures the quintessential struggle of binge-watching: the negotiation of control between viewers and broadcasters, between viewers and society, and between viewers and technology, which has existed since the first commercial televisions were plugged into homes. So, while the word and practice appear relatively new, the spirit of that struggle was felt with every utterance of "We'll be right back," and "Now a word from our sponsors," and "Tune in next week..."

Digging Up Roots

How are definitions decided? In dictionaries, lexicographers often examine an array of sources and contexts to present examples, both historic and contemporary, of how a word or term can be used. Journalism and literature are the often-cited sources, and those articulations can provide a story of how words have evolved in popular (non-recorded) usage. When I first began studying the phenomenon of binge-watching in 2012, there was no dictionary definition, but people had some sense of what the term meant. It wasn't until 2013, when the Oxford English

Dictionary (OED) named binge watch one of its Words of the Year, that we were provided with this rather unsatisfying codification:

binge-watch, *verb*:

to watch multiple episodes of a television programme in rapid succession, typically by means of DVDs or digital streaming. [ORIGIN 1990s: from BINGE + WATCH, after BINGE-EAT, BINGE-DRINK.]

    The word *binge-watch* has been used in the circles of television fandom since the late 1990s, but it has exploded into mainstream use in 2013.

The current online OED definition of binge-watch (as a verb) claims it first appeared in an AOL X-*Files* fan group in December 1998—Greg-Serl's post. But was that really the first time it appeared? As I dug into this research, I discovered two crucial issues in the OED tracing: (1) while lexicographers had been searching for instances of binge watching, they had overlooked a nearly identical synonym that had been in use since the 1980s—binge viewing—and (2) there appears to be an assumption that marathon and binge in relation to television are synonymous. GregSerl's usage—Do you ever binge watch (marathon)?—so indicates. But TV marathon and TV binge appear in journalism throughout the second half of the 20th century, and they, unlike "binge watching" and "binge viewing," are frequently used to mean different things related to perceptions of healthy behaviors and cultural status. Why, for instance, was expansive coverage of sports events described as "binge TV" in the 1960s and 1970s, while large-scale broadcasts of theater and multi-episode documentaries were referred to as marathons (4 Games, 1967; Kirk, 1978; Vogue, 1970)? As a researcher of binge-watching, I found it frustrating that there was no source that traces the history of these words or accounts for the difference in usage. Furthermore, I believe that the lack of such a history contributes to the ongoing difficulty that media scholars have studying this phenomenon (Pittman & Steiner, 2019).

In this chapter and in Chapter 3, I explore how journalists have written about binge-watching/viewing and TV marathons from 1948 to 2016. I first chronicle that history through an exhaustive archival analysis of all journalistic references to binge and marathon in association with TV prior to mid–2012. The history I have drawn sets the stage and provides context for Chapter 3 in which I show how journalists shaped what binge-watching came to be understood as from 2012 to 2016. Originally, my goals were to (a) provide a history of the terms' origins and (b) to provide an organizing framework of how binge-watching has been defined in journalism. What I discovered through this painstaking archival research is a larger story about what TV is: the struggle

for control of our entertainment experience. Over this 70-year history, we see that power shift from broadcaster to viewer and then back
to streamers as Peak TV exists in the 2020s: a post-network, diffuse,
power-sharing pastiche of content creation and consumption.

What Journalists Can Tell Us About Binge-Watching

This chapter is an attempt to understand what the phenomenon of
binge-watching is by exploring how journalists have used it. The rationale for this approach is rooted in the ideal that "journalists above all
are information providers"
(Zelizer, 2005, p. 67) and that
their work serves to inform
the public (Patterson & Seib,
2005). While the extent of that
service is a matter of debate,

If you are not interested in the theory and
in the methodology of this history (why
and how I executed the project), you can
skip ahead to "Chronicle of Binge" on 27.

people use the work of journalists—primarily news articles—to gather
information about the world (Blumler & Katz, 1974; Lazarsfeld, Berelson, & Gaudet, 1944). Park (1940) argues that "news performs somewhat
the same functions for the public that perception does for the individual" (p. 677). This is particularly the case when phenomena and technology are new and when there is tension around their understanding
(Marvin, 1997). The public use journalists as their eyes and ears to gain
knowledge about subjects they are curious about and which they don't
have the access or expertise to acquire on their own (Lazarsfeld, Berelson, & Gaudet, 1944).

Gaines (2007) notes that "journalists contribute to social discourse
by using words, sounds, and images to represent stories" (p. 81). It is
in these word choices that definitions are
couched, made common, and, through
omission of explanation, accepted and normalized. Words that arise from technology
like "blogger," "email," and "binging" aren't

For more in-depth analysis on
this topic, turn to 201 (note 1).[1]

usually the creations of journalists, but their popularization and codification, in part, are. Changes in language affect meaning and meaning
in effect changes language (Torfing, 1999). News editors struggle with
word choices for this reason, and style manual updates are a deliberative
and lengthy process (Seigel & O'Connolly, 1999, p. vii). The language of
journalists also indicates which words and ideas need explanation and
which do not. To paraphrase the mythical maxim of news writing: If a

seventh grader needs a word explained, then the editor will replace that word with one that doesn't require explanation, unless that word is necessary to the story, in which case an explanation of some kind will be provided. Shifts and amendments to word shapes and to grammar provide clues about how journalists think the public, or at least their collective seventh grade-level readership, should understand any word and its significance to other aspects of the story (Seigel & O'Connolly, 1999, p. viii).

One indicator of a new term's familiarity is its position in the compounding process. "Database" and "online" were once spelled "data base" and "on-line"; they were new terms, like "micro-wave" before it became kitchen appliances. Compounding—merging two words to create a new word through agglutination and/or fusion—is a process of linguistic normalization (Shaumyan, 1987, p. 290). The more normal the word, the closer the parts get. There are conventions about word-type hyphenation, but generally, the process moves through three forms: "open" compounds like "data base," hyphenated compounds like "data-base," and closed compounds like "database."

Language is always evolving, and the "one character in grammar who demonstrates the constantly evolving nature of the English language [is] the hyphen" (Hyphens, n.d.). The hyphen is like the engagement ring for two words, while the closed compounding is the marriage. Studies have shown that language learners have greater facility in acquiring closed compound words than open and hyphenated, and so the process of word normalization can often move from "open" to "hyphen" to "closed" (Beshaj, 2015; Cheng, Wang, & Perfetti, 2011).

The move from open to hyphenated in journalism is an indication of a word's public familiarity but not necessarily agreement on its definition. Often, the more popular a word becomes, the more complex its definition grows (McLuhan, 1964, pp. 22–24). This is certainly the case with binge-watch. Examining compounding and grammar shifts of journalists over a period of time can illuminate the cultural and the technological understanding around new words like binge-watching. While not a complete picture, such an examination can shed light on how "binge-watching" evolved from TV binge and how that evolution relates to shifting perceptions about television-watching.

To explore journalists' influence on our understanding of binge-watching, I also analyzed news articles containing their historical usages and definitional articulations to catalog what frames and shapes have been used over time. Looking at their word choices, descriptions, and news frames across 70 years of news articles can animate a corpus of texts into an "informant in the anthropological sense" (Kelty

& Landecker, 2009). The movement of these elements leaves trails of meaning-making that slither through the decades. To interpret and to contextualize binge-watching's journalistic trails, I analyzed word choices based on the overt descriptive meaning, the implications through omission, and the contexts of usage within the articles' greater frames as well as concurrent coverage.

To date, the only scholarly work examining the definitions of binge-watching through journalistic articulations is "Just One More: How Journalists Frame Binge Watching" by Ri Pierce-Grove (2017). Recently, De Keere, Thunnissen, and Kuipers (2021) found that journalists reframed the moral panic around television consumption by the "legitimization of new cultural boundaries" (p. 630). Their project uses binge-watching as a case study in the reversal of moral panics around cultural practices once perceived to be dangerous through 631 news stories. Pierce-Grove (2017) builds a definitional framework in her excellent article, which uses "the archives of the *New York Times, Atlantic, Wall Street Journal, Daily News, New York Post, Slate*" as a dataset to "track the normalization" of the term from 2003 to 2016. She finds that "journalists participated in the construction of 'binge watching as an all-consuming experience'" but that they also "contradicted this construction by using the term to represent practices of serial media consumption that fit seamlessly within existing patterns of work and leisure" (Pierce-Grove, 2017). She concludes, based on her analysis of usage, that "the episode, not the hour, is the fundamental unit of the 'binge watch.'"

Pierce-Grove's article is a valuable contribution to the literature on binge-watching, not least for the fact that she includes "binge-viewing" in her search. Its structure as an article for the online journal *First Monday* provides a focused scope. Her sampling of the press is limited to four New York City–based newspapers, two with international readerships, and two prestigious online magazines. She also focuses her analysis on articles written by American-based "arts and entertainment critics" with less exposure to domestic and international journalists covering the TV industry and technology. While she rightly notes that use of "binge-watching" before 2011 was sporadic, that period of binge-watching history is relevant and thus the focus of this chapter. Journalistic articulations of "binge" in association with "TV," which began as early as 1948, provide a background for how journalists began constructing binge-watching. Their shifting constructions during the 20th century speak to the discourse around and understanding of television watching. The 55 years prior to Pierce-Grove's first cited usage (Nussbaum, 2003) contain the history of binge-watching's linguistic development, a history that may give context for her finding that journalists have "multiple uses" for the term. An important consideration in that history is the more common term "TV marathon" and its relation to how journalists would later construct "binge-watching." Though some literature suggests that these are functionally synonymous (Lotz, 2014), other scholars, such as Perks (2015), disagree. Pierce-Grove (2017) writes, "'Binge' was frequently paired, especially in early coverage, with 'marathon' and 'addiction.' It exists midway between them on a spectrum of self-control and intention" (Pierce-Grove,2017). However, it is difficult to discuss how and why usages differ without an examination of the early journalistic usages of marathon.

Methodology aka How the Sausage Gets Made

It took me more than two years to gather, to organize, and to categorize the 10,000 articles and to conduct the multi-level analysis that constitutes the journalistic history in this chapter and in Chapter 3. The aggregation and the organization of archival news stories is tedious, frustrating, repetitive, and occasionally astonishing. Though moments of astonishment may spring from small oases in deserts of tedium, often mirages, they sustained this researcher on his journey toward a more fertile understanding.

Even more challenging was determining whether the available older entries, often scans of newspaper pages, contained an article with the keywords, an article without them but with an ad on the page that had the keywords, or a typo. Poor newsprint resulted in several hours of futile searching after a TV schedule page in a late 1950s *Los Angeles Times* indicated that KCOP 13 had a 30-minute

If you are interested in learning more about the search terms and process, turn to 202 (chap. 2 note 2).[2]

show on Tuesdays and on Thursdays at 11:30 a.m. called *TV Binge.* There is no record of any such show ever being on TV in L.A. or in any other city, though in my opinion it could now be pitched. After a thorough investigation of other scanned TV schedules I discovered that I had spent these hours hunting down a smudged "o"; the show was called *TV Bingo.*

Despite other distractions, like Marathon TV Film News Reel Inc. and the *Gentile and Binge TV Frolic,* and the manual parsing of articles that discussed binging unrelated to television, I was able to organize several data sets for my textual analysis of the articulation of binge-watching in journalism. I should note that the process of scanning through titles and abstracts, and sometimes reading whole articles, to determine whether the journalist was discussing an eating disorder or a TV binge was extremely time-consuming but also enlightening. Journalistic framing of addiction, obsessive behavior, and mental illness share similarities to the framing of 20th-century TV-watching, and, in some articles, they overlap. GergSerl's (1998) prescience emerged again when Agent Mulder portrayer David Duchovny acknowledged real-life struggles with pornography addiction (Serjeant, 2008). While slightly outside the scope of this project, the process of determining which articles were excluded from my analysis influenced my analysis of the articles that were included.

For Chapter 2, I conducted an intensive survey of the terms' usages prior to the behavior's popularization in 2012. This involved a close reading of every news article mentioning "binge" or "marathon" and "television" or "TV" from the first article in 1948 until the first articles defining "binge watching" began appearing at the beginning of 2012 (BW = 251 articles) (MARA = 1,530) (there was some overlap of these articles, particularly with telethons: Category 1 [see Table 1 on 38]). Through these 1,781 pieces we can see how journalists articulated mass consumption of television during the mid to the late 20th and early 21st centuries. Those articulations form the history of how we came to understand what binge-watching is.

To chronicle and to analyze that history, I considered the technological and cultural events that framed the usages. I accounted for the news contexts surrounding the appearances of these terms in relation to the tenor of the article and to the frequency of their appearance over periods of time. I also noted the geographic locations, usage characteristics, discourse between other sources, and the linguistic shifts over that period from noun (TV binge/TV marathon) to gerund (binge-watching) to active verb (binge-watch). I organized the periods into categories based on themes that I coded to address changes in the relational understanding of television and viewership from 1948 to 2012.

I chose July 11, 2012, as my cutoff point for two reasons. First, it is my general approximation of an inflection point in the journalistic usage of binge-watching, after which there is an exponential increase in articles using the terms based on the frequency of news articles found in my search (jump to "Binge-Watching Reaches a Tipping Point" on 64 for full story). The terms became "hot" around the summer of 2012, and journalists shifted their focus to contextualizing and explaining them. Journalists used the term more than 100 times more frequently from July 2012 to July 2013 than they had from July 2011 to July 2012. Second, July 11, 2012, is the last day before the verb or gerund forms were used in news headlines (Jurgensen, 2012). This was helpful for my filtering of articles in my textual analysis of journalistic definitions from 2012 to 2016 (Chapter 3). Every choice in research has its drawbacks, but I feel that this was a sensible one based on the goals of this project.

Through this textual/contextual analysis of binge-watching in journalism, I chronicled a history of the term's usages and development, articulated a defining framework (see Chapter 3), and illustrated the cultural value of the media ritual in relation to journalists' professional roles and sourcing practices. My findings illuminate the borders that journalists shaded around binge-watching through their numerous articulations across 70 years.

Chronicle of Binge

Television of the 1940s was really a spinoff of radio. Its invention, propagation, promotion, and success are often attributed to the Radio Corporation of America (RCA). As CBS director of programming Gilbert Seldes (1950) wrote, "If [RCA TV pioneer Vladimir Zworykin] had been working for any part of the movie industry, the control of television might have been rooted in Hollywood; if he had been a researcher for the Navy, the course of television again would have been altered" (p. 162). But Zworykin worked for RCA, and RCA applied its vertical monopoly and the blueprints for content creation and advertising to build the technical, economic, and cultural infrastructure that became network television—the most pervasive mass medium in history.

Philo Farnsworth publicly demonstrated functioning TV technology in 1927, but the Great Depression and World War II slowed its diffusion. By 1945, America had emerged as a global superpower, and its burgeoning middle-class citizens were hungry for peacetime entertainment after years of austerity. In 1945, less than 2 percent of U.S. households had televisions; 10 years later, 65 percent had them (DiMaggio & Cohen, 2003). From 1946 to 1948, the FCC issued more than 100 licenses increasing the coverage, by 1950, to more than half the country. This was the decade when *Meet the Press*, late night talk shows, and the idea of binge-watching were born. It was during this period of growth that binge was first used by journalists to describe television.

First Uses (1948–1949)

The first journalistic uses of "binge" in reference to television appeared in *Variety* under or around the byline of TV industry reporter

George Rosen. Because some articles have no bylines, it is difficult to say that he coined the usage, but if he didn't, he was close to the coinage. During December of 1948, the weekly entertainment magazine went on something of a *binge* binge, using the term to describe TV programming seven times over three issues. On December 1, an uncredited TV writer asked whether NBC would have to go on a "creative programming binge" now that CBS was shifting to shows built around celebrities poached from 30 Rockefeller Center (*Variety*, 1948a, p. 22). Later in that issue, an uncredited reporter described how NBC's Philadelphia affiliate, WCAU, was going on a "daytime binge" with "a solid hour and a half of commercial programming" (1948b, p. 31). Portions were smaller back then! On December 8, TV broadcasters' upcoming Christmas line-ups were titled a "Yuletide Binge" (1948c, p. 31). Rosen (1948) wrote on December 22 that New Orleans was going on a "video binge" with the debut of its first station, WDSU, and the preceding installation of 1,500 sets "thanks to the initiative of local Philco and Admiral dealers who romanced customers by putting on live demonstrations in the show rooms" (p. 26). TV demonstrations were spectacles for towns across America, with residents crowding the streets outside the dealers to stare at the glowing boxes. Rosen had a couple more mentions in 1949, and then "binge," in reference to "television," disappeared from journalism until 1952.

During the early *Variety* period, "binge" was used as a modifier of elements of TV. There was no mention of a "TV binge." The meaning of "binge," in all usages but Rosen's credited article (1948), was a large quantity of programming. The quantity was of no fixed amount, but the binge was always modifying a specific type of TV programming—daytime, Christmas, and so forth. The binges belonged to networks or to programmers. It was their action rather than the viewers' action (as we conceptualize binge-watching today). Broadcasters controlled the signal, the content, and the flow of television for America's growing audiences.

Rosen's use was the exception. He used the term "video binge" (p. 26) when describing the medium more broadly, including TV technology and culture for a viewing area. He meant that the entire New Orleans area, from the local channel to its electronics dealers to those first 2,000 buyers, were all getting jazzed about the new technology. He also detailed how WDSU would be a uniquely New Orleans station. Benefitting from a freeze on FCC licenses, a strong signal, and flat bayou terrain, the non-interconnected, local channel had a monopoly on TV eyes for a 150-mile radius until 1950. As such, the programming had a "strictly local flavor and atmosphere" (p. 26)—Mardi Gras, the Sugar

Bowl, and so on. The audience for this "video binge," if it can be imagined, was totalizing and yet limited in its viewing to the 8,000 sets that optimistic dealers predicted would be sold by the end of 1949.

Early Usages (1949–1959)

The 1950s have been described as television's first golden age (Kristoff, 1995). By 1956, 70 percent of U.S. homes had sets, and the major networks poured resources into near-round-the- clock content to grab the attention and the dollars of a growing and increasingly affluent American consumer audience. Central to this growth was the broadcast of live sports. In the 1940s, the greatest hurdle for television's adoption "was not the size of the screen or the cost of production or the reluctance of sponsors; the essential thing was to get into Madison Square Garden" (Seldes, 1950, p. 162). Sports leagues had been resistant to the new medium, fearing a decrease in attendance. Ironically, it was the poor quality of TV technology at that time that led to increases in attendance for sports like Major League Baseball. Due to the still primitive camera technology, televised sports looked better at night under artificial lighting than in the glare of the day. This led teams and leagues to increase the number of night games, which, because of typical work schedules, were more easily attended and viewed at home than day games. Just as it had with radio, live sports became bait for selling TV sets in the 1950s, and Americans bit (Serazio, 2019, p. 43).

Perhaps it's not surprising, then, that the term *"TV* binge" first appeared in an American newspaper's sports section. On July 27, 1952, the *Atlanta Journal-Constitution* sports editor Ed Danforth used the term to describe a Bob Hope–Bing Crosby telethon to raise money for the U.S. Olympic team (Danforth, 1952). As you may remember, 1953 was the year that "idiot box" first appeared in a newspaper (Wolters, 1953). Fellow Atlanta sportswriter Marion Jackson of the *Atlanta Daily World* (1952) described the U.S. Olympic fundraiser as a "TV marathon." Jackson's use of "TV marathon" in reference to a telethon was common during the 1950s, but "TV binge" did not appear again until 1955, when *Variety*'s Rosen used it to describe Coca-Cola's advertising rollout of the family-sized 26-ounce bottle; today's large soda bottles are around 68 ounces: again, portions were smaller back then. "Coca-Cola," he wrote, "like the cigarette companies is on a 'king size' TV binge. The Coke company had designated four markets to try out spots for its upcoming national video campaign" (p. 21). After that, "TV binge" did not appear again until 1959 when Jackson wrote, "The National Football League is on a TV binge. Sixty-six games will be screened this fall by a 24-man announcing staff." By 2019, the number had grown to 256 games with production crews in excess of 200 per game.

TV Marathons

Journalists used "TV marathon" nearly 10 times more than "TV binge" (with all configurations) from 1948 to 2011; therefore, to contextualize how binge-watching usage evolved in the press, it is valuable to examine how "marathon" and "TV" were used, particularly during the early years, when "binge" was less common.

As TV sets became household appliances and as TV culture entered its first "golden age," journalists used "marathon" and "TV" together 228 times (1949–1959). Their usages fell into the following six categories: (1) *Telethon*, (2) *Political Stunt/Punditry*, (3) *Lengthy Oratory*, (4) *Plus-Sized Show*, (5) *Plus-Sized Series*, and (6) *Plus-Sized Programming*. Those categories fall into two distinct master usages: Sender-Focused Marathons and Viewer-Focused Marathons. The vast majority of Sender-Focused usages (93 percent) are most often news reports on (1) a public figure or figures (2) who have accomplished televised feats of endurance (3) in the past. Viewer-Focused usages are most often (1) previews or reviews of (2) larger than normal amounts of television (3) informing viewers of potential participation in or effects of the consumption.

If you want to learn about the history of how journalists used TV marathons, keep reading.

Tired of TV marathons? Then jump to "Early Uses of TV Binge" (1959–1986) on 38.

These six categories and two master usages set the stage for journalistic usages of binge and marathon in association with television for the next 70 years. While those categories remained constant, the contexts in which journalists used them changed with technology and with culture. Collectively, they demonstrate how public understanding of the roles and the relationship of broadcaster and viewer evolved during the 20th century and the shifting power dynamics over television's flow and entertainment experience. Through this organizing lens we can more clearly see how consumption and control of television were instantiated in the press, which contextualizes and foretells the rise of binge-watching in the 21st century.

Telethons and Political Stunts (1949–1952)

As with Jackson (1952), journalists first used "TV marathon" to describe what soon became known as telethons, the portmanteau of television and marathon. This seemingly wholesome, if not healthy, humanitarian activity accounted for 89 percent of all uses of TV marathons between 1949 and 1953, despite the *Chicago Daily Tribune* critique that called telethons "Revolting Appeals" (Voice, 1950). Starting with Milton Berle in 1949, numerous celebrities donated hours of their time to persuade the growing population of viewers to contribute to charitable causes. Berle reportedly lost nine pounds during his first 22-hour, $1.1 million drive for the Damon Runyon Cancer Fund (Cancer, 1951). "TV marathon" remained associated with live fundraising events through the early 1950s, with celebrities like Bing Crosby, Dean Martin, and Bob Hope raising money for various charities, hospitals, and other causes. This remained the most frequent journalistic usage of "marathon" until the 1980s, though the frequency really began falling in 1952, as journalists and style guides began using telethon instead. The portmanteau saved typesetters between two and 10 letters per mention of the most common usage of "television/TV marathon." In 1956, the *New York Times* wrote that "the Yukon 5 designation is a special call-dispersion rig dreamed up by telephone company engineers just for 'telethons'" (Berger, 1956, p. 47). Note that it was still in quotes.

However, before the end of 1953, there were only four news stories, across 21 articles, that used TV marathon to describe something other than a telethon. These stories instead focused on politicians blanketing television and radio airwaves for hours on end to inform and to persuade the public to vote. The first came during the final days of the 1950 New York State elections. In a political stunt that *House of Cards* fans may find reminiscent of Will Conway's 24-hour streaming video call-in, the incumbent governor John Dewey participated in a live TV broadcast from 6:00 a.m. on Monday, November 6, until midnight Tuesday (Election Day). Broadcast from the WOR-TV studios near Central Park West, with audio available over the radio, the marathon "relied heavily on Q&A" and featured roving reporters with camera crews patrolling the city streets to gather questions from local residents (Conklin, 1950). Both TV and radio audiences were encouraged to phone their questions for the governor into the studio, a first according to the *New York Times* (Conklin, 1950). A *Los Angeles Times* story titled it the "New Idea in Politics," a "TV Talkathon," and reported that the Republican candidate "drank many cups of coffee ... taking time out only to wash up, apply new television make-up and confer with his campaign aides" (*Los Angeles Times*, 1950).

Dewey's idea spread south for the 1951 Philadelphia mayoral race (Miller, 1951, p. 2). Then, in November 1952, Dewey rebooted the stunt, this time to drum up votes for Republican presidential candidate Dwight D. Eisenhower. With the General Election approaching, the New York governor took to the radio and to TV for another binge in support of General Eisenhower's bid. Starting at six in the morning, Dewey went for 18 straight hours on WOR-TV. He was countered that evening by a rather succinct "television marathon arranged by the labor division of the Democratic State Committee … over Station WPIX (Channel 11) from 9 to 10:30" (Ingraham, 1952, p. 11).

On January 16, 1953, Philadelphia mayor Joseph S. Clark, Jr., and Transport Workers (TWU) Union Local 234 president Paul O'Rourke went on a "radio and television marathon" to avert a crippling transit strike (McCullough, 1953, p. 1). Along with TWU International president Michael J. Quill, they took the airwaves in "a combined barrage of more than five hours of radio and television pleas … all in favor of ending the 'wildcat' walkout" (p. 1). There were nine more such walkouts from 1955 to 1960, but this was the only reported TV marathon to end one (TWU 234, 1970).

The Ironic Outlier (1953)

In December of 1953, a "haunted" television set was behind what the *New York Times* called "the longest TV marathon." For 51 hours, the frozen face of Francey Lane, a singer from *The Morey Amsterdam Show*, appeared trapped on the screen of a Long Island family's set. Her face took up most of the display, eyes half open as if "the woman was sad or singing a torch song" (Newport, 1953, p. 7). Changing the channel could not exorcise her! Reporters, engineers, and eventually the singer herself flocked to the Blue Point, New York, home to marvel at the spectral countenance that remained whether the TV was on or off. According to investigators from a local appliance store, "an explosion of electrons burned the image of a face into the fluorescent lining of the picture tube" (p. 7). While perhaps outside conventional understandings of what would constitute a TV marathon, this was the first instance where the term was used to describe something other than a telethon or a political stunt. Here we see the term being used to characterize what on the surface would be an exceptionally long broadcast of a single pre-taped show, ironically disguising a technological glitch.

This marked an important shift: for the play on words to work, there needed to be a public understanding of what a "TV marathon" normally meant and the possibility that records for duration were kept. The article coincided with an expansion of journalistic usages into non-telethon descriptions of TV marathons over the next year. Interestingly, only a few months later, the city of Los Angeles announced that it would "no longer sanction marathon television shows to raise money for charities" (Hill, 1953, p. 29). A civil ordinance was passed requiring applicants to obtain a solicitation license to host telethons in L.A. after it came to light that more than 75 percent of the money raised went to "overhead expenses" (p. 29).

Politicians and Pundits (1954–1959)

Political reporters began to use "TV marathon" more frequently in the mid–1950s for the increasing number of candidates engaging in multi-hour stunts, à la Dewey. In July of 1954, the *Philadelphia Tribune* described how Congressman Pat Sutton had "created quite a sensation with his radio-television marathon appearances" in his bid for the Democratic senatorial nomination (Halliburton, 1954). The term was used without explanation, indicating that readers would understand that what was implied by a TV marathon, was not a telethon. Furthermore, it described the simulcasting across radio and TV as a marathon rather than as a biathlon.

Marathon television _____ *construction.* Across the pond in 1955, *The Observer* described David Butler's "marathon television commentary" on Britain's parliamentary elections as "the most lucid and apt thing in the campaign" (Pendennis, 1955, p. 5). The Oxford psephologist's live coverage of polling day (and night) results may not have been the first of its kind, but it was the first to be described by journalists as "marathon television." In this case, the marathon was not so much describing the lengthy coverage as it was Butler's individual performance over that long period, similar to Milton Berle's telethon endurance. This is the first instance where marathon was used to modify television commentary of an event.

In the late 1950s, "marathon TV" began to be used for lengthy political speeches, often by leaders of non–NATO countries. Reporters regularly described Cuban president Fidel Castro's many and verbose public addresses as "marathon TV talks" (Cooke, 1959; Walter, 1961). The lengthy speeches were not only coming from communist leaders like Castro and Khrushchev (Crankshaw, 1960); critics also predicted marathons of TV speeches from British parliamentarians if television cameras had been allowed into the House of Commons (Kennedy, 1962). In 1979, C-SPAN televised its first session from the U.S. House of Representatives, and a decade later, in 1989, cameras began live broadcasts from the British House of Commons.

Sender/Receiver Hybrid Outlier

On February 25, 1954, the *Los Angeles Times* described how celebrity chef Joseph Milani would be busy taping a "radio and TV marathon" (p. 30). That day Chef Milani was slated to appear on KMPC at 9:30 a.m., KFI at 11:00 a.m. (helping Bob Hope), then back to KCOP to prep afternoon meals for a 3:00 p.m. show, and then at 8:00 p.m. he was scheduled to "wrestle with his Juvenile Talent Patrol" (*Los Angeles Times*, 1954, p. 30). This usage described not only a long TV schedule but the multiple non-sequential Milani appearances as a "TV marathon" (p. 30). It also indirectly addressed the audience's role, leading with "If anyone misses Chef Milani today it will be because his sets aren't turned on" (p. 30). This acknowledgment of the choices afforded to audiences across channels and across media is a nod to the potential of viewer agency and at the same time an acknowledgment of the lack of choice that viewers and listeners of the era had. On the one hand, you can't miss Chef Milani; on the other hand, the only way to avoid him is by unplugging your devices. Besides Francey Lane, this is the only story that didn't fit neatly into the two master usages. It is sender-focused with a personality performing a feat of endurance across media. But it also addresses the audience's participation in the marathon and is reported on prior to the event taking place.

Receiver-Focused Marathons

Plus-Sized Serials

In July of 1955, the *New York Times* described *I Remember Mama* as a "marathon TV serial" on account of the CBS comedy-drama entering its seventh season (Zolotow, 1955, p. 24). This is the first instance of a collection of episodes being modified with "marathon" due to the show's longevity. Live event broadcasts like telethons are discreet entities: TV marathons. In this case, "marathon TV" is modifying a TV series which, given the available technology, could not be consumed in one sitting. In 1962, a similar usage can be found in the description of *Coronation Street*, then only two years old. In *The Observer,* Maurice Richardson (1962) wrote, "all marathon TV serials with fixed settings and regular characters are cunningly designed and processed to be like comic strips which aim with slight variations on a familiar pattern to turn the viewer into an addict." That *Corrie* remains the longest continuously running television soap opera, with more than 10,000 episodes, may speak to the alluring force of that structure though, as Richardson notes, it may also be the show's "realistic" and "matter of fact" depiction of everyday life in Northern England that has hooked fans for seven decades.

Plus-Sized Episodes

A prescient *Chicago Tribune* article about the future of TV programming was published in December of 1955. Hubbell Robinson, CBS's vice president in charge of programming, predicted the following: "Television is going to get much better" (Wolters, 1955). Viewers, in his estimation, were demanding quality, and that was exactly what the networks intended to provide them. The mid–1950s was a period some TV scholars consider to be the first "Golden Age of TV" (Kisseloff, 1995, p. 227). For Robinson, the improvement in quality meant an increase in episode length, with the 90-minute show as its flagship. ABC was reportedly following the trend by "going into the marathon TV program field next season with *Dramaculars*"—a weekly dramatic series with feature-film length episodes. This idea was in lockstep with television's technological advancements, as seen in ad slogans like Emerson's "Now, a TV picture so clear, so sharp … you'll think you're at the movies" (Spigel, 1992, p. 107). It also indicated the sharp cultural demarcations between the silver screen and the small screen that continued into the early 21st century.

Robinson determined that dramas work better in 60- or 90-minute formats as opposed to comedies that tend to "go flat after a half-hour" (Wolters, 1955). *Tribune* columnist Larry Wolters, however, seemed skeptical of the impending cultural upswing, opining, "Wish I could believe this because each week I see an awful lot of glop." His distaste may have been reflective of the rapid ubiquity of TV adoption and the growing fears of its social consequences (see "Cultural Boogeyman" story on 5). His use of marathon here implies that any show that breached its "customary" temporal boundaries (30/60) might be considered a marathon, particularly if a number of networks were choosing to do so. It was not just the length of single episodes that made up Wolters's marathon but also the confluence of many plus-sized shows in the upcoming season. This use was the closest to *Variety*'s (1948) uses of "TV binge" as a mass of programming rather than as a single program.

The next year, a correspondent in the *Baltimore Sun*'s London bureau described a scheme by the British tabloid *The News of the World* to avoid Britain's advertising restrictions by creating a weekly television series composed entirely of the content found in the paper—mostly "lurid court dramas." It was billed as "the biggest advertising campaign this country has ever seen" (Sun, 1956). While the Church of England might disagree, this certainly stands out as an innovative marriage of media. The goal of this "marathon TV commercial" was to "demonstrate all the paper's attractions except its suitability for wrapping up fish and chips." It is notable that such a form of inter-media branded content was considered to be a marathon; the scheme pairs with contemporary blended product placement and with native advertising that binge-viewers prefer over commercial breaks in the current streaming video era (see Chapter 5).

Plus-Sized Programming

Although the Republican and Democratic national conventions were broadcast on television in 1952, the production was sloppy and plagued by technical issues. By 1956, both parties realized the potential power of TV and adapted their conventions' lengths, formats, and venues to accommodate live broadcasts (Jarvis, n.d.). In response to this technological pandering, a *Washington Post* (1956) editorial sarcastically previewed the plus-sized Chicago Democratic Convention coverage as a "quadrennial TV marathon." The description and the tone were echoed in a September 25 editorial on voter registration from the *Chicago Defender*. In it, the editors chastised election apathy and the numbing effects of round-the-clock convention coverage on audiences. Rather than inspiring political participation, all the "marathon TV presentations ... [had] done was to bore the listening public to death with the rivers of double talk and the fervent wish of most viewers was 'Let's get this thing over with and get back to baseball and *Strike It Rich*" (*Daily Defender*, 1956, p. 1). The editorial board managed to be critical of the motives and the values of networks broadcasting political conventions and dismissive of viewers' potential interest in the democratic process. This dominating depiction of television's flow has the networks controlling the limited scheduling options, flooding the airwaves with poorly produced political theater to a bored audience who apparently can do nothing else but stare at the screen. It foreshadows the dystopian Las Vegasization of America described by Neil Postman (1985) in *Amusing Ourselves to Death*.

The 1960 U.S. presidential debates between Richard Nixon and John F. Kennedy are often cited as the touchstone moment for television's influence on elections. However, in 1959, Britain's Grenada Television launched its first "Election Marathon," which came to be called "TV Marathon." Since then, televised debates have become cornerstone media events of U.S. presidential election years. Even in this age of diffused viewership, the 73-plus million people who tuned in to watch Joe Biden debate Donald Trump in September 2020 were a ratings windfall, second only to the Super Bowl (Adalian, 2020).

Marathon Peak

Throughout the 1950s, journalistic usage of "TV" with "marathons" fell roughly into six categories: (1) *Telethon*, (2) *Political Stunt/ Punditry*, (3) *Lengthy Oratory*, (4) *Plus-Sized Show*, (5) *Plus-Sized Series*, and (6) *Plus-Sized Programming*. The only notable exception to these usages was the faulty frozen face of Francey Lane, which was intentionally ironic, and Chef Milani, who bridges several categories and both master usages. After 228 appearances in the 1950s, journalists' use of "marathon" with "television" cooled in the 1960s to only 81 mentions. Usage crept up in the 1970s (102), in the 1980s (135), in the 1990s (107), but no decade surpassed the 1950s total mentions. While "movie marathon" appeared as early as 1948 (Gould, 1948), journalists did not describe viewing them as "TV marathons." Even when televised movie marathons began becoming common in the 1970s, journalists modified marathons by the content's original medium. Films and TV shows were separated, and journalists stuck to these six usages. It wasn't until the turn of the last century, when technology and fan culture began to turn "marathon" and "binge" into more viewer-centered gerunds, and then active verbs, that terminal meanings expanded.

The six categories of journalistic usage can roughly be subdivided by two constructions—"TV marathon" and "marathon TV _____." One-off shows and events like telethons, political stunts, and political conventions are described as discrete TV marathons. Collections of shows, advertising, programming, speeches, and series are described as marathon TV _____. In the first construction, "marathon" is a noun modified by the adjective "TV." The marathon centers on an individual or on a specific event, with deference paid to performers who can be on air that long—often for a supposedly worthy cause. The viewer experience is rarely part of the story until late 20th-century constructions of film and later TV marathons.

What is perhaps most telling about these usages is that categories 1–3 are all news reports about earlier performances of live television endurance. Whether it be Jerry Lewis riffing for hours to fight muscular dystrophy or Nikita Khrushchev railing against Western imperialism for hours before the United Nations, these TV marathons were news because of the grueling activity of individuals on TV.

	Sender Focused			Programming/Receiver Focused		
	Telethon	Political Stunt	Oratory	Plus-Sized Episodes	Plus-Sized Series	Plus-Sized TV Programming
TV Marathon	161	22	2			6*
Marathon TV [___]	14	4	9	6	1	3

Table 1: 1949–1959 uses of marathon in journalism (n = 228).

Viewers had a clear and active role in telethons—donating money—but the celebrity hosts on screen were the marathoners. Even when journalists used marathons to describe the endurance of those covering lengthy elections, the accomplishments were of TV correspondents, not of TV audiences. While viewers may have caught every minute of Mayor Dewey, Chef Milani, or David Butler, they, by journalistic omission, are at best passive observers of these historic televised feats.

By contrast, categories 4–6 use marathons to describe abnormally large quantities of prerecorded content or, in the case of the 1956 Democratic primary and the 1959 British parliamentary elections, previews and reviews of the programming and its implications. Since most were published prior to airing, they acknowledge the potential role of viewers. They are instructive of how to tune in and the implications of doing so. Such uses were rare, but they at least acknowledge the audience's involvement in the marathons, even if sometimes portraying them as couch potatoes yearning for bread and circus. Furthermore, they were increasingly critical of network television's motives and its effect on audiences, which coincided with the popularization of the term idiot box in the late 1950s. Those uses of *marathon* shaped the understanding of practices that would soon become referred to as TV binges.

Early Uses of "TV Binge" (1959–1986)

While the first journalistic uses of "binge" with "TV" predate the uses of "marathon" with "TV," they were scarce after Jackson's 1959 description of the NFL's move into television. "TV marathon," in various constructions, seemed to meet most of the lexical needs of journalists during the next 30 years. From 1959 to 1986, TV binge or television binge were the only constructions of the terms found in journalism, and they were rare. When journalists used them, they did so to describe only three categories of the receiver-focused master usages from TV Marathon: (4) *Plus-Sized Episode*, (5) *Plus-Sized*

Series, and (6) *Plus-Sized Programming* (see list on 30). Speeches, political events, and telethons were rarely characterized as binges. The American TV viewer, it would seem, was capable of binges, not marathons. Journalists' critique of the effects of such binges on viewers and of the powerful forces behind them may have been less clear had they used the healthier-sounding, charity-associated term *marathon*. Additionally, *binge TV* was used generically at times to describe a large quantity of something related to television, such as advertising. In this section I provide a chronological breakdown of the journalistic usages highlighting shifts and exceptions from early constructions.

In 1961, the *Wall Street Journal* described how the Ideal Toy Company, maker of such popular dolls as Betsy Wetsy, Shirley Temple, and Miss Revlon and later the Rubik's Cube, was rolling out a new line of toys for the spring season. Staff reporters quoted Ideal chair Benjamin Michtom, who said the company was "going on a half-million-dollar television binge" to promote the toys (*Wall Street Journal* Staff, 1961). This usage is similar to Rosen's (1955) description of Coca-Cola's advertising campaign. While increasingly less common after the 1970s, journalists as late as the 1990s used "TV binge" to describe a blanketing ad buy as in the case of the California Democratic primary between Gray Davis and Diane Feinstein (Matier & Ross, 1998; Shuit, 1992).

In 1962, a *Time Magazine* article on education discussed a potential technological solution for South Carolina's underfunded school system: video learning. There were myriad articles written during the late 1950s and early 1960s on the pros and cons and fears and fantasies of supplementing classrooms with filmstrips (see Chapter 4) and even airplane broadcast television feeds for rural and for understaffed school districts. The author of this 1962 piece stated that "South Carolina's TV binge is drastic—as well it might be" (Salvation, 1962). The focus was on the producers creating a cross-disciplinary library of educational content that could be shown to large audiences across the state. Fifty-eight years later this would become the new normal, as schools and universities around the world were forced to move learning onto screens in the wake of the COVID-19 pandemic.

In December of that year, a theater review in the *Chicago Tribune* contained the first use of "television binge" addressing audience behavior, buried in the final paragraph. Claudia Cassidy (1962) factiously suggested that Stravinsky may be considering a televised opera "if he can find a libretto. Possibly a Greek theme." She then broke down the potential revenue that could be generated by viewers of this "closed circuit television binge for national culture," a precursor to pay-per-view events. This marks the first time a journalist indicated the audience as the primary actor in a "television binge." While not direct, individual viewers were the ones going on this binge by purchasing access to the closed-circuit broadcast. The Cassidy piece also marked the last time binge was used in association with the theatrical arts (politics aside) until 1988.

Sporting events, particularly those with expansive coverage by networks across multiple games, were the most common category of "binge TV" usage by journalists during this period. Interestingly, live sports are most often categorized as non-bingeable content by contemporary journalists (see "Binge Hierarchy" on 80) though viewers do use the term when describing some sporting events (see "Bingeable Content" on 146). The first article to use "TV Binge" in the headline was a December 30, 1967, primer on the upcoming college bowl games. It led with "Football starts off today on a three-day, 10-game binge that figures to strain more marriages than horse-playing husbands" (4 Games, 1967). Beyond the gender stereotyping, which continues throughout the piece, this article is notable for constructing the audience of "fathers and sons" as the lead actors in the binge, with their fuming wives and mothers in the background. Such constructions of the male sports TV fan began to take root in the next decade with the couch potato caricatures (see Chapter 4) as well as TV dads from Archie Bunker in *All in the Family* to Kevin McRoberts in *Kevin Can F**k Himself*. Here we see that by the mid–1960s, the viewer's role in binge-watching was established and further explanation by journalists was not necessary.

While the article was titled "4 Games Kick Off TV Binge," its subtitle was "Gator, Sun Bowls, Blue-Gray, East-West Tilts Open Marathon" (4 Games, 1967). Articles on plus-sized sports broadcasts contained "binge" more often than "marathon" (perhaps because in the sports section, marathon might be confused with running or because sports are understood to be primarily entertainment rather than informational or wholesome like politics and charity). Journalists were more likely to choose marathon when describing broadcasts of plus-sized cultural events such as musical theater (Kirk, 1978), lengthy commercial-free documentaries, such as economist John Kenneth Galbraith's epic *Age of Uncertainty* (Stigler, 1977), and some of the coverage of patriotic events such as the Fourth of July (O'Connor, 1976).

The use of TV binge to describe massive consumptions of televised sports content grew in the 1970s. *Vogue* even featured it in its "People Are Talking About…" section—the fashion magazine's pop culture, trend-spotting page. Above the talk of "trashed" being used as a verb for destroying a hotel room, and "cool out" as the new term for drug overdose, we learn that people were talking about "the television binge of sports with more networks finding live action healthier than canned plots" (1970). Health, in the case of TV networks, correlates with ratings. Still, sports journalists over the decades tended to use TV binge as a side effect of technological improvements in broadcast television and around such multi-game sporting events as the NCAA (National Collegiate Athletic Association) tournament, the Olympics, and the World Cup (Isaacs, 1984, Jackson, 1959; Klein, 1984; Maisel, 1982).

Gonzo Binge-Reporting

During the 1960s and 1970s, journalists began conducting binge-watching experiments on themselves. These subjective dispatches bucked established newswriting norms of the 20th century by positioning the reporter as the subject of the report. Like New Journalism of that era, feeling and interpretation were favored over objective coverage. Think Electric Kool-Aid Binge-Watching Tests. Not unlike Tom Wolfe, these dispatches from the couch carry a tone of colonial anthropology through their patrician lamentations on the decay of American culture. The first such viewing experiment came in 1960, when three *Esquire* writers watched a full Wednesday of programming and found it to be "an inherently bad idea, like morning alcohol" (Rovere et al., 1960, p. 114). Charles Sopkin (1967) described conducting a weeklong binge with a seven-TV array in his book *Seven Glorious Days, Seven Fun Filled Nights*, something that he recommended all citizens try once. These usages depict, through first-person POV (point of view), a specific viewer on a binge (rather than a generalized mass audience) using technology to potentially create political action and/or critique culture. However, the "average viewer" is othered—an unwoke automaton of idiot box culture who needs protection. In a 1971 *New York Times* op-ed, Paul Harper, Jr. (1971) used "TV binge" to describe how he had spent a day watching TV nonstop. "A few Sundays ago I went on a TV binge, watching the tube from noon till midnight. I recommend this exercise to everyone who is concerned with the great pressures being exerted on business today by the Government and consumer groups."

While such self-induced binges may result in greater civic engagement by an enlightened few, the language implies that prolonged viewing carries negative consequences reflective of post–World War II American society. These binges are recommended not because the viewers will enjoy the content but so viewers can learn how bad things are. "TV is a mirror. What it reflects is, to me, principally an appalling picture; but however distressing, it reflects what is the life of a hundred and twenty-eight million people on an average day, and I think that it is incumbent on a writer to look at it" (Rovere et al., 1960, p. 114). The erudite journalist serves as a guardian of high culture and as a guide for the couch potato masses navigating the vast wasteland. Similar narratives reappear 40 years later in reports of tech savvy cord cutters demanding better content and conquering network television (spoiler alert: see Pamer, 2006, p. 78).

The language of addiction and the shared assumption of TV dangers were woven into a 1973 *New York Times* editorial titled "Withdrawal Pangs." Following the conclusion of the first Congressional Watergate hearings, the writer noted that "it will take some adjusting and post-partum exercise to get back to normal after this national binge of watching and wondering" (p. 30). The idea of engagement with political processes through TV was thus couched ambivalently. On the one hand, journalists herald an informed electorate as the primary benefit of an independent press (Patterson & Seib, 1995, p. 190) but also cast the idiot box as a poor source for the electorate to gather its information. This narrative lives on in the mainstream media's castigation of former president Donald Trump and the general public for using television as a primary source of news (Lahut, 2020). In November 1993, a Canadian journalist "spent most of the past week of a largely misspent life—so nothing really new there—following the North American Free Trade debate on U.S. television, mostly on CNN" (Camp, 1993). Journalists positioned a cable news binge as more productive than a random binge, but information seeking on TV still necessitated acknowledgment of a modicum of shame. The shame was excused, though, since they were news professionals doing their job (Pierce-Grove, 2017).

Binge Consumption and Children

By 1980, television had been a fixture in American homes for nearly 30 years, and its content began to reflect nostalgic fantasies for the simpler, happier days of the 1950s, when kids played outside and *Leave It to Beaver* was as offensive as TV got. Journalists increasingly used "TV binge" in evergreen articles on the dangers associated with children's exposure to media. While such news reports were born in the 1950s, improved technology (larger screens, color TVs, and remote controls) available at lower prices during the late 1970s coincided with an increase in news articles on potential dangers for young people. Journalism profiled families whose children were voracious watchers and described how those habits had "dramatically altered the pattern of family life" (Ricklefs, 1976, p. 1). As cable television expanded the number of channels and the variety of content beyond what network-era parents were used to, journalists increasingly raised alarms about the dangers prolonged exposure posed for youngsters. Syndicated columnist Carl Rowan (1984) feared that abundant coverage of suicide might breed copycats: "I have never swallowed the argument that television portrayals of murders and bank robberies provoke more people to perpetrate homicides or hold up banks. But I confess to a special worry about the impact of a television binge about teenage suicides."

Seattle Times columnist Geoffrey Cowley (1985) wrote an alarming piece called "Care Scare" about the mistreatment that working parents might not be aware of in Washington State's 7,600 daycare facilities. Beyond the more publicized sexual and physical abuse, he reported that daycares often neglect children by parking them in front of television sets: "Day care should be an enriching, educational experience," according to one quote, "not just a television binge." After spending months cooped up with their children during the Great Lockdown of 2020, many COVID-19 parents may agree!

In addition to warnings, 1980s journalists also offered nervous parents solutions to combat television's alluring power over impressionable minds. Allan Thompson (1988) reported on the salubrious effects experienced by a 10-year-old who took a one-year hiatus from TV. Despite his "worthwhile" sacrifice, the fourth grader "figures he'll go on a bit of a television binge in the next few weeks catching up with the new shows he missed." The paternalism in these pieces tacitly suggests that TV in large quantities is inherently dangerous and that children cannot be trusted to control themselves around it. Parents who "in the womb [were] exposed to Milton Berle ... sucked baby formula with Captain Kangaroo ... and by the age of four watching anything put before [them]" (Kamenetz, 1979, p. A19) were not reassured that the abundance of choices from cable TV would improve the culture. Instead, they were offered strategies for TV detox and TV abstinence.

These "just say no" uses of "TV binge" reinforced, through omission of explanation or counter argument, the narrative that television watching is a distraction with the potential to harm children. Binges were framed as large doses of a passive activity. There was no mention of healthy content that might be binged; all TV is unhealthy and, in the case of Rowan (1984), potentially lethal. In these articles, "binge" was meant literally, and abstinence from TV was always tacitly and sometimes overtly encouraged. Without irony, journalists identified viewers as the agents of TV binges and impressed on authority figures the goal of limiting viewer agency and "TV time" for fear of the negative outcomes of exposure to the seductive medium. While the novelty and the uncertainty of cable television may have driven newspapers to publish these stories, their language indicates no ambiguity as to the meaning of a "TV binge." When a term is unclear, journalists should provide explanation. The absence of a terminal explanation implies understanding. In 1980s journalism, the meaning of "TV binge" was fixed and uncomplicated: a lot of a bad thing. Marathon TV and TV marathon came to be increasingly used for shows with adult audiences. Journalists eschewed "binge" in highbrow previews of broadcast movie marathons and of plus-sized episodes like the two-and-a-half-hour Lehigh Valley, Pennsylvania, premier of the British soap *East Enders*—the "Cockney saga is closer to 'Hill Street Blues' than it is to 'Dynasty'... Britain's most popular television marathon" (Lawler, 1988, p. T01). A patina of shame coated binge articulations for the remainder of the 20th century, even as the term transformed into the ironic foil for early binge-viewers in the 1990s (GregSerl, 1998).

Control and Consumption

During the 1990s, the diffusion of cable reached ubiquity. I remember when my family final got wired in 1992. Fears from the war on drugs gave way to fears of American overconsumption and obesity. Journalists increasingly linked threats to Americans' health and culture with binge food and with TV consumption. This increase coincided with the spread of cable and satellite access, with the expansion of available channels, and with an increase in national obesity rates (CDC, 2006). There were hundreds of articles addressing American consumption habits that didn't specifically use the word combinations of "binge" and "television," but they nonetheless reinforced the frames of a collective understanding about idiot boxes and about couch potatoes (see Chapter 4).

Turnstall's (1988) piece titled "In France the Pleasures of Eating Are More in Talking" painted a morbid tableau of Americans living "in the land of the late-night binge and the television-snack marathon." In 1990, a *Minneapolis Star Tribune* story described how a United Church of Christ parent group took "a week of television abstinence ... to discover what family life is like without TV" (Freeborn, 1990). The *Grand Rapids Press* columnist Charles Honey (1993), profiled local teenagers who chose not to watch in a piece titled "UNPLUGGED In a Land of Couch Potatoes, a Few Bravely Disconnect and Declare, 'Out, Darn Set.'" That year, Chris Cornell (1993) reported on a Florida father who commoditized his children's TV watching time through a technology called TV Allowance. The device hooked up to a television's power source and could be programmed to cut off after a preset number of minutes each week. The piece led with the following proclamation:

"parents are waging war to wean the children from a diet of TV, TV and more TV." This seizure and regulation of the TV set was needed because "children had a tendency to go on a TV binge." Cornell reported that the TV Allowance technology, available for only $29.99, brought families closer together, though some enterprising teens would save their allowance for weekend binges. Again, the meaning of a TV binge during this period was rarely contextualized beyond the modifier "cable." It was still a noun meaning too much TV, any of which was accepted to be indulgent and too much of which was potentially pathological.

Rewinding to Find the Easter Egg Gerunds (1986, 1988, 1991, and 1999)

Prior to 1986, journalists had used "TV binge" to describe plus-sized programming and content and then to describe the plus-sized TV sessions journalists and viewers could go on. Such sessions were akin to riding a paternoster elevator. Viewers could get on for as long as they liked, but they had no control over the direction their TV experience moved. The increase in channels during the 1980s did give them an array of different paternoster elevators, which they could nimbly hop between with their remote controls. But content flowed in one direction (start to finish) from timeslot to timeslot, from day to day, and from season to season. Viewers had no control over when a show aired and no ability to stop or to change direction; they just went along for the ride. A broadcast TV binge could be defined solely by quantity—how long you watched whatever passed in front of you.

VCRs empowered viewers to disrupt that flow. The elevators could now be stopped, moved backward, and even accelerated past those pesky advertising floors. Through VCR technology, viewers became their own micro-broadcasters with increased control over their personal viewing experience. This dismayed powerful production studios, like Universal and Disney, which sued the Sony Corporation, maker of the Betamax video recorder, in 1977 for copyright violations (Bianculli, 1984). Like some sports leagues feared in the 1940s, if the entertainment was available at home, ticket sales might decline. Studios alleged viewers would be less likely to go to the movies and, as the technology developed, purchase their movies on tape. After lower courts sided with Sony on First Amendment grounds, the Ninth Circuit Court of Appeals overturned that ruling and held that such recordings were a violation of the studios' copyright protections. In 1984, the U.S. Supreme Court gave a definitive answer. In a 5–4 decision, "the justices concluded that the private taping of a TV program by consumers for viewing at a later time amounts to 'fair use' of the material and is therefore permitted" (Mann, 1984, p. 1).

While production companies lost, the ruling did not hurt their bottom lines as they had feared. It did, however, legalize "time-shifting." By allowing viewers to capture the content and to consume it when, where, and how they wanted (provided it wasn't for profit), VCRs transferred some control over television from broadcast networks to viewers. It was through them that underground fan groups cropped up and engaged in proto-binging activities, sharing their home video libraries through fanzines (Stevens, 2021). That power shift required different terms to articulate more clearly how TV could now be watched. Non-early adopters of technology may first encounter new terms and innovations in technology journalism during the "awareness stage" of diffusion, and they often rely on that journalism to gather information during the "interest stage" (Beal and Bohlen, 1956). So while VCRs were marketed as machines to take control of viewing experiences, journalists who used terms such as time-shifting were forced to provide brief explanations each time they used them as the technology became more and more common (Pothier, 1981). Just as TV marathon was a hot term in 1950–1952, so too was "time-shifting" from 1981 to 1984. *Philadelphia Inquirer* technology reporter Andy Wickstrom described the practice in a 1983 piece on the viewer control afforded by VCRs: "Their most popular use is called time-shifting. You can't be in front of your set at 10 p.m. for 'Hill Street Blues,' so you start your recorder at that time, manually or via the timer. Your TV is dark, but the recorder is on. The next day you have a free hour before dinner, 'Hill Street' is at your command."

While these kinds of articles on time-shifting were common in the early 1980s, few described using a VCR to consume multiple episodes of a show in a single sitting—binge-watching as we now conceive it—because of some challenges. (1) VCRs and blank tapes were relatively expensive and intimating for many people. (2) The Supreme Court did not rule on the legality of recording content from televisions until 1984. (3) The ability to capture an entire season of a show would require waiting until the season was over and ensuring that the VCR was set to record each episode each week and ensuring there was sufficient tape on each VHS to capture the entire episode. (4) As I described in Chapter 1, the perceived value of most broadcast television at the time did not justify the risks or the effort. Note, it was Hollywood film studios that sued Sony, not television networks. The real value of time-shifting in the 1980s was reported to be in-home movie libraries and "freeing viewers from helpless dependence on TV schedules, programming practices and wasted time while waiting or sitting through mediocre TV (which is most TV) while waiting for a specific program" (Pothier, 1981, p. L9). After the lawsuit, JVC and other VHS VCR companies (Sony's Betamax technology never caught on) used the decriminalization of home movie libraries to flog their wares. TV shows were the secondary benefit—a convenience for those who could not be there to watch a single broadcast.

Perhaps this is why the first TV/VCR-related binge-watching usage didn't appear until December 21, 1986, when Wickstrom wrote about last-minute Christmas presents for VCR enthusiasts. In a paragraph under his most luddite gift suggestion—Scotch tape—the columnist asked readers the following question: "Are you a confirmed weekday time-shifter, saving up the soap operas for weekend *binge viewing*?" (p. 11; emphasis added). This is the first printed usage of the term *binge viewing*, which is a far closer synonym to binge-watching than marathon. And while the term only appeared three times more times in newspapers before 2002, Wickstrom, in addition to Bob Donahue's "MASSIVE binge watching" in the 1996 X-Files Usernet group, should be recognized for first using the gerund.

Wickstrom meant something different than a "traditional" 20th-century TV binge when he wrote about "binge viewing" and about "time-shifter." We know this because (a) the terms were associated with relatively new television roles and practices with VCR technology, which (b) required Wickstrom to provide an explanation. Additionally, he imagined viewers controlling their binge experiences, which differentiates them from those watching live wall-to-wall political or sports coverage. Furthermore, unlike the 1970s TV binges these were non-linear binge-viewings of binge-serials with sequential story arcs. Importantly, Wickstrom gives the viewers identity beyond the channel-surfing couch potato or the self-dosing cultural critic. He positions "time-shifters" as savvy TV viewers and VCRs as the technology through which they gain the affordance of "binge viewing." His meaning making was more complicated than previous uses of "TV binge." The viewer was controlling their television-watching experience, outwitting the broadcasters and the sponsors, while gorging so voraciously on serials that they needed Scotch tape to mend the VHS tapes.

That complication could not be conveyed as simply by a "TV binge" or as precisely by a "TV marathon." The gerund "binge viewing" connotes a freedom to move outside the confines of traditional understanding. While still a noun, a gerund takes the shape of a present progressive verb (watching and viewing). In this form, it is a potentially continuous and temporally movable activity, rather than a discrete event (getting on and off the elevator), which active viewers control to manage their time beyond the constraints of the networks' fixed schedules. By time-shifting, the viewer controls when, where (on other VCRs), and, to some extent, by what they will be entertained. Binge-viewing is a demonstration of control over the content, and yet the language ironically conveys pathology in that choice as if that power has gone to the viewers' heads. The tapes are being used so frequently that they have frayed, yet the insatiable binge-viewer continues watching freely.

The next appearance of binge-viewing was in an August 28, 1988, *Toronto Star* article about the Vancouver Fringe Festival (Masters, 1988). John Masters used the term to describe attending multiple theatrical performances over 10 days to create a cultural experience tailored to the viewer's tastes. "The Fringe idea was to offer groups performance space based not on artistic merit, but on who asked first. As a result, Fringes are weird and woolly affairs with a few real gems tossed in.... A Fringe is a cultural crap shoot, but an inexpensive one" (p. D4). He captured the excitement and joy of being able to immerse one's self, at one's own discretion, in a variety of stories. This was one of the first articles I came across during my research of journalistic articulations, and it evoked a Proustian flood of memories of my first binge-viewing experience, which I discuss in Chapter 6. Then and now, theater inhabits a higher cultural stratum than television. Masters (1988) exalted the "appeal" of such "cultural binge viewing" without mention of the negative side effects that accompany journalistic description of TV binges. Beyond theater's cultural higher ground, the navigation of more than 600 plays in more than 30 locations involved a level of physical activity that 1980s television binge-watching, because of its spatially immobile technology, lacked.

"Binge viewing" next appeared in a newspaper on May 31, 1991, when Virginia Hall wrote: "The prospect of 300-plus TV channels is oddly reassuring, all considered. After a few dozen lost weekends of binge viewing, Americans may be ready to pull the plug" (p. C9). The *Kansas City Star* columnist used most of her 742 words paraphrasing Neil Postman's (1985) *Amusing Ourselves to Death* to depict the dangers of an expanding number of cable channels. Unlike Wickstrom (1986) or Masters (1988), she did not specify a specific show or genre in her usage. Instead she argued that the available variety on cable television would lead to mindless channel surfing through a vaster wasteland. Any agency the viewer may have had, in Hall's estimation, was traded for the pleasure of passive amusement. As she saw it, "the nature of public discourse has been altered, fragmented and trivialized by [television], as well as the nature of public institutions and events." Some 26 years later, critic Brooke Gladstone (2017) made a similar, if more nuanced, argument about social media.

The final journalistic appearance of binge-viewing in the 20th century turned out to be a most likely unintentional pastiche of many of the previous uses over the previous 52 years. On December 1, 1999, *New Orleans Times Picayune* TV columnist Mark Lorando penned a pre–Christmas viewing guide titled "It's a Wonderful Month." His 25-day schedule for linear consumption of holiday programming also captures the joy and the shame of binge-watching that would become the hallmark tone of 21st-century journalists. It is written as an ironic cautionary menu for those prone to kitsch Yuletide compulsion: "In order to prevent binge viewing and an overdose of what my colleague Benjamin Morrison calls 'TTMoC'—short for 'The True Meaning of Christmas'—we're recommending a strict diet of one Christmas special per day." He leads with the following admission of "addiction" for the cloying, predicable happiness of holiday TV: "A jingle bell junkie. A deck-the-hall-ic. It's sap, but true: I never met a Christmas special I didn't like.... Which makes today the official start of The Most Wonderful Time of the Year on TV—and for us yule fools, the most dangerous" (p. E1). While viewers' consumption is based on broadcast schedules, Lorando has curated an intentional sampling of Christmas-related content across a variety of channels. The result is a light-hearted acknowledgment of the ambivalence that has come to characterize binge-watching—control and excess, joy and shame. Lorando's article contained the final appearance of the gerund in 20th-century journalism. Its usage captures much of the 20th century's categories of TV binge and marathon, and its irony portends 21st-century uses of binge-watching.

Binge as Defiance

Besides these first four instances of "binge-viewing," journalists continued to use "TV binge" during the last two decades of the 20th century, as in the recommended Al Roker TV binge during the Blizzard of 1993 (Gay, 1993) and a TV binge of JFK Jr.'s funeral (Goldberg, 1999). These 30 articulations follow the traditional 20th-century norms that connote "TV binge" as a lot of some kind of TV content, related to the fourth, fifth, and sixth master usages of TV and marathon (see list on 30). When HBO re-ran Season 1 of *The Sopranos* in the run-up to the Season 2 drop in December 1999, journalists reported that the premium cable channel "would pre-empt a large portion of its prime-time schedule for a week to run a marathon of the first 13 episodes of the series" (AJC, 1999). HBO was running the marathon, not the viewers.

After the ball dropped on the new millennium, and Y2K came and went without apocalypse, reports began appearing of Americans binge-watching as an act of defiance. Perhaps these were, as the OED claims, rooted in the rebellious ideas bandied around late 1990s online fan communities. The expansion of internet access, as a new, albeit primitive portal, for seemingly endless consumption of video, may have help spread those ideas. In 1995, 42 percent of U.S. adults hadn't even heard of the internet and another 21 percent "knew it had something to do with computers and that was about it" (Fox & Raine, 2014). A decade later, nearly 70 percent of them were online. However, based on the journalistic coverage, it was DVRs and especially DVDs that empowered viewers to watch and to re-watch episode after episode of popular and long-forgotten shows with a growing alacrity that was somehow both nostalgic and disaffected with the past. The reporting appeared in first-person accounts of journalists and their families attempting to understand viewers' role in 21st-century television while still bound to the idiot box narrative of the previous 50 years.

In 2000, critic Heather Seggel journaled her week of TV attendance as a Nielsen viewer for *Bitch Magazine.* While she used "binge" to refer to watching several episodes of *Ally McBeal* on live TV, her writing indicates greater viewer control through her power to influence as a Nielsen viewer and also as a blogger: "If I don't watch, *V.I.P.* could be canceled. Oh, the freedom, the responsibility, the temptation to just cheat and fill the whole thing in now! But no. I'll be strong ... and I'll strategize." At the same time, Nielsen ratings were no longer entirely capturing television viewership, rendering the standard by which advertising revenue was measured inaccurate (Lotz, 2017, loc 312).

In the early 2000s, reality television and interactive game shows sprang to prominence across network television as broadcasters went on something of an *Idol-Survivor-Millionaire* binge. Critics have analyzed and lamented this era of "factual television," but the surge in reality programming served to sharpen the distinction between traditional advertising-driven linear TV and so-called quality TV (Hill, 2005). While similar to the film/TV cultural divide of the 20th century, technology was now empowering viewers to curate a more à la cart TV experience that could be as highbrow or lowbrow as they wanted. In 2001, Andy Smith cataloged his summer viewing habits, including a "reality TV binge" of contestants eating live crickets, from networks indulging "their odder impulses" (p. G-03). But the *Providence Journal* TV critic also praised the unexpected quality of HBO programming, calling the subscription-based, premium channel "an oasis," with "characters who become deeper and more interesting as the show progresses" (Smith, 2001). He also marveled at his ability to control his binge-watching experience across an ever-widening range of television culture.

Conversely, *Rocky Mountain News* critic Dusty Saunders (2001) described his "reality-TV binge" as blurring the lines between news and entertainment, leading us deeper into a 21st-century simulacrum. Television, he argued, is "caught in a reality warp" (p. 2D). This sentiment was echoed by many in the wake of the terrorist attacks of September 11, 2001. *Badger Herald* columnist Jay Senter (2001) admitted that he'd "skipped classes, neglected homework and become antisocial so that I can take in the non-stop, never-ending coverage" (p. 1). He discovered through his multi-day "television binge" that he was less interested in the actual events than he "was in observing the way the media were covering them." For Stenter, being able to switch between different angles and commentaries within the wall-to-wall coverage, which he compared to action movies, gave him perverse feelings of control and entertainment.

Fears of kids watching too much TV continued during these years, but now parents were noticing how the digital divide made controlling consumption harder. Kathleen Rizzo-Young (2002) described her children's rebellious "binge viewing" during a seven-month prohibition on weeknight TV. In the frame of earlier idiot box critiques, Rizzo-Young leads with nostalgia for the passive watching of the network era while decrying the contemporary television scourge: "In the 70s, there was a background soundtrack—the TV ... but back then, what was the worst that could happen from too much TV? You'd become the office pop culture junkie? Or really good at trivia. Today, depending on whom you listen to, the consequences for a kid of too much TV can range from obesity to a predisposition to violence."

Because her children began watching news, the only TV allowed during the week, she concluded that "it's the TV itself that's addictive, not the content." But it is the use of technology for "binge viewing" that Hall finds most problematic: "We've noticed that during the winter our son has attempted to 'even the score' by 'stocking up' on TV shows on the weekends to prepare for the week ahead. And to make the joy of viewing last longer, he has been known to repeat his favorite threads of TV dialogue for days afterward. (If someone could plug the multiplication tables into the 'SpongeBob Square Pants' theme music, we'll have a genius on our hands)" (p. A6). While not a definition, this description indicates that binge-viewing can be the act of a single viewer through technology to control consumption, a role reminiscent of 1980s time-shifters and of parental regulation of the hours. The language also implies that it was an act of defiance by less powerful but more savvy teens whose quick wits should be redirected toward more productive endeavors than staring at the idiot box. Ironically, Hall may have unintentionally enhanced her son's viewing experience by forcing him to binge-watch *SpongeBob SquarePants* on weekends. As Perks (2015) argues, "Stockpilers are not mindlessly hoarding content; rather, they are mindfully choosing to engage the content in a time and manner that will enhance their gratification" (p. 70).

The journalistic narrative of technology as a tool for rebellion against both parental authority and network control coincided with the rise of prestige television (Leverette, Ott, & Buckley, 2008). While DVRs and more streamlined on-demand options allowed viewers to time shift, they were less reliable for the multiple sequential consumption of serial television. Both protocols left viewers reliant on networks to supply the content they would curate. TiVo could only record what was broadcast and required fast-forwarding through the commercials as well as clunky navigation between episodes. On-demand variety from MVPDs was becoming more robust, but it could be spotty and ephemeral. I remember the frustration of attempting to binge *Weeds* on-demand and discovering mid-season that Comcast offered episodes 6 and 8 but not 7. DVDs gave viewers better control and commercial-free variety, which may be why they are the technology most associated with early binge-watching.

As DVD players became increasingly popular, studios increasingly began marketing and distributing the content of their vast libraries (Pamer, 2006). At first, films mostly populated the DVD market, but, as I discuss in the Binge Technology section of Chapter 1, things were about to change. In 2003, more television shows were released on DVD than movies. While not surprising given the numbers of available titles that had previously been perceived to be unworthy of such an august format, this industrial shift was an indication of the changes in TV's reputation that were to come during the next decade. Journalists' coverage reflected this new abundance of texts and the associated changing habits of viewers.

The first usage of the term "binge-watching" in journalism reflects that preference. On April 12, 2003, the hyphenated gerund appeared in the *Frederick News Post*, which the Oxford English Dictionary (OED) recognizes as the first usage. "Fox Aminated Series 'Family Guy' Finds a New Home on DVD" was written by Zap2It.com managing editor Brill Bundy and distributed by Knight Ridder Tribune News Services; it appeared in papers such as the *Frederick News Post* as well as the *Beaver County Times* and the *Press-Register* of Mobile, Alabama. In it, Bundy captured the pseudo-hacker satisfaction that fans, myself included, got from using DVDs to enhance their entertainment experience. Her tone indicates an understanding of the practice beyond the sheer quantity of episodes or the amount of time spent. Bundy speaks to the qualitative enhancements of binge-watching while demonstrating the sense of viewer empowerment. It wasn't just the consumption of multiple episodes; it was the use of technology to enjoy a show in a way that was better than what a broadcaster could provide. It was also an act of defiance and a muscular yet reclined demonstration of pop cultural savvy.

Viewers were using technology to make a show flow better, while telling the broadcaster, in this case Fox, that it had screwed up. Despite winning multiple Emmys during its first 49-episode, three-season run, Fox cancelled *Family Guy* in 2002, favoring less expensive, less offensive (to sponsors) reality programming, much to the chagrin of its fans. The release of the first two seasons on DVD became "one of Amazon.com's top sellers, [showing] that demand for the Griffin family ... hasn't diminished" (Bundy, 2003, p. C10). Paradoxically, the purchase paid Fox while apparently defying the network. As Bundy notes, "While binge-watching an entire season's worth of a series in a couple of sittings can lead to such revelations as network meddling (cough, cough, 'Sports Night'), 'Family Guy' has the opposite effect." For "diehards" this new kind of viewing experience was a way to show Fox what a mistake it had made. I was one of those rabid *Family Guy* fans, and I purchased this DVD box set in 2003 and binge-watched it religiously and repeatedly. Dialogue from the show became the shared slang among the young adults I lived, worked, and played with in Boston. It became, as the pan-genre fandom literature suggests, a dialogic password whose use could instantly connect strangers in a familiar and subversive narrative (Robertson, 2014). That that collective viewer rebellion was eventually rewarded served to reinforce the narrative of empowerment. Because of the popularity and cult following of the show through DVD binge-watching, Fox brought *Family Guy* back to the airwaves where it continues to entertain and to offend millions to this day.

Bundy's usage was significant because it was instructive and also because it contained binge-watching in its hyphenated form. OED cites this as the first journalistic usage, and while I argue that Wickstrom's "binge viewing" deserves recognition as a nearly identical synonym, Bundy's was the first hyphenation of binge and watching. That little line marked the significance of the connection of the two words; it was their engagement. The process of compound words going from open to hyphenated to closed also indicates a term's commonality (Bragg, 2003). The open form of "binge viewing" as a compound indicated how rarely the term was used. As stories about binge-watching increased over the next decade, hyphenation of the compound word became more common. From there, the emergence of other more active forms of binge began appearing in journalism, while (spoiler alert) the narrative of viewer empowerment would be increasingly co-opted by newer disruptive video platforms.

Binge-Viewing to Binge-Watching to Binge-Viewer to Binge-Watch (2003–2011)

It took nearly 40 years, from Rosen to Wickstrom, for TV binge to become a gerund. It took another 17 years for the gerund to be hyphenated by Bundy (2003). But from 2003 to 2011, the term began morphing more quickly as usage of the noun "TV binge" gave way to "binge-viewing" and from there to the definable role of binge-viewer and the active verb binge-watch. This morphological transformation coincided with three important TV advancements—DVDs (texts), DVRs (hardware), and improved on-demand programming (software). Not surprisingly, journalists' new constructions during that eight-year period often came in articles focusing on these new technologies as drivers of changing viewer uses.

New York Times TV critic Emily Nussbaum (2003) provided one of the first instructive rationales for DVD binge-watching of specific shows. In "Taking Back Television, One Disc at a Time," she writes: "DVD's are perfect for fast-paced arc shows like '24,' increasing the intensity of the action and introducing the sickly pleasures of binge-viewing." This was the first hyphenated compound usage of "binge-viewing" in journalism. Her brief articulation of the viewer's role was machine dependent ("DVD technology can allow viewers to act like scholars instead of passive recipients") and couched by addiction language ("it's 5 in the morning and time to call in sick for work"). Interestingly, she used "marathon" to describe "the junkiest shows," such as "reality television," that were broadcast in large sequential batches on commercial networks. This choice implied a technological separation between viewer-controlled binge-viewing and broadcaster-supplied marathons. While both may be "hypnotic," DVDs afforded the former, allowing viewers to "take back the television" from the control of the latter.

DVRs existed in the late 20th century, but MVPDs remained stubbornly outside the DVR marketplace until the early 21st century. Successful corporations are loathe to move quickly, especially when the movement puts their proven revenue-generating models at risk (Lotz, 2014). For a cable provider, the potential loss of ad revenue from sponsors, who prefer viewers not be able to skip ads, was an obvious disincentive. Their hesitance to offer DVRs allowed TiVo to gain significant market share. The result was that viewers were skipping ads anyway with expensive equipment that cable companies could have been leasing or selling to customers. As Lotz (2017) points out, "strategies built upon the constant flow from one program to the next were so entrenched in the lived experience of television that they came to seem inherent to the medium rather than as protocols of broadcasting as a distribution system." Consider the network practice of hammocking—airing a less popular show between two popular ones in the hopes of catching new viewers who were too lazy to change the channel. To compete with TiVo, MVPDs began to offer DVR systems to subscribers that allowed them to record live content while containing that usage and capturing the resulting data within the companies' ecosystems.

The proliferation of DVR technology beyond early adopters allowed for the mainstreaming of new viewing habits—including binge-watching—reflected in the news coverage of that time. The novelty and the growing popularity coincided with journalists in early 2003 providing rough proto-definitions of these activities. Paul Davies (2003) described 10 new viewing behaviors among London subscribers to Telwest's new DVR system. These included "'buffering,' where favourite programmes are regularly moved to a more favourable time slot, and 'stacking,' where several episodes of a programme are stored for a later 'binge viewing session.'" While this usage is adjectival and unhyphenated, it indicates the growing recognition of binge-watching as an act of viewer control made possible by technologies.

Birth of the Binge-Viewer

Perhaps it was the new millennium, but journalists of the early 2000s often described new viewer practices and new TV technologies through contrasts to older TV practices that were limited by old technology. This was also the beginning of what NPR TV critic David Bianculli called *The Platinum Age of Television* (2016) and television scholars call TV III (Jenner, 2014; Lotz, 2017). The "out with the old, in with the new" motif began carrying hints of disdain for broadcast practices. Journalists also described TV's improved content quality in contrast to its low-brow past. "When did American TV get like this?" mused an astonished British critic (Dalley, 2004). *Newsday* TV writer Diane Werts (2004) argued that the content of TV's long-derided vast wasteland should be "regarded as kitsch classics." It was also around this time that journalists began hinting at a narrative in which technologically empowered viewers were affecting the industry. The narrative of viewers disrupting broadcasters' control of flow was similar to the news stories that hailed VCRs as revolutionary. But these early 2000s stories went further, with reports that viewers might themselves be advancing television culture through their use of technology. Rosenbloom (2005) argued that "binge viewing of [a] TV series is creating a new breed of aficionado." Werts (2004) cited those aficionados and described their DVD empowerment as "a viewing revolution." Without calling them "binge-viewers," she interviewed tech-savvy cult fans who jokingly used drug addiction language to describe their binging. It was in those uses that the public heard the language of superfan subcultures that had been covertly undermining broadcast network control since the late 1970s. Now those change agents—devotees and real artists—were being quoted, albeit sparsely, by entertainment journalists as sources behind a rebellion that was about to disrupt 50 years of TV industry orthodoxy (Stevens, 2021).

Gayle MacDonald (2005) was the first journalist to use "binge watcher" and "binge viewer"—neither hyphenated. Like Werts (2004), she spotlighted techie superfans as demonstrators of the new affordances of DVDs, including Gord Lacey of Edmonton "who runs the website tvshowsondvd.com" and "Toronto TV producer Anna-Lea Boeki [who] is a self-confessed TV-DVD binge viewer." Boeki used tongue-in-cheek addict lingo to describe her viewing and reported similar symptoms from binge immersion as depicted in the binge-viewer ads of media companies after 2012 (Chapter 4) and as described by viewers (Chapter 5). Thanks to early blogging technology and DVD-enabled binge-watching, binge-viewers were performing roles once reserved for TV critics. MacDonald (2005) also interviewed Steve Cohen, owner of Videoflicks in Toronto, who explained that "there's [a] huge demand for nostalgia titles." Cohen stated that superfans flock to "cult-TV-DVDs" like *Freaks and Geeks* (1999). The critically acclaimed comedy-drama was a show about misfits whose misfit fans believed had been cancelled too early by CBS because it was "too smart" for mainstream TV audiences. As with *Family Guy*, journalists spun the narrative that clever binge-viewers and online fan groups were beginning to dismantle the structures supporting the idiot box.

A 2006 *Chicago Tribune* article titled "Binge TV: New Breed of Couch Potato" described how binge-viewers were disrupting studio publishing norms: "DVD box sets of TV shows are now blockbusters, filling 15 of the top 20 slots last week on amazon.com" (p. 52). That same year, Michelle Griffin (2006) penned a first-person feature for Melbourne's *Sunday Age* titled "Turn On, Tune In, Pig Out," which evaluated the addictive qualities of binge-watching across a range of content.

She describes viewing patterns illustrative of the viewer taking control of their consumption and losing control of it:

> AS SOON as I finished watching the season one finale of *Veronica Mars* on Channel Ten, I went online and bought the second season on DVD from Amazon. My favourite show had been shunted to the fag-end of Friday nights, and I didn't know when the show might be aired again.
>
> As it happened, new episodes screened on Ten, unpromoted, in weeks, but by then I had my six-DVD fix of the next 22 episodes. What followed wasn't pretty: I watched more than 18 hours of the show in three weeks, alone, and often on the DVD drive on my computer. My weekly treat had become a binge [p. 13].

She consulted Dr. Andrew Campbell, "Australia's foremost expert on cyber-psychology," who assured her that she doesn't "have a problem. Yet...." provided she can eschew the temptation to hum the *Veronica Mars* theme song in public (p. 13). Dr. Campbell went on to tell her how he binge-watched *The West Wing*. The upshot of this piece is that with the new viewing powers comes responsibility, not just in how much we watch but what. This differentiation of quality meant that not *all* TV content is bad. In fact, show quality may even be a psychological diagnostic consideration. She quotes new media scholar and *24* binger Mark Pesce, who advises, "Our media diet needs to be as rounded as our food diet.... There's always the temptation to consume junk all day. We need to learn how to pick and choose" (p. 13). Prestige dramas are positioned as gourmet and reality shows as junk.

The narrative that binge-gourmands were raising TV's cultural standards continued subtly circulating in entertainment sections of mid-aught newspapers. In the run-up to the 2006 Emmy awards, Melissa Pamer (2006) wrote that "some DVD fans live for the binge, and the industry seems to like their choice." The *Los Angeles Times* TV critic asked, "Is a populist cabal of remote-control-wielding DVD-obsessed fans controlling the Emmys?" While she answered, "OK, not quite," Pamer did note that "it's impossible to look at these series showing this year without noting the intersection between Hollywood awards culture and this evolving consumer behavior"). Gilbert Seldes (1950) had lamented that television reduced viewers to robots and culture to a Pandora's box. In 2006, it seemed a rebellious, obsessive faction of those robots were smashing open the box and reprogramming its contents.

Pamer profiles these anti-establishment binge-viewers who used technology to enhance their TV experience despite the addictive side effects. Bodily sacrifice for improved viewing is valorized as sports fans valorize athletes who play through pain "going to the limits of endurance ... drunk with 'animal' fatigue" (Brohm, 1978, p. 23; Serazio, 2019,

p. 171). Through a series of interviews, readers were introduced to a sub-
culture of self-described "addicts," whose quotes sound on their surface like an AA meeting: ""This show is like crack"; "We're like junkies";
"I was hooked" (Pamer, 2006). These subversive "21st Century [sic] TV
watchers" grew up reading books instead of watching television. They
chose not to "subscribe to cable or satellite TV. Some don't even own
a TV, instead watching on computers or video iPods. Yet this group
has the devotion of the recently converted." Netflix's chief content offi-
cer Ted Sarandos was also quoted in the article calling binge-watching
(hyphenated) "a new behavior." He described the abundance of TV content his company was shipping to subscribers before admitting that he
too "has succumbed to binge-watching."

Pamer's description painted binge-viewers as rebellious freedom
fighters wielding technology as a weapon against a monolithic industry that could no longer ignore their cries for TV liberation. By 2006,
increased bandwidth allowed networks to experiment with streaming
content. But these initial ventures were reportedly insufficient: "Unfortunately, each episode stays up for only one week, which discourages
binge viewing" (Setoodeh, 2006). Journalists began writing about the
demise of network TV through the kind of piracy that they had speculated would kill the music industry a decade earlier and TV a decade
before that: "Web TV is the medium of the future. Can traditional sta-
tions keep up?" (Harlow, 2007).

Even as MVPD on-demand variety grew, binge-viewers reportedly demanded more. Commercial interruptions were a common complaint, but the "rebels" also began associating most network content
with the 20th-century identity of an idiot box in a vast wasteland. By
the time "binge-viewer" earned its hyphen, news articles appeared with
longer descriptions of the growing rebel group's rejection of the television industry and its "low brow" commercial content through cord
cutting:

> Unless I'm sucked into a Philadelphia Experiment–style tear in the
> space-time continuum and find myself back at age 20, unemployed and
> with bags of weed to smoke, I don't need 50 TV channels.... Don't get me
> wrong, I've watched loads of telly, and I'm not anti–TV at all, but people
> often assume the fact I haven't seen Australia's Next Top Model is a form of
> snobbery. It's actually just that I'd rather binge-watch three episodes of *The
> Wire* on my own terms, without the Doors Plus advertisement—the cheap
> ad agency equivalent of waterboarding—interrupting the narrative arc at
> 12-minute intervals [Northover, 2009].

Journalists during this period differentiated "binge-watching"
from "TV binge" based on content and ritual. A kind of terminal

hierarchy began to take shape—the order was an indication of both taste and control. Several articles in the early 2000s mentioned "reality TV binges." Journalists in these usages were addressing the exuberance of networks in producing reality programs. Their meaning was more akin to early uses of "binge" and "marathon" in reference to advertising buys (Rosen, 1955; Wolters, 1955; WSJ Staff, 1961). Viewers were rarely the ones going on the binge, and, when mentioned, they were homogenized into "the public" or "TV audience" as in this *Entertainment Weekly* review: "The skimpy ratings generated by summer fiascos like Fame and Paradise Hotel indicate that the American viewing public's reality television binge has led to an inevitable purge. For those who feel like they've overindulged in the genre, the ideal remedy may be a show that's almost 100 percent artificial: The Hollywood Squares" (Fretts, 2003).

Even when journalists turned binge into an active verb, placing "TV" in front of it indicated commercial broadcast viewing: "I sometimes TV binge on 'The First 48,' 'Intervention,' 'Dog the Bounty Hunter,' 'I Survived,' 'Snapped' and anything else on Discovery Channel" (Bearden, 2008). These uses are closer in meaning to broadcasters airing an anthology, like a James Bond marathon, rather than fans intentionally binge-watching a sequential series, like a box set of *24*. Again, order indicates flow control. A TV binge was also used to mean general watching—journalists sometimes wrote the term to mean any and all content over a period of time. A review of Bill McKibben's *Age of Missing Information* described the author's months-long, daily consumption (eight hours per day) of every show available through his Virginia cable provider as a "TV binge" (Knifton, 1992). The culture critic had recorded 24 hours of content from each of the 94 channels providing him with a diversity of texts, the order or selection of which was determined by the broadcaster. His experiment was a super-marathon of TV-watching as constructed by journalists in the 20th century, but it fell outside of 21st-century usages of binge-watching. In the early 2000s, as the verb "to binge-view" began to appear in news articles, journalists reserved the action of binge-watching to refer to the consumption of a single series in television (Werts, 2006) or a single auteur or oeuvre in cinema (Rochlin, 2003).

Medium Is the Messenger

By 2011, journalists' descriptions distinguished a "TV binge" from the active verb "binge-watching." The word "television" became conspicuously absent, implying that modes of viewing had moved beyond the tube. When it appeared, it was subordinated by the action. Prestige dramas, particularly those available to stream on Netflix, were labeled "Binge TV" (Simons, 2011). Before, TV had been modifying the kind of binge; now binge was modifying the kind of TV. Journalists of this time seldom used "TV binge" when describing a viewer-controlled, non-broadcast TV consumption. While not quite mainstream behavior, binge-watch was an active verb that was disrupting television.

Binge-watcher and *binge-watching* began appearing in journalism from 2006 to 2011 and their hyphenation became more regular after 2012. Rather than providing formal definitions, journalists gave personal accounts of their experiences and stories of "the techno-savvy" while discussing how the TV industry was attempting to adapt (Harlow, 2007). Their tone was more curious than the patrician New Journalism binges of the 1960s and 1970s. "After subscribing to Netflix, I discovered that I'm a binge-viewer of television. When we had cable, I rarely watched a show regularly because I didn't keep track of television schedules. With Netflix, though, an entire season of a show is just sitting there, waiting to be watched" (Collier, 2011).

Viewer-controlled time management and viewer-curated content became essential to the action of binge-watching as an increasingly personal entertainment experience (Jenner, 2015). With that, journalists focused more on the viewers' specific uses of the technology rather than on the technology itself with a generalized audience. Technology and service, in particular streaming OTTs (over the tops), were still an essential part of the story, but their declination moved from nominative to instrumental and the viewer from accusative to nominative. This took the form of first-person accounts from journalists shaping definitions based on their experiences and those of other binge-viewers. While there were some explanations and descriptions given, prior to 2012 no journalists attempted to offer a formal definition of what the term binge-watching meant. As early TV binges did not need explanation, the nicheness of "binge-watching" did not necessitate formal definitions from journalists yet. As the technology advanced and quality

Binge-Watching/Marathon TV Timeline

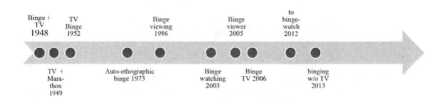

Binge + TV 1948   TV Binge 1952   Binge viewing 1986   Binge viewer 2005   to binge-watch 2012

TV + Marathon 1949   Auto-ethographic binge 1973   Binge watching 2003   Binge TV 2006   binging w/o TV 2013

TV was increasingly prized, there grew a palpable need for the general public to understand what was happening to TV. The narrative of binge-watching disrupting television was primed for viral contagion. It was ready to become the talk of the town. In Chapter 3, I explore how journalists took up the call of reporting on that story through articles that defined binge-watching. Through them we see the struggle for control between creators and consumers shift again as emerging media companies capitalized on inefficiencies in broadcast TV and journalistic conventions to co-opt binge-watching for great profit while cancelling the idiot box identity.

3

High-Definition Control

Newspapers Navigate the Netflix Narrative

> The root of all evil in public and civic affairs of the world lies, in my opinion, in the fact that people either call the same things by different names or different things by the same name
>
> [Karel Havlíček Borovský, 1850?]

What's in a Name?

On January 6, 2014, Dan Jordan, Spencer Larson, and Chris Laughlin sat down in white leather armchairs at the Las Vegas Convention Center. Over the next 87 hours they were surveilled by hundreds of people at the Consumer Electronics Show: medics measured their vital signs and proctors logged their food consumption and bathroom habits. Former NFL quarterback Tim Tebow even showed up to offer them encouragement. On January 10, they got up from their seats and were awarded the Guinness world record for "the longest marathon watching television" (Lynch, 2014).

The event, sponsored by TiVo, marked another milestone in the hyper-adoption and mainstream acceptance of binge-watching. It also demonstrated the liminal space that the word and behavior inhabited. The old-school Guinness (née *The Guinness Book of Records*, 1955) described the 87-hour record as a "marathon" of television-watching (Lynch, 2014). However, TiVo plastered signs on their booth at the convention center promoting the event as "TV binge viewing" (TiVo, 2014). The practice of watching television for extended periods of time is nearly as old as television itself (Dulles, 1940; Felix, 1931; Ives 1928). And for as long as advertising dollars have been tied to ratings, television networks have wanted viewers to watch for as long as possible (McDonald, 1958). But is that binging?

In March 2012, comedian Mark Malkoff tested how many movies

he could watch on Netflix in one month. Over 30 days he watched 252 films, averaging more than 13 hours a day, for a grand total of 404.25 hours. Some reporters called his stunt a "binge" (Woodruff, 2012), while others called it a "marathon" (Kooser, 2012). The stunt earned him a handshake from Netflix CEO Reed Hastings. But was it binge-watching? Movie marathons have been around since the mid–20th century and are still called marathons when they air on broadcast television or even stream (HBO). When Suresh Joachim watched 121 straight hours of movies in 2015, Guinness (2015) called it "the longest marathon watching films." Joachim's record was set in a Johannesburg pop-up cinema, so are the venue and medium what differentiates the two?

Jordan and Larson's record did not last long. In April 2016, Alejandro "AJ" Fragoso shattered their mark, logging 94 hours of viewing. The 25-year-old Brooklynite screened an array of programming, including back-to-back episodes of *Battlestar Galactica*, *Bob's Burgers*, *Curb Your Enthusiasm*, and *Game of Thrones* (Spangler, 2016). For context, the record a decade earlier had stood at 47 hours, eight minutes (Barrett, 2004). Fragoso's record, which still stands, "was achieved by Cyber-Link, using PowerDVD, with the support of Diffusion PR ... in support of CyberLink's new video optimization software for streaming media" (Guinness, 2016). While Guinness still calls it the record for "longest marathon watching television," journalists reporting on the feat used the term "binge-watching" except when referring to Guinness's official name. CNBC actually renamed the record by combining the terms, writing that Fragoso had secured "the Guinness World Record for the longest television binge-watching marathon" (Gibbs, 2016), while *Variety* ran the headline "TV Binge-Watching World Record Set" (Spangler, 2016). Why would journalists use a different term than Guinness? Why do only a handful of the news headlines contain the word "marathon" while nearly all have "binge-watch"? If they are synonyms, why would editors choose "binge" over the official "marathon"? And if they are not synonyms, what is the difference and how is that distinction made? What does binge-watching mean precisely? To date, a clear definition, even among TV scholars, remains elusive (Pittman & Steiner, 2019). In this chapter I provide a functional, multi-part definition based on the work of journalists from 2012 to 2016. I also trace a definitive history of binge-watching's revolutionary narrative through the descriptions, accounts, and sources of those journalists across nearly 10,000 articles. The definition is divided into four parts: (1) Binge Parameters; (2) Bingeable Content, (3) Binge-Watching Rituals; and (4) Binge-Watching Consequences/Significance. In the pages ahead I provide the background and context of this phenomenal period in television history, but if you choose you can cut to the chase.

Although academics have yet to agree on a formal definition, journalists have been offering them since 2012. They suddenly had to. In Chapter 2, I chronicled the news reports on TV binges and marathons starting in the mid–20th century. At first, journalists used marathon and binge interchangeably, but usage distinctions by culture and control (high/low, broadcaster/viewer) began appearing in the 1960s. As the century turned, news reports of binge-viewer subcultures using DVDs to control their experience appeared, and the journalists writing them chose "binge" to refer to an oppositional act in defiance of traditional TV power structures. The early 21st-century narrative of the rebellious superfan reclaiming power from the broadcaster through asymmetric DVD conflict had flown mostly under the public's radar.

If you would like to jump to the binge parameters, turn to 76.

If you would like to skip to the bingeable content hierarchy, turn to 80.

If you want to try the Binge-Watching Rituals, turn to 81.

If you want to discover the consequences and the significance of binge-watching, turn to 85.

By 2010, a broader perception of television content improving the technology existed but the terminology that linked it to culture hadn't yet caught on. Binge-watching remained an extremely rare, insider term, appearing in fewer than 100 articles during the first decade of the 2000s. The act itself may have been happening quite frequently, but the word was seldom printed. Similarly, people had been taking pictures of themselves for centuries, and they even began calling them selfies as early as 2002 (OED). But it wasn't until smartphones with front-facing cameras and the data capacities to post to and view on social media sites became ubiquitous that the term "selfie" entered the zeitgeist. Both binge-watching and selfie were among the OED's 2013 Words of the Year. Binge-watching—with its complex dynamics of creation, consumption, and control—required considerably more explanation. Journalists stepped up en masse to provide that explanation and by so doing shaded not only the contours of what constituted binge-watching but also mainstreamed the narrative of upstart streaming companies enabling viewers to take control of their televisions by binge-watching. Whether journalists were reflecting the phenomenon or fueling it or both, hardly any chose to call it "marathon."

Binge-Watching Reaches a Tipping Point

From 1999 to 2011 "binge-watching" (or other versions) were seen in no more than 11 news articles per year. In 2012, the term suddenly leaped from obscurity to journalists' pens worldwide. Between 2012 and 2016 nearly 10,000 articles mentioned the terms "binge" and "watch" or "binge" and "view" (see Chapter 2 database search note for specifics). In that period, Google queries and n-gram frequencies of those keywords soared. Shares of Netflix (NFLX), the fourth most popular related topic, and the fifth most popular related query, to "binge watch," in Google searches soared 1,380 percent (Yahoo! Finance, n.d.); the number of global users more than tripled (Watson, 2020). Binge-watching became a buzzword that journalists flocked to cover, creating a global fascination fueled by what economist Robert Shiller (2019) called "narrative contagion" (p. xvii).

Isolating the causes of a viral tipping point can be more art than science, but the timing of binge-watching's angle of repose, in terms of news report frequency, coincided with the following key events:

(1) Netflix's first full season release of original programming (*Lilyhammer*, 2012),

(2) the majority penetration of in-home broadband internet among Americans over 30 (Pew, 2017),

(3) the mass shooting in an Aurora, Colorado, movie theater (July 20, 2012), which preceded a sharp decline in American cinema attendance (McClintock, 2012), and

Results of a Google Books Ngram Viewer query of binge-watching from 2006 to 2016. The graph shows the exponential growth in occurrences of the term between 2012 and 2016.

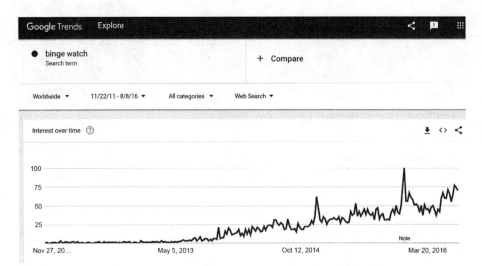

Results of a Google Search Query of binge-watching from November 2011 through August 2016. The graph shows the growth as well as peaks and valleys of searches during the period when binge-watching became a buzzword.

Results of a Google Search Query of binge-watching from November 2011 through August 2016. These are the related topics as they pertain to the above Google Search Query. Notably, Netflix is the number 1 related topic and number 1, 2, and 5 related query indicating a public association between binge-watching and the streaming video company among the public during the mainstreaming period of the term.

(4) AMC's two-part release of the final season of *Breaking Bad* (July 15, 2012), which caused so many people to catch-up binge the first four seasons on Netflix that ratings for the final season "skyrocketed an astounding 442 percent" (Hibberd, 2013). The effect of binge-watching was apparently so profound that, after accepting the 2013 Emmy for Best Drama, *Breaking Bad* showrunner Vince Gilligan actually thanked the streaming video company, saying, "Netflix kept us on the air" (Weisman, 2013). And so the story grew.

By the 2020s, Netflix's role as a savior of quality shows, a disruptor of broadcast television networks, and an architect of Peak TV had been branded in our collective consciousness (Epstein, 2020; Paskin, 2015). The activity most commonly associated with Netflix remains binge-watching, though since 2018, the company has been less enthusiastic about the term (D'Souza, 2020). Netflix, along with the growing panoply of streaming services, now provides such a variety of complete, ad-free, mobile television (2.2 million minutes as of March 2020 [Moore, 2020]) that the vast wasteland is but a faded memory of the 20th century. Being jarred from a riveting show by commercial breaks can seem like a dirty anachronism—the TV equivalent of collect calling or indoor smoking.[1] However, the process by which public perceptions of television consumption shifted from shameful habit to proud hobby was neither simple nor organic. The idiot box died through a complex matrix of intersecting technological, economic, and cultural shifts, which for a time were connected to binge-watching and by proxy Netflix. News reports from 2012 to 2016 provide the broadest and in some ways the most comprehensive accounting of that process through their well-circulated public discourse on the new media behavior. In this chapter, I interrogate that discourse through the definitions and descriptions of journalists in roughly 10,000 news articles published during this phenomenal period when binge-watching tran-

If you are not interested in the theory and methodology (why and how I did this aspect of the project), you can jump to "Binge Defining" on 71.

sitioned from obscurity to ubiquity. And while perceptions of television's value had been improving for decades, this was the period when the plug was finally pulled on the idiot box.

The Other Power of the Press

Journalists help shape public understanding of new things because they have public trust and greater access than the public to sources of information. But a less conspicuous power of the press is its influence on which new things the public pays attention to (Hall et al., 1978). This may sound upside down. News organizations are supposed to be objective reporters of important information, not selectors of what is important. And yet that is what they do. Journalists have the power to determine what is circulated and recirculated through their channels and what is not. Social media has redistributed some of that power, but mainstream media still largely sets the news agenda—what is mostly considered to be newsworthy information in a given news cycle. And while journalists do pay a great deal of attention to their readers' traffic and preferences, the standard by which they most often validate their gatekeeping is to observe "the work of their colleagues, especially the work of those at elite organizations" (McCombs, 2005, p. 164).

The more a word, an idea, or a narrative is printed, broadcast, and shared the more relevant it can appear to be in society at large (Price & Tewksbury, 1997). Such relevance can drive both more coverage and a greater need for understanding. Agenda-setting theorists suggest that uncertainty most often occurs about new topics that appear relevant (Iyengar & Kinder, 1987; McCombs & Reynolds, 2009). If people you know are talking about and sharing news stories about a topic that you don't understand, it is natural to feel at least curious about it. In such circumstances, people often seek more information to develop a better understanding about the word, the idea, or the narrative, and to do that they turn to trusted information sources such as news organizations (Beal & Bohlin, 1956; Blumler & Katz, 1974). News coverage begets news coverage.[2] The more a news story is covered, the newsier it can appear. As a result, it is conceivable that (1) a rapid proliferation of news stories (2) containing a new term to describe a new phenomenon (3) could increase the perceived relevance of that term and thus (4) increase the need for understanding it. At the same time, new terms like binge-watching are, by definition, less understood. When a newer topic has a perceived high relevance because of its prevalent coverage, and a high uncertainty because of its novelty, the public is likely to have a high need for orientation (McCombs & Reynolds, 2009). Under such circumstances, individuals are more likely to "reflect the salience of the objects and attributes on the media agenda" (McCombs & Reynolds, 2009, p. 9). Binge-watching rarely appeared in the news from 2000 to 2011, and, therefore, the term, if not the act, appeared less relevant, thereby reducing the public's need to understand it. Since few people had heard of it, few people were curious about it. And then things changed.

In the summer of 2012, binge-watching was suddenly everywhere at once, and journalists rushed to cover it. From July 11, 2012, to July 11, 2013, there were 1,235 news stories that included some mention of it. At the same time, the more journalists covered it, the more audiences were exposed to the term and thus the more it was discussed and written about. That created a binge-watching feedback loop, which amplified the term's salience: the more something new is reported on, the more relevant it seems, and the more relevant something new seems, the more news coverage it will likely get. But because binge-watching was a new word and activity to most people at the time, and because it involved newer technologies that required more explanation than using a cell phone to take a selfie, journalists were not only reporting on the phenomenon but also instructing the public on what it was and how to do it as they did with VCRs in the early 1980s (see Chapter 2).

As coverage increased, journalists struggled to identify the contours of the term and also its socio-cultural, technological, industrial, and health consequences and significance. From 2013 to 2014, many articles included some form of explainer of "binge-watching," be it a single sentence or an entire article. By 2015, the articles began to stabilize thematically, and by late 2016, the definitional discourse had largely died down while the term's popularity remained strong. As illustrated, "binge-watch" was a popular Google search in 2016, so editors driven to acquire pageviews often included it in titles of articles that provided little explanation of the behavior. Binge-watching, to borrow from an often-cited Netflix study, had "become the new normal" (Seitz, 2013). Journalists assumed reader understanding and ubiquity of the behavior, and they used it with diminishing elaboration.

Sampling the Discourse

But how did that happen? In order to understand what binge-watching is and how it killed the idiot box, I examined the definitions and descriptions provided by journalists during the period when it transitioned from obscurity to ubiquity (2012–2016). To do so, I conducted a purposefully sampled, multi-level analysis of the roughly 10,000 binge-watching news articles from July 12, 2012, to August 9, 2016. Building on Ri Pierce-Groves' (2017) initial analysis of press definitions and De Keere et al.'s (2021) analysis of journalists' reframing of moral panic around TV, I focused on the language and framing in news stories. Additionally, I explored the sources journalists relied on to shape their definitions as well as the timing and frequency of when the articles were published from 2012 to 2016. Doing so provides context for understanding the normalization process as it relates to the TV industry as well as cultural, economic, and technological influences. This process allowed me to capture the history of binge-watching in the press and articulate a more comprehensive definition of the term.

For more information about the sampling process turn to 202 (note 3).[3]

Initial Frames and Categories

My multi-level analysis of how journalists defined binge-watching focused on their language choices, framing, and sourcing. To organize the vast number of articles, I started with framing. Editors often make the frames clear by an article's title or section within a newspaper or a site. A reader knows what to expect when clicking on a piece titled "What Is Binge-Watching?" and how it differs from a piece titled "What to Binge-Watch This Weekend." Two defining articles that appeared online in January 2012 contained initial frames that

A deeper explanation of those three categories and my methodology in this analysis can be found by turning to 203 (note 4).[4]

nearly all 2012–2014 definitional journalism on binge-watching followed: McNamara (*clinical*) and Choi (*ephemeral*). A third frame, *review*—often titled or written around "What to Binge"—became increasingly popular as the definitions grew more normalized. Review frame articles often offered recommendations of shows. They provided scarce articulation of the behavior other than to indicate what kind of content may be bingeable at certain times, and from those times they suggested an indirect articulation of rituals, i.e., what to binge-watch during Christmas.

Mary H. K. Choi's piece "Can't Stop, Won't Stop" was published in the December 2011 issue of *Wired* (I read this in hard copy at that time—the online version is dated 2012, which I use for reference accuracy). It was my introduction to the term "binge-watching," one which I discuss in greater detail in Chapter 6. Choi's article was structured as a first-person account of the author's pleasures and pains with the emerging phenomenon. It articulated a definition through ephemeral language that transported the reader into what Pierce-Grove (2017) calls "a different state of consciousness" (p. 2). Articles using this frame emerged in the early 2000s (Seggel et al., 2000) and began to diminish by 2014, as reporters increasingly wrote articles on the buzzword within clinical and review frames, with the author largely removed from the story. Journalists using the ephemeral frame articulated definitions of binge-watching through evocation of mood and attitude. In addition to their first-hand accounts the writers often cited binge-viewers' personal experiences and focused on rituals and health consequences as well as on the industrial disruptions of binge-watching as related to viewer empowerment.

McNamara's (2012) article "The Side Effects of Binge Television" was more clinical, though at times still humorous and personal. It provided a formal, dictionary-style definition and discussed the changes to television story structures (culture)—quality versus quantity—as well as potential impacts of binge-watching on the television industry. Articles using the clinical frame tended to use declarative statements and followed traditional U.S. news-reporting conventions. Rather than quoting personal binger experiences, journalists more often cited official sources—experts and insiders—and referenced polling and survey data. Such sourcing increased after 2013 as more "professional" data became available. Some articles had elements of both these frames—ephemeral and clinical—though most are distinguishable from each other by their tone, structure, and sources.

I coded the content of these two frames (ephemeral and clinical) of articulation into the following four overlapping categories: (1) Binge Parameters, (2) Bingeable Content, (3) Binging Rituals, and (4) Binge-Watching Consequences/Significance. Using Burke's (1966) scientistic method (see methodology note) of defining through negation, illuminated binge parameters, rituals, and content. While I gave weight to what journalists defined binge-watching as, I also paid close attention to what they defined it as *not*. The dramatistic method of defining was also useful for analyzing the consequences and significance of binge-watching through the journalists' tone and humor in ephemeral and clinical articles. Their attitudes and instructions were indicative of what properties and values of binge-watching they intended to convey as impactful or not based on emphasis in relation to others. Both frames contain these categories which, when taken together, shape the definition of binge-watching articulated by journalists from 2012, when the term became "hot," to 2016, when the term became normalized.

Binge Defining

Parameters

In the summer of 2012, binge-watching became a buzzword that demanded definition. Unlike ponderous academics, journalists can offer a formal definition (for cultural phenomena) with an official sounding study, a few good quotes, or, if they're qualified, their own opinions. While descriptions during the first decade of the 21st century laid out rough parameters, journalists now began to specify what exactly constituted binge-watching beyond the technological affordances of DVDs and DVRs and focused instead on the term's boundaries as a viewer practice. Quantity (of time and/or episodes) was the salient metric journalists initially chose. McNamara (2012) offered the first formalized definition in the third paragraph of her article, which was syndicated in at least six different newspapers with titles such as "The Pros and Cons of Binge TV Viewing": "Binge television: any instance in which more than three episodes of an hourlong drama or six episodes of a half-hour comedy are consumed at one sitting. *Syn.: Marathon television and being a TV critic.*"

While she used it as a noun, the *Los Angeles Times* television critic was describing an activity ("consumed") of a viewer. Unlike future definitions (Porter et al., 2016), McNamara didn't set parameters around technology or location (other than indicating a sedentary viewer). Her definition was shaped by length of time—around three hours—and content—any episodic drama or comedy. Because the norms of American broadcast TV had long stipulated that (including commercial breaks) drama episodes are 60 minutes and comedy episodes are 30 minutes (Wolters, 1955), her three or six parameter indicates that after three hours a viewer is binging. An admittedly unscientific poll of *The Atlantic* newsroom determined that binging started at "four episodes, if you're watching dramas. If you walk away before the fourth episode, people I've spoken with generally agreed, all you did was have a little TV time" (Feeney, 2014). As Pierce-Grove (2017) notes, the matter of time versus episodes becomes complicated in the coming years when television texts broke beyond linear TV norms. However, three or six became approximately the mainstream understanding of binge-watching by 2016, in contrast to Choi's "all at once" binge, which was characterized in later journalism with terms like "heavy binge-watching" (Pearlman, 2015).

Ephemeral accounts linked the parameters of binging to sensations of immersion and rates of consumption of whole series, though not necessarily all in one session: "Speed is just distance divided by time, and binge consumption of a TV show collapses both—the time it takes to watch a whole run, the distance between you and the people who made it" (Choi, 2012). Transportation and escape have long been uses of television (Rubin & Perse, 1987), but with binge-watching, time management and destination selection are the defining parameters of ephemerally-framed articles (Wong, 2013): "Only four more nights (less if you call in sick) and you've logged the whole run of Breaking Bad" (Choi, 2012). Choi was less concerned with hours or episodes unless their duration affected the binge-viewer's experience: "Only one season of Downton Abbey on Netflix? Only three episodes of Sherlock? Even at 89 minutes long, that's not enough to tune into the wave length. I want more faster." Nicole Rogers (2012) specified the number of episodes, but her parameters served as a management of time to enhance her viewing experience. "Instead of jumbling up your mind with multiple shows and plotlines, blending characters from one show into situations of another and generally overtaxing your brain, binge viewing (what would that be, consuming four or more episodes of the same show in one sitting; three if you're a woman? For me, it's anything more than two in a row) is way more efficient for the busy television connoisseur." Rogers' principle of singular shows/plotlines would become a defining aspect of binge-watching rituals (see "Binge-Watching Rituals" on 81).

Official Sources Shape Parameters and Penetration

Two-hundred sixty-seven (40.2 percent) of the 664 news articles (binge title group, 2012–2016) referenced a poll, survey, or study, with 157 of them coming prior to 2015. Journalists cited these official-sounding data during this initial upswing in usage (2012–2014) not only to instruct the parameters of what binge-watching was but also to demonstrate how popular binge-watching had become. Trying to define the practice and penetration of a niche behavior is difficult to do through large-scale sampling. For instance, if researchers asked 300 people in 2000 how they typically "binge-watch," they might get 290 instances (my guess) of the exact same answer: "What do you mean by binge-watch?" As the word's usage expanded across journalism and mainstream media, it became possible for researchers to gather national user data. Starting in 2012, and increasingly in 2013–2014, clinical-framed articles relied on industry data to define the parameters of binge-watching and demonstrate its pervasiveness. An examination of those articles reveals that many of their parameters were based on this research finding about viewers: "A majority (73%) defined binge watching as watching between 2–6 episodes of the same TV show in one sitting" (PRNewsWire, 2013).

That finding came from a Harris Interactive poll, which was commissioned by Netflix. Forty-eight of the 157 news articles written from

2012-2014 (30.6 percent) mentioned the Harris poll. It was cited, linked to, referenced, and repurposed more often by journalists than by any other research on binge-watching from 2012 to 2016—the entire dataset. And while at first journalists noted that it was Netflix-sponsored research (Jurgensen, 2013), as the story circulated and the results were repurposed, that sourcing caveat was sometimes dropped (Hewitt, 2013). Other times Netflix itself was cited as the source, with little scrutiny as to why the notoriously secretive company would be releasing these particular nuggets of internal research: "According to Netflix, of those who watched a full season within 30 days, 25% completed watching a 13-episode series in two days. Meanwhile, 73% of TV streamers said they have 'positive feelings' about the habit" (Spangler, 2014).

While the Harris poll represented 30.6 percent of the "hard data" used between 2012 and 2014, journalists cited other "official sources" when articulating their parameters of binge-watching. Twelve of the 157 articles cited a study by Frank N. Magid Associates—media consultants for Amazon and Disney. Among them, Chmielewski (2013) stated that the binge-watching "phenomenon is so pervasive that a majority of Americans ages 8 to 66 say they've engaged in this sort of copious TV consumption." One Ohio news article citing the study put the percentage of binge-viewers at 70 percent among those aged 16 to 35 (Grindrod, 2013).

Ten articles cited a survey of 1,000 U.S. internet users conducted by Netflix. Another 11 cited a Canadian survey conducted by Head Research for its client, Netflix. It found that "81 per cent of respondents watched three or more episodes of a series" (Oliveira, 2013a). The Head poll appeared to be a response to six articles that cited Solutions Research Group's polling of Netflix penetration in Canada. The Toronto–based media consulting company, which lists NBC-Universal as a client, found that binge-watching *House of Cards* was not popular in Canada. The article (Oliveira, 2013b) stated that less than 30 percent of people were binge-watching the show. If the number seems low, it is because the article defined binge-watching as completing an entire season of a show rather than Harris's 2-6 episodes standard. Interestingly, both articles were written by the same author. Five articles cited research from Miner & Co., which counts Viacom among its many media clients. Miner's poll found that "seven out of 10 American TV viewers call themselves bingeviewers—watching three or more episodes of one series in a single sitting" (Tribbey, 2014, p. 7). Five more articles cited a variety of other media-consulting research: a TiVo-sponsored poll, one sponsored by Roku, and an internal Cox Communication user survey (Cox, 2013).

It should be noted that not all of the articles cited industry-sponsored studies. The four that didn't include media critic Brian Stelter's (2013) article on how binge-watching was altering the way stories get written and broadcast, which cited Nielsen's new surveying model. There was also a mock piece in *Variety,* which cited a U.S. Department of Education "study" finding binge-watching to be the leading cause of death among college students (Hollywood & Swine, 2013). One article cited a University of Pennsylvania study on "the effect of parental television viewing on children's television viewing" (Melnyk, 2013). The study itself, published in the journal *Pediatrics,* did not specifically address binge-watching, so this may have been an instance of an opportunistic editor using a buzzword in the headline for SEO (search engine optimization). And finally, there was a cantankerous opinion piece from John R. Nelson (2013) in the *Poughkeepsie Journal* that led with "Binge, cram, repeat. The new TV-watching craze sounds very painful, no? Most commonly known as binge-watching, it refers to taking in an entire season of television in one viewing…. As for me I don't get it." Nelson's was an ephemeral piece, describing the odd new behavior of young people in his life. It found its way into my sample because it included the keyword "study," which Nelson (2012) used to describe how he likes to watch TV: "Watching a series shouldn't feel like you're cramming a few hours before a college final. How exactly is that enjoyable? I'm a nerd, so I always preferred to study throughout the semester and thus feel confident that as I took (and aced) the final test it would resonate and stick with me years later. I was never one for an all-night study marathon. I didn't understand the masochistic appeal of cramming. That transfers right into television watching. Why cram?"

These polls, particularly the Harris one, continued to be referenced from 2014 to 2016 (108 articles). While the percentage of binge-viewers continued to grow (a popular Deloitte [2015] study put the number of millennials who binge-watch at 90 percent), the parameters of what constituted binge-watching did not. In all, 95 percent of the "official" data cited by journalists in the 2012–2014 binge-titled sample came from research firms that work for media companies, and 65 percent cite Netflix-sponsored data. While some non-industry studies began appearing in 2015, the parameters of what constituted binge-watching were largely set by that point. Even when surveys associated binge-watching with loneliness, the positive perception tied to the non-disputed parameters seemed fixed. That positivity or at least ambivalence from the 2012–2014 industry sourcing spread beyond the parameters and penetration of binge-watching into

content recommendations, rituals, and consequences (see the following section).

Defining Parameters

Based on my multi-level analysis of this sample, journalistic parameters of binge-watching normalize around the following definition:

> Binge-watching is the liminally intentional act of viewing at least two con-
> secutive episodes of the same show when the episodes are longer than 60
> minutes, and three in a row when the episodes are shorter.

This constitutes "a binge" and is the point after which a viewer is "binging." Based on the dramatistic definitional method, I found the following principal binge-watching parameter in journalism: "The fewer
episodes that are watched consecutively and/or the shorter the episodes are, the faster a season and more exclusively an entire season or
series should be consumed, so as to maintain immersion in the show's
world." By negation and omission, no definition of binging from this
period allowed for an entire season to be consumed in more than 30
days unless episodes were re-watched. Three hours remained the modal
time when binging starts. And since shows with episodes longer than
90 minutes are rare, in most circumstances the time is sufficient for the
minimum two episode requirement.

Bingeable Content

Twentieth-century journalists used TV binge and TV marathon
to describe large amounts of television. As the usage transitioned to
gerund and then to active verb, the types of television that should or
could be binged began emerging in line with better technology and
more available channels. By 2012, journalists defining binge-watching
through both clinical and ephemeral frames (and later in all review
frame pieces) were also articulating a hierarchy of bingeability through
inclusion and omission in their articles. That hierarchy instructed
viewers how to use the new technology to enhance their viewing experience. It was also notable because it defined binge-watching in a way
that associated it with higher culture prestige television while differentiating its streaming delivery from network-controlled appointment
television.

McNamara (2012) stated that "certain types of shows" are more
bingeable than others. "The big dramas," she wrote, "are the most

obvious, especially those in which a season tells a precise story—'The Wire' is a perfect example." In this case, bigger means better. Her delineation between shows that are better when taken in large, uninterrupted doses and others that can be watched more sparsely was in line with the parameters set by Nussbaum (2003) and other journalists from the DVD binge era. Similarly, ephemeral articles described a preference for sprawling shows with complex characters, plots, and dialogue, like *Lost*, that allowed viewers to experience a richer sense of immersion (Wang, 2013). It could be easily inferred that a streaming provider that allowed viewers to binge-watch all six seasons of *Lost*, like Netflix did until 2018, was improving the viewer's experience and the show in opposition to its network broadcaster ABC.

"More and more viewers are turning on to elaborately scripted shows, tuning in via digitized devices and not dropping out: They're watching marathons of their own making," CNN arts and entertainment critic Aaron Riccio (2013) wrote. His usage connoted standard marathons were controlled by broadcasters but binging was about controlling the path, scenery, and distance. In contrast, choosing more pedestrian scenery could result in worse viewer experiences. *Minneapolis Star Tribune* columnist Bill Ward (2014) profiled an "unabashed binge viewer" who stated, "If I binge-watch a reality show, I feel like I have wasted a ton of my time." Rogers (2012), a proponent of HBO dramas like *The Wire*, wrote, "I used to think it was a bad thing, especially when I found myself watching hour after hour of VH1's 'I Love the 80s' or 'Top 100 One-Hit Wonders.'" Her change of content from linear VH1 marathons to self-directed prestige drama binging illustrates a change of meaning and attitude about the practice, perhaps through viewer control. Binge-watching was for quality TV, albeit in large quantities.

So were viewers making TV better? Narratives of the improved content that catered to viewer tastes were rampant in the binge-watching journalism from 2013 to 2015. During that time there were spikes in coverage that focused on the quality of programming afforded through binge-watching around the releases of Netflix's flagship original programming. Season 2 of *House of Cards* was released in February 2014. Despite being the shortest month, February saw the most articles on binge-watching that year, many speaking directly about *House of Cards*. TV critics covering the release of prestige shows on HBO, Showtime, AMC, Amazon, and others also brought up binge-watching in their articles. While binging was mentioned in reference to other shows, journalists most commonly associated it with hour-long dramas, regardless of whether the shows were released all at once or, as in the case of cable network shows, released one episode at a time. In cases of the latter, critics suggested binging to catch up before the start of the new season (Stelter, 2013) (see "Binge-Watching Rituals" on 81).

Non-Bingeable Content

Journalists indicated the programmatic boundaries of binge-watching by the shows they omitted from their defining articles. Despite being prevalent in earlier uses of "TV binge" (see Chapter 2), sporting events were conspicuously absent from the content discourse among journalists from 2012 to 2016. When they mentioned televised sports, journalists positioned such consumptions as other than binging. In his piece "Binge-Watching: To Stream or Not to Stream," Brendan O'Brian (2015) wrote that "binge-watching is definitely possible on all three media services [Netflix, Hulu, and Amazon]. So what's holding people back from making the switch? The lack of live news and sports options, I would presume." Live sports made broadcast television a household medium in the 20th century and thus far have preserved it in the 21st century (Serazio, 2019).

While TV audiences for major sporting events such as the Super Bowl and the NCAA men's basketball tournament continued to grow during those years, reporters rarely described the hours spent watching them as "binging." Instead, they created a distinction between passive appointment viewing and active binge-watching (Conlin, Billings, & Averset, 2016). Often, they wrote that all that prevents universal cord-cutting is "the fact [that] sports is largely not available anywhere other than [in] live broadcast television" (Szklarski, 2013). In 2015, White Sox pitcher Chris Sales was quoted as saying that he had "had enough with binge-watching." His statement was not an indictment of cord-cutting fans abandoning live sports but rather an admission that he had been binge-watching during a prolonged injury and was look-ing forward to returning for the 2015 season (Kane, 2015). The last functioning vestige of media events remain live competitions, usually sporting or political.

Journalists of the period repeatedly reinforced differentiation of live from binge-watching. *Orange Is the New Black* actor Paulo Sch-reiber is quoted stating, "I don't watch a lot of TV, unfortunately. I watch zero live TV except for sports. It's all DVR or On Demand" (Bazilian, 2015). The narrative of binge-watching being distinct from television often hinged on commercials and the interruptions they caused to a story's flow. Since U.S. broadcast television is built around (and largely supported by) commercial interruptions, shows airing with that traditional format were less likely to be mentioned in articles defining binge-watching. Televised news, for instance, was never described as bingeable, even though 20th-century journalists characterized extensive news coverage as both "marathons" and "binges" (see Chapter 2). By omission, these 21st-century journalists clearly distinguished extensive live TV consumption from binge-watching. Even though it was never explicitly written that binge-watching had to be on Netflix, a reader might deduce this by subtracting the content journalists omitted from binge definitions (sports, news, anything live, anything with commercials, and shows you had to wait to see more of). Essentially, any content on Netflix could potentially be binge-watched, with serialized prestige dramas like *House of Cards* being the most binge-worthy (see "Binge Hierarchy").

Movies, which culturally and narratively align with some of what makes binge-watching attractive, often fell outside of the content reporters described as bingeable. This makes some sense for single movies, which are typically less than the three-hour parameter many journalists set. However, the omission of multi-episodic film sagas is more curious. How could sitting through the six hours and 28 minutes of *Star Wars* Episodes IV–VI not be binge-watching? What about the 9.2 hours it would take someone to screen the *Lord of the Rings* trilogy? Surely going toe-to-toe for nearly 12 hours with *Rocky I–VI* would be mentioned in news reports on binge-watching. Instead, movies are conspicuously rare in the binge-defining journalism from 2012 to 2016.

Their cinematic content omissions indicate that journalists were differentiating traditional movie marathons from the new phenomenon. The underlying cultural superiority of the silver screen over the small screen is enmeshed in the ironic use of binge and television. Recall that early binge-viewers made their control of lower-culture TV the defiant act, which streaming companies seized on and co-opted. Netflix, which started out as a DVD rental company, had long sought to be a disrupter of inefficient commerce through technology. Why pay late fees and go to a video store and wait in line to rent what was left on a shelf when you could sit on your couch in pajamas, order any content you want and keep it for as long as you'd like? While the company did stock and ship pricey movie titles, Netflix recognized that it could make more money with cheaper and more popular box sets of old TV shows (Jenner, 2018). When the company transitioned to streaming, its licensing model continued to exploit the inefficient pricing model of production companies that were still locked into the 20th-century mindset that television had less value than cinema. And therein lies the irony. Netflix was not so much a disrupter of TV culture as it was an amplifier of a cultural realignment quietly developing among fan groups since the late 1970s (Stevens, 2021, p. 31), which it exploited for great profit through streaming technology. Rather than unpacking the corporate motives behind this growing narrative, journalistic coverage of binge-watching instead emphasized the content distinction, which served as evidence of television's revolution, while implying it was made possible by Netflix (see "Reported Binge-Watching Consequences and Significance [BCS]"). It should be noted that while movies were mentioned less in early binge-watching articles, they were not completely omitted. They came up sporadically in quotes or when journalists cited certain non–Netflix research:

> According to a recent omnibus survey conducted by Research Now for Roku, Inc., maker of the popular streaming platform for Roku players and Roku TV, 75 percent of Americans plan to watch holiday movies and TV specials this season.... This unfiltered access to entertainment through streaming has also ushered in a new term for how people consume entertainment today, "binge-watching," which refers to watching multiple TV episodes or movies in one sitting [Binge Becomes, 2014].

Social media and user-generated content from sites like YouTube, Instagram, and Vimeo remained outside of the journalistic discourse on binge-watching before 2016. At that time, the delineation of social media from television was clearer. While journalists did describe binge-watching on technology other than on television sets, the sources of the content determined bingeability. Today this has changed, as YouTube, Apple, and Facebook enter the "TV business," but during the period when binge-watching was defined (2012–2016), journalists most frequently omitted them. Streaming providers, particularly and at first Netflix, had the most bingeable content libraries; they were the tech companies that journalists most associated with binge-watching.

Binge Hierarchy

Collectively, these articles created an instructive content hierarchy for what could acceptably be binge-watched and what could not. I explore the extent to which readers followed those instructions in Chapter 5. It should be noted that the show differentiations of the hierarchy have grown increasingly opaque. Technically, a procedural is supposed to resolve its conflict (traditionally who committed the crime and/or a jury verdict) by the episode's end while series extend that tension across an entire season. But of course procedurals stretch themes and sometimes even storylines over multiple episodes (like *The Good Wife*) while serialized dramas can have seemingly stand-alone episodes (*The Sopranos* episodes "College" 1.5 and "Pine Barrens" 3.11). Comedies are often dramatic (*BoJack Horseman*) and dramas can be full of comedy (*Orange Is the New Black*). A show like *Shameless* forces the awkward portmanteau of "dramedy," while 30-minute shows like *Master of None, Lady Dynamite* and *Louie* have been dubbed "comedies in theory" (Mason, 2015; Seitz, 2016). In 2021, *New York Times* chief television critic James Poniewozik cited *Ted Lasso* as evidence that television comedy had fundamentally changed, but the generic distinctions had long been in doubt. Even in 2012, and soon after very much so, these lines were blurring, in part because binge-watching allowed for the disintegration of television genres and forms that were most profitable to commercially-sponsored broadcast TV. Nevertheless, this is the definitional content hierarchy journalists provided from 2012 to 2016, from most binge-worthy to least binge-worthy based on frequency and tenor.

Binge-Worthy Hierarchy

1. Prestige serialized dramas (*House of Cards, The Americans*)
2. Miniseries/limited series (*True Detective, Fargo*)
3. Comedies in theory (*Unbreakable Kimmy Schmidt, Transparent*)
4. Episodic anthologies (*Black Mirror, American Horror Story*)
5. Procedurals (*The Good Wife, Law & Order*)
6. Situation comedies (*The Office, Parks and Recreation*)
7. Reality TV
8. Movie series
9. Sports
10. Online videos
11. News
12. Talk shows
13. Commercials

Binge-Watching Rituals

Since the word "binge-watching" was less familiar to people in 2012 than what it actually involved, the rituals journalists described were both informative and instructive. Viewers could now compare how they watched to this new phenomenon and, ideally, employ binge-watching rituals to improve their TV experience or at least not feel left out. The "how to" binge-watch service journalism normalized newer practices within the context of Western society, encouraging a broader reimagining of what television could mean.

Some journalists with clinically framed definition articles avoided lengthy descriptions of binge-watching rituals. Instead, they provided step-by-step guides, like Casandra Porter's (2016), which through ritual delineates appropriate technology:

1. A subscription to a television streaming site is crucial....
2. Have a device....
3. Have snacks ready....
4. Find a comfortable spot....
5. Know the shows. Verse yourself on the top binge-worthy shows to choose from....
6. Schedule breaks....
7. Find a new show for when you finish the old....

Others cited data on viewer habits, demographics, and group sizes. Snyder (2015) wrote, "In the U.S., solo binge-watching happens across all age groups, but it is highest among those 16 to 24 years old." They also cited accredited experts such as Grant McCracken. Netflix hired the Canadian cultural anthropologist, who was cited in at least 35 articles, to study binge-watching. His articles and press releases normalized once-taboo rituals thus: "Getting immersed in multiple episodes or even multiple seasons of a show over a few weeks is a new kind of escapism that is especially welcomed today" (Matthew, 2014). It was McCracken, in conjunction with the Harris Interactive study, who also encouraged the notion of solo binge-watching of a single show (Jurgensen, 2013). While new research has demonstrated more positive emotional outcomes when binge-watching is social (Pittman & Steiner, 2021), the emphasis of focusing on a single show is critical to the notion of an evolved and attentive viewer. The ritual of a viewer advancing at that viewer's pace through a story is also crucial to binge-watching definitions and to Netflix's model—full season and limited series drops, the auto-play function, algorithmic suggestions of future viewing based on user preferences.

At first, the rituals described came with a modicum of guilt, as if there needed to be external reasons for binge-watching. Times and places were selected that would allow the binge-viewer to remain a responsible, working member of society—the TV equivalent of the functional alcoholic. Some journalists presented generalizable situations for binging that outlined acceptable rituals:

Once an outlier rite of professionals, the brokenhearted and the ailing—honestly, is there any better way to spend those first numbed-out, post-surgical days than with the last two seasons of "Sex in the City"?—binge television is now mainstream. Caught between overstocked DVR queues—when you're so behind already, why not save all those "Mad Men" episodes for a rainy day and then simply watch them one after another?—and the increasing availability of entire seasons on DVD and the Internet [McNamara, 2012].

More ephemeral definitions focused on feelings people had about binge-watching in association with the times and places where ideal binging happens. Many journalists mentioned binging on weekends and vacations, indicating that those are the preferred times to binge-watch. This evokes a sense of transportation away from day-to-day responsibilities, positioning Netflix as a kind of streaming travel agent and tour guide.

I'm not proud to admit that with each break from school, I'm swept into the binge-watching culture. As each episode of my current series obsession winds down, I patiently wait as the Netflix 15-second clock winds down, and, viola, the next chapter starts up seamlessly. Three bags of popcorn later, three seasons of my current show are gone [Fisher, 2014].

Solitary TV consumption guilt melts away when binge-watching is reimagined as self-care (Da Costa, 2021). You're not being a lonesome, pathetic slob; you're treating yourself to a restorative cultural retreat without getting off your couch! The experience, according to McCracken (2013), should be seen as a ritualistic, virtual mini-vacation so sought after in today's attention-deficient world: "Such relocation is powerful for creating meaning for the self and for the family, especially as TV has taken on a new role in our lives. It has become the structural equivalent of our place in the country, our second home." That narrative is interwoven in the journalist's explanations of how people binge-watch, thereby elevating the cultural and cognitive connotations above the vast wasteland and its lingering shame:

It's not just what they choose to watch that makes binge watching restorative. It's how they watch, too: Binge watching is more like going to a movie or play than watching Russian dashcam videos. They talk about watching "with compete attention," being "fully immersed," "completely in a different place," or "filtering out everything around me." Many turn off their phones or ignore email. One knits through Homeland, but that occupies her hands, not her eyes. Even people who can't arrange such complete immersion use the technology to keep interruptions from becoming impediments. One stay-at-home mom says her four children make it hard to "give something at home the same concentration that I can at the movies," but with streaming services, "any distractions can be dealt with without missing anything.

For many, binge watching is a break or reward: They wait until major projects are done or grades turned in, and they have time to spend a day in another world. As one musician put it, she and her colleagues "binge rehearse and binge perform," so it's "no coincidence that once the semester and final performances end, I go plop down on the sofa and watch hours and hours of Miss Marple" [Pang, 2014].

One ritual that journalists often described was the (un)intentional continuation of viewing. Articles in the clinical frame cited research from viewers: "They start out intending only to watch one or two episodes, but then get 'sucked-in' to a much longer viewing session" (Study, 2013). The ritualistic immersion—losing one's self in a story so deeply that control over the time spent there was lost—was another defining aspect of binge-watching. Whether the viewer lost control or not, the tension around losing control was woven into journalists' descriptions of binge-watching rituals (see also "Reported Binge-Watching Consequences and Significance [BCS]"). "Before you know it, watching a couple episodes of your favorite show can turn into six hours of time lost to inertia" (Allan, 2015).

Certain journalists framed that loss of self (control) as a benefit of binge-watching, in the right circumstances: "For quality binge-watching, you have to go solo and go hard. Getting strung out on the tension of long-arc narrative is private.... Seen on a laptop screen at 4 a.m., microprocessor superheating the bedsheets" (Choi, 2012). Wood (2013) takes the Boy Scout approach: "Come prepared. You don't just get smelly watching hours of TV. You get hungry. And like most things, binge viewing isn't as enjoyable fun on an empty stomach, so stock up on snacks beforehand." The rituals here make binging a series sound like a spirit walk as much about self-discovery as about completing the show.

Journalists often credit Netflix's single season release model and vast library for creating new viewing rituals that viewers use to improve television. "Netflix has ton[s] of television programing available, and their users binge watch seasons in the matter of days. They have the stats to prove this. Why change what's been working for them? Why not challenge the status quo of releasing an episode a week with an original series?" (Scieretta, 2013).

Based on these articles, journalists articulated binge-watching rituals as follows: (A) The typically solitary viewing of a single serial story, (B) preferably done during nights, weekends or vacations (times when professionals, rather than the lazy and unemployable, aren't working), (C) often at home, with food, on a couch or in a bed, (D) most likely on a TV, though other devices were acceptable, (E) always involving some degree of tension around losing control, but (F) when intentional, the goal being often to catch up, complete or experience a show in a way not possible on linear TV.

Reported Binge-Watching Consequences and Significance (BCS)

Nearly all of the articles from 2012 to 2016 made some reference to the impact of binge-watching on individuals, society, and/or the TV industry. Some articles focused on the consequences and significance the phenomenon was having; most included a few sentences on them, while others, particularly reviews, reflected on them without deeper commentary. What is clear from the reporting is that binge-watching was significant and consequential from 2012 to 2016. What is less clear, or at least less simple, are their answers to the question so many readers were seeking clarity on: *Is binge-watching good or bad?* Instead of affirming the idiot box narrative of 20th-century journalists, those writing about binge-watching consequences and significance from 2012 to 2016 presented a decidedly ambivalent story. And that ambivalence spoke volumes about how far television had come.

It is important to note that ambivalence varied depending on the category of consequence. What journalists had to say about the impact of binge-watching for individuals was different from its impact on the TV industry, but, when taken together, their ambivalence conveys a larger narrative about how television was evolving. To illustrate this, I first present the reported binge-watching consequences and significance (BCS) into three overlapping subcategories: (A) Sociocultural BCS, (B) Industrial BCS, and (C) Personal BCS. I then bring the three together for a broader discussion of the reporting.

Sociocultural BCS

The sociocultural consequences of binge-watching described by post–2012 reporters stand in stark contrast to those of the 20th century. Articles titled "Binge-Watching Makes TV Better" (Riccio, 2013) and "The Revolution Will Be Televised and Binge Watched" (Verini, 2014) speak to the reported evolution of TV's identity from its idiot box roots. At least 45 articles post–2012 referenced the Golden (or other precious metal) Age of TV. The significance of binge-watching was reinforced by journalists who cited viewer behavior, in congress with Netflix's full season release model, as the catalyst for better shows (Barney, 2013): "For those who think television is a brain-rotting, time-wasting toxic box of depravity, this is the beginning of the end. But for those who believe television is our next great art form, this is the beginning of the future" (Goldstein, 2013).

After being immersed in 20th-century articles about TV (Chapter 2), I found the journalistic transformation about television's role in society jarring. It felt as if the fears of the past had mutated into fantasy, leaving only a vestigial tail to be chuckled over. That tail gives shape to the half-hearted warnings about the death of water-cooler conversations (Rainey, 2015)—as if American office socializing would cease because co-workers watched different shows. The Atlantic's Nolan Feeney (2013) argued that Netflix and on-demand services might actually be saving water-cooler conversations. He cites Comcast's senior vice president of digital and emerging platforms Matt Strauss, who found that live ratings go up when earlier seasons are made available to binge. The trick is knowing which water coolers where you should hang out and when. This is related to another social consequence of binge-watching reported in journalism of the period: *the spoiler*. McCracken (2013) explained that "spoilers are no longer accidental, they're things we 'must actively avoid,' sometimes going to great lengths to avoid social media and apps, not to mention instant-recaps and classic news feeds." Spoiler alerts and water-cooler conversations may have been changing, but compared to the dire warnings of societal obliteration (Postman, 1985)—from the "Western Flu" (Wolters, 1955) and "insidious narcotic" (Gould, 1948)— these "consequences" are laughable.

While acknowledging the potential loss of traditional social capital, journalists also celebrated the diversity of available content. As audiences grew increasingly individualized, journalists argued that minorities and subcultures were changing the complexion and gender of TV (Littleton, 2016). The actual impact of this is still debatable. While the faces of hit shows may have been changing—from "the age of Difficult Men" to the "age of Difficult Shows" (Seitz, 2016)—journalists spent little ink describing binge-watching's impact, or lack thereof, on the off-camera social and economic structures that were producing and distributing the "groundbreaking" culture. This remains an area of struggle in the television industry.

Other cultural consequences of binge-watching discussed by journalists included its effect on the critical viewing of texts. While many argued that binge-watching improved the viewer experience through immersion (see "Personal BCS"), some pointed out that the rate of rapid consumption might cause viewers to miss flaws they had previously caught (Krey, 2016). Traditionally, viewers had an entire week to dissect, discuss, and perhaps re-watch a single episode. Gaffes, plot holes, and other errata were parsed by fans, and future predictions were made (remember those X-Files Usernet groups?). Binge-watching reportedly changed these social practices. Furthermore, journalists argued that the impossibly large volume of available content was leading to broader, shallower cultural analyses (Rainey, 2015). Reviewers also complained about disruptions to their professional practices, particularly the increased speed of consumption. This is evident in the early adaptations from appointment viewing to full-season drops as with the *Arrested Development* Season 4 release. As Jenner (2018) points out, "the most common complaint is that they felt compelled to watch the series very quickly to produce the review by their deadline" (p. 168). While celebrating the variety and abundance of content (Ryan, 2015), traditional critics described being overwhelmed with trying to keep up, and, like many non-millennial journalists, were put out by the new generation of non-professional fan critics who might sway a show's discourse through social media banter and SEO savvy. Often these complaints were tinged with nostalgia for a time before everyone was a critic.

> There used to be a time when, once a week, colleagues would gather around the water cooler to discuss the previous night's episode of a certain television show. When you would be left, mouth gaping, as a bombshell was dropped at the end of an episode of your favourite series; knowing you had to wait a full seven days to find out what happened next. When nobody but TV critics could publish spoilers; when all anyone could talk about for months on end was how on earth that season's drama was going to conclude. Those days are long gone [Rainey, 2015].

Industrial BCS

Journalistic discourse about the consequences and significance of binge-watching on the network TV industry were the least ambivalent of these subcategories. It is clear through the historical articles that I have analyzed in Chapter 2, and the more contemporary ones addressed in this chapter, that these reporters had (have?) at best a cordial relationship with the powerful corporations that own and control television. While journalists had for decades enjoyed special privileges and insider access from broadcasters and studios, they expressed little loyalty to them. In fact, from 2012 to 2016, they sounded joyful that the networks were struggling to catch up with TV's new world order (Plaugic & Miller, 2015). They positioned themselves with savvy viewers and TV creatives (actors, writers, and directors) in mutual celebration of the decline of commercial broadcast television. By default, this also aligned them with the "upstart" streaming tech companies and left little editorial space to check their sources, practices, and motives.

I found no articles in which a reporter wrote that commercial breaks enhanced the quality of binge-watching or in fact any television—except the Super Bowl. At the same time, "Netflix's refusal to make viewership numbers available has thrown a wrench into television's ratings-driven business models" (Lev-Ram, 2016). However, the imminent death of interstitial advertising initially raised concerns for some journalists who feared the free ride would soon end with the empire of broadcast networks striking back: "I stress about cash-poor, business challenged Netflix, because I need my streaming fix. I'm wringing my hands about Hulu's new owners" (Choi, 2012). Yes, only a few years ago journalists worried that Netflix might have to resort to commercial breaks in order to survive! But the allure of commercial-free TV also hinted at a fantastic future: "Industry observers, noting the growing popularity of binge-watching, have speculated that Netflix ultimately could wreak havoc with television's long-running, tried-and-true model" (Barney, 2013). SPOILER: in 2022, Netflix caved to ads.

Journalists were also initially uncertain about the financial consequences of releasing a whole season at once. On the one hand, "Netflix management has said their release-as-a-package approach reflects their desire not to be bound by the tired strategies of network TV. A worthy goal." On the other hand, "from a buzz-based, water-cooler community point of view, it is hard not to wonder whether Netflix is cutting itself off at the knees.... That is how TV works. It builds a community among its viewers.... By releasing all 13 episodes of 'House of Cards' at once, Netflix has in many ways blocked the formation of any sort of community" (McDermott, 2013).

By April 2013, around the time Netflix's stock price began a meteoric surge, journalists began calling Netflix the pioneer of binge-watching and crediting binge-watching with driving TV's Golden Age (Lacob, 2013). Ross Miller (2015) wrote, "Gone are the days where you have to write/shoot/edit around commercial breaks and—this is my favorite—you can choose to build an episode around the idea of people binging." Journalists often cited creative insiders to justify their claims of TV revolution. *New York Times* TV columnist Dave Itzkoff quotes *Daredevil* (a Netflix original) showrunner Steve S. DeKnight to illustrate the industrial significance in contrast to TV's older models.

> "When you're working on a network show, especially a pilot, the notes you get are, basically, 'Cram the entire first season into that first episode, so everybody knows what they're going to get,'" he said. On Netflix, Mr.

DeKnight said: "It really is the exact opposite. It's more, 'Slow things down, let it breathe, explore it.'" The Netflix model also means that subsequent episodes don't have to spend time recapitulating what happened in previous installments [Itzkoff, 2015].

As I discuss in Chapter 4, Netflix deployed its acclaimed show-runners to promote its full-season release model as improving the flow of television by encouraging binge-watching and for providing shows the freedom to develop outside the traditional commercial constraints through surrogates like Kevin Spacey (Jenner, 2018). Journalists quoted these surrogates who explained that before Netflix showrunners where always under the gun to keep ratings up, but now they "get to tell their full-season story without the fear of cancellation or having to react to changes in viewership" (Plaugic & Miller, 2015). This new paradigm and the demand for more and innovative content was significant for writers trying to sell challenging scripts and actors and directors trying to find work in an industry of limited access (Lev-Ram, 2016). Consequently, journalists participated in the celebration of viewer and creative liberation against network oppression. What Netflix was charging for admission and extracting from attendees was less discussed than the endless champagne they were supplying.

Netflix was also celebrated in the press for resurrecting shows that could not survive on network TV (Sims, 2015). Whether for better or for worse, *Arrested Development* was a structurally and narratively different show on Netflix than it was on Fox according to its creator Mitchell Hurwitz (Manjoo, 2013). Journalists even argued that Netflix's success had pushed MVPDs to rethink their programming and services. For instance, Comcast's X1 operating system interface seems remarkably similar to Netflix's and Amazon's (Swisher, 2016). In 2016, America's largest cable provider decided to stop losing viewers who had been exiting its ecosystem to stream by allowing its customers to access their Netflix accounts through the X1 interface (King & Goldman, 2016). Comcast was no longer marketing a cable service but inviting viewers into their own "entertainment experience." Since then, almost all legacy media companies have created their own streaming apps to compete with Netflix (see Chapter 6).

Through all the celebratory journalism of this period, criticism of binge-watching and articles predicting dire consequences for television itself were rare. While quick to dance on the grave of the network era, journalists were remarkably welcoming of the new industry leaders. The narrative that binge-watching made the TV industry better was rarely challenged. And while journalists prior to 2012 focused on the binge-viewer rebels who were fighting against the evil empire of broadcast TV, after 2012 they tended to depict Netflix, and other streaming companies to a lesser extent, as the disrupters of a backward and inefficient industry (Lacob, 2013).

Personal BCS

Journalists' descriptions of individual viewer consequences were rife with irony and ambivalence about how to handle TV's new Golden Age. While most celebrated the viewer control of time and content, they just as frequently fretted about how to handle the freedom—though never enough to want to relinquish it. Their tone and attitude can be summed up by this Jerry Seinfeld (1995) joke:

> I gotta say that I'm enjoying adulthood. For a lot of reasons. And I'll tell you reason number one: as an adult, if I want a cookie, I have a cookie, okay? I have three cookies or four cookies, or eleven cookies if I want. Many times I will intentionally ruin my entire appetite. Just ruin it. And then, I call my mother up right after to tell her that I did it. "Hello, Mom? Yeah, I just ruined my entire appetite ... cookies." So what if you ruin.... See, because as an adult, we understand even if you ruin an appetite, there's another appetite coming right behind it. There's no danger in running out of appetites. I've got millions of them, I'll ruin them whenever I want!

What I continually sensed while analyzing their words was that almost all the reporters in my sample came of age in the 20th century, when the consumption of television was a treat and its mass consumption was viewed as an unhealthy indulgence. That idiot box narrative was like a scar bulging beneath their descriptions, so that despite the medium's apparent cultural and cerebral evolution, personal pleasure derived from TV still required some admission of guilt, as if their parents' warnings about the idiot box might yet come true. "One-quarter of respondents in a December 2013 Harris Interactive admitted they'd watched an entire 13-hour season of a series in two days, raising specters of glassy-eyed adults, misused sick days, and neglected pets. But to me, the experience of binge watching *Lost, Breaking Bad*, and *Avatar: The Last Airbender* has always felt more complicated" (Pang, 2014).

When the apparent evolution is recognized, it usually comes across with an almost defiant pride for the new-found control. "Yeah, I just ruined my entire appetite ... cookies." *Tech Radar* columnist Chris Smith summarized the situation with a lengthy allusion to Roald Dahl's *Charlie and the Chocolate Factory*:

> With the advent and mass adoption of on-demand portals like Netflix, Lovefilm and Spotify we've all been given the keys to the proverbial Chocolate Factory and boy have we gorged ourselves silly like an insatiable army of

Augustus Gloops…. Streaming services have broken down traditional barriers, democratised the best content and empowered the consumer. Quite frankly, we've never had it so good.

But is this instant gratification offered through high-speed internet, Smart TVs and mobile devices really such a Golden Ticket? Or are we becoming a bunch of spoilt "don't care how, I want it now" Veruca Salts, whose collective compulsions and sense of entitlement are lessening our appreciation and dumbing down our cultural and emotional responses to great content? [Smith, 2014].

No journalists fully embrace Willy Wonka's parting words from the 1971 movie adaptation: "But Charlie, don't forget what happened to the man who suddenly got everything he always wanted…. He lived happily ever after." Instead, there clearly is underlying fear and guilt about the consequences derived from television pleasure. On the other hand, neither are strong enough to preclude binge-watching. While journalists used addiction language throughout their articles from 2012 to 2016, they rarely do so in what could be considered a dangerous way. For instance, *Mercury News* TV columnist Chuck Barney (2013) described a Bay Area mother's habit thus: "Cheney embraced it a few years ago, after she had kids…. Now, Chaney is hooked on binge-viewing, pointing out that it allows her to be in control." Swap any dangerous substance with "binge-viewing" in that sentence, and concerned readers might consider calling child protective services on Cheney. Instead, the "addiction" is a tool that allows a working mom to find some pleasure around the demands of her career and children: "Bogged down during the week by workplace and parental obligations, she realized that she had precious little time for TV and was missing entire seasons of her favorite shows." To get her fix, she and her husband would sneak *Supernatural* binges after putting the kids to bed.

Some take a subversive pleasure in flouting the supposed dangers and addictive drive of joyful immersion:

Weird stuff happens after about eight hours of watching the same TV show. Your eyes feel crunchy. You get a headache that sits in your teeth, the kind that comes from hitching your free time to a runaway train of self-indulgence—too much booze, food, or sleep. Of course there's also the sense of accomplishment, of smugness, that comes from blowing through years of television in mere days [Choi, 2012].

The smugness is a nod to the original binge-viewers and a call to Mom about ruining your appetite. But it is also a celebration of freedom and a reimaging of the previous decades of shameful pleasure now maturing into cultural pride. As Goldstein (2013) put it, "Ah, nerd glaze. It's not something you get when you watch television. It's something you get when you binge." For others, the guilt is offset by ritual and climate. Ward (2014) admitted that "realizing you've wasted an entire weekend away on the couch doesn't necessarily make you feel like the most productive person in the world. But especially during a cold Minnesota winter, it's nice to hole up and escape into a riveting drama."

While feeling guilty about spending his holidays binge-watching, Nathan Fisher (2014) also claimed that "as each season of a show finished, I had a sense of accomplishment and closure." Choi (2012) also referenced *Willy Wonka* (1971), writing that when you complete an entire show in one sitting "you get the world of pure imagination, if you can handle mainlining it." Her drug terminology harkens back to the VCR proto-binging language found in 1980s fanzines (Stevens, 2021).

When journalists initially brought up fears of isolation and loneliness from hours spent alone binge-watching, they were met with rebuttals (Martin, 2013). Anthropologist McCracken (2013) penned an eloquent explanation for rethinking the isolation as a virtual vacation with only your favorite people. "Contrary to what others may argue here, we don't lose that 'shared cultural space,' the shared experience of everyone talking about the same shows. We just narrow the space to an island inhabited only by ourselves instead of all of America watching the same show at once."

In 2014 and 2015 a smattering of articles cropped up connecting overindulgence to binge-watching with potentially negative outcomes. Some were published after the holiday season and preceded by December lists of shows to binge (Pierson et al., 2015). Because health and television continued to be an evergreen topic, these articles were syndicated and appeared multiple times in the dataset. After the initial wave of streaming industry sources, some journalists began to quote psychologists and media scholars who offer ambivalent answers to the consequences of binge-watching. The debate of connoisseur versus glutton creates an enticing tension that fueled binge-watching appeal during this period. Once again, Roald Dahl's fable of chocolate scarcity and abundance provided context for readers: "While the experts we consulted had their own preference, they all saw merits in both consumption models—ultimately it's up to you whether you are the Charlie or the Augustus of the new Netflix world we live in" (Smith, 2014).

By mid–2015, preliminary scholarship on binge-watching came to academic conferences. Some journalists defining binge-watching through the clinical frame referred to these academic studies, most often the University of Texas survey (n=316) on isolation (Sung, Kang, & Lee, 2015). Unlike the Harris poll and other industry research, which reported people having generally favorable experiences with binge-watching (PRNewswire, 2013), the news stories citing potentially negative consequences tended to have shorter-lived penetration. After 23 citations in January and February of 2015 (mostly wire story reprints), the Texas survey fell off the radar of journalists, at least in terms of attribution. But that survey's findings, which are obliquely referenced during the next two years,[5] may have spurred journalists to examine and write about ways to binge-watch less in late 2015 and into 2016. These few articles are also notable for their ambivalence—their authors are quick not to condemn binge-watching outright, merely to control binge by setting limits and selection purity standards. For instance, in December 2015, Patrick Allen wrote a piece for *Lifehacker* titled "How to Break Your Netflix Binge-Watching Habit." He leads with two paragraphs of binge-watching equivocation before offering tips on pacing yourself: "Vegging out in front of the TV can be a fun activity for a lazy Sunday, but.... Watching TV isn't inherently bad and it's a great way to relax after a long day, but too much of it saps your productivity."

Besides the Texas loneliness paper, none of the other academic studies were cited more than two weeks after the first appearance in an article from 2012 to 2016. After some prominent initial coverage, Sung, Kang, and Lee's (2015) study was mentioned more often as a passing statement below the fifth paragraph to balance an article's exuberance for the pleasures of binge-watching. Journalists seldom sought secondary opinions on health studies and often linked to other news stories that mentioned a study rather than the study itself. Their passing references indicate a lack of interest in these potential consequences compared to their repeated emphasis on potential positive or ambivalent personal outcomes of binge-watching. Sometimes binge-watching and addiction were exploited (presumably to drive traffic) in the headlines of articles that were barely related to the topic, such as "5 Ways to Stop Binge-Watching Netflix and Actually Get Sh*t Done" (Bilyk, 2016). I ended up wasting time I could have spent getting this chapter done by reading and re-reading that article in order to figure out what it had to do with binge-watching. The answer: nothing besides the title.

While the tone of journalists was most frequently ambivalent, the underlying sentiment leaned toward this perspective: "Binge-watching is only unhealthy if you consider exuberant freedom of choice unhealthy" (Meyer, 2013). The overarching consequence found in the definitional binge-watching journalism from 2012 to 2016 was a complication of the television experience. Enthusiasm about reimagining the idiot box as technology that could turn a guilty pleasure into a culturally enriching enterprise while undermining broadcasting structures precluded reporters from digging too deeply into the new systems of delivery and the tech companies behind them.

Instead, there was a kind of adolescent glee, like first-semester college students discovering that their parental control had been overbearing and was now lifted. That glee was most often tempered by ambivalence, as if they suddenly remembered that they were journalists and not fans. Across these thousands of news articles, binge-watching was described simultaneously as empowering and disempowering, as addictive and liberating, as transportive and vegetative. That complicated and contradictory nature no doubt drove further fascination with the new phenomenon during this period. It's rare that journalists articulate such ambivalence, and rarer still when that ambivalence involves transformative consequences of a common household item. Yet that is what binge-watching did for television, and journalists around the world speculated on the outcomes with extreme ambivalence.

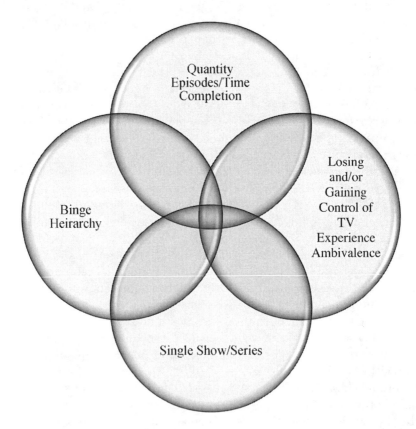

Binge-Watching News Definitional Venn Diagram.

Netflix Narrative Disrupts Journalism Conventions

Journalism's authority is often a product of its sources. Traditionally, journalists are authoritative voices on a topic because of professional experience in newsgathering and personal expertise about certain subjects. Also, and perhaps more importantly, journalists have greater access to sources of information than readers do. As Gans (1999) describes it, "the news is shaped above all, by the sources on which journalists rely" (p. 236). Their words are a record, which, ideally, readers can rely on to understand the aspects of human experience that interest them. Sources serve as evidence that shape the boundaries of that understanding. News can be seen then as "the exercise of power over the interpretation of reality" (Schlesinger, 1972, p. 4) and, therefore, an influential part of public discourse.

Most 20th-century usages of "binge" in reference to "TV" came with little explanation. Sources were not needed to justify common knowledge. Journalists instead relied on a shared understanding that a binge meant an excessive amount, and that TV was, for the most part, a unidirectional broadcasting medium of commercial content shaped to capture the attention of a homogeneous, passive audience. When VCR technology began complicating viewer agency and consumption in the late 1970s and early 1980s, journalists provided informative reporting to help readers' understanding of the new technology (Wickstrom, 1983). Just like with the crush of reporting around home video libraries and time-shifting during the early 1980s, the 2012–2016 binge-watching articles were both informative of the new technological practices and also speculative about the potential disruption of commercial television. They differed in that the speculation of VCRs' disruptive powers had been written as opinion with quotes from optimistic manufacturers like JVC and Sony. The binge-watching reports contained opinions too, but they were often written in a more authoritative tone, with quotes from experts and official studies that instructed and normalized the behavior while reinforcing the narrative of a streaming video revolution.

The single-season release model disrupted journalistic norms of information acquisition and distribution. For decades, TV critics had been part of an elite group granted access to an entire season of a show, often before it aired. Netflix's full-season release model "thoroughly interrupted ... the temporal regularity of television" (Grandinetti, 2017, p. 11) and the elite access of those reviewing it. Prior to 2012, critics could know a lot about the show a lot sooner than the audience could;

after 2012, the information gap shrank. Viewer experience aside (see Chapter 5), this shrinking information gap raised professional questions about how journalists should report on a show that their readers may have already seen (Greenwald, 2014). Not only that, but for TV critics, binge-watching was news that affected their organizational routines, authority, and livelihoods. If, to paraphrase Walter Gieber (1964), news is what gatekeepers make it, after 2012 the news was making the gatekeepers news. While historically entertainment writers are less averse to first-person narratives than so-called "hard news" reporters, their critiques have historically not focused on their personal sleep habits or hygiene. But in 2012, their personal and professional lives became news. The mainstreaming of binge-watching through the single-season release model was reflected in the abundance of first-person narratives of journalist binges replete with the tongue-in-cheek addiction language and ambivalent pride-shame of staying up all night to watch groundbreaking TV. Was this newsworthy? Sure. But the impact of news authorities as cultural shapers also contributed to the public acceptance of binge-watching as an acceptable and a desirable form of cultural consumption.

Journalistic criticism of binge-watching is rare and never matches the 20th-century screeds on the dangers of TV. As Mary McNamara's (2012) second synonym indicates, it is "being a television critic." While not all readers of TV commentary aspire to be professional commentators, the choice to read about TV from a news source implies a desire to learn about some aspect of television from an authority. Binge-viewers did not become binge-viewers because journalists were doing it. But the way journalists described how they binged was an influence on how the public understood it. As with any official review, it's not just the content of the review but how the reviewer consumes the content that matters. This is particularly true when the new rituals of consumption are shaping the content being reviewed. In this sense, a critic is an expert on not just what to watch but how to watch it, and in 2012, it became increasingly possible for their followers to do both.

Since binge-watching was widely reported to be a (wink-wink) dangerous hobby, there was no need to seek contrary sources to its viewer-empowering narrative. However, by rarely seeking them, journalists positioned opposition opinions as antiquated and outside the realm of debate. The past narrative of TV addiction leading to America's downfall was passé—a quaint 20th-century concern that, like smallpox, had been overcome through technological advancement. Fears about the idiot box were replaced by official data supporting fantasies of streaming viewer empowerment. Of course there was irony and ambivalence throughout coverage and often playful tones: this was TV, after all, not heroin. Perhaps as a result of journalists' fanciful and celebratory attitudes, their discourse on binge-watching came to be influenced by a few unchecked sources connected to powerful, interested stakeholders. This is not to say that the Harris Interactive poll or any of the others were methodologically unsound. It does mean that Netflix and other media companies, through various proxies, became regular, and supposedly reliable, sources for journalists articulating the new behavior when binge-watching was becoming part of the zeitgeist. In 1955, Wolters used CBS's Robinson as a source, but when he included Robinson's claims about TV getting "much better," Wolters was quick to voice skepticism of them. Whether due to professional demands or personal interests, TV critics from 2012 to 2016 were conspicuously uncritical of streaming companies in their binge-watching coverage and remarkably credulous of their sources. While Netflix may not have set the news agenda at that time, it certainly had a hand in steering the journalistic narrative about TV. And that narrative went viral, much to the benefit of Netflix and the other streaming tech companies that steered it (Shiller, 2019).

Marathon versus Binge

So were Jordan, Larson, and Laughlin binge-watching or were they engaged in a TV marathon? Based on my analysis of journalistic coverage, what differentiates binge-watching from other forms of extended video viewing is (1) the content of what is viewed, (2) the technology for viewing the content, and (3) the manner in which the content is viewed. While TiVo can be used to binge-watch, the trio watched multiple programs during those 87 hours. By content and ritual, journalists defined it as the focused completion of a single program. Channel surfing falls outside their definitions of binging. So while the trio may have binged-watched certain shows, the act of watching TV for 87 hours straight does not by itself meet the initial journalistic criteria of binge-watching.

But if TV has gotten so much better, shouldn't we use the healthier "marathon" to describe it? Lisa Perks (2015) would certainly agree, and she is not alone. Constructions such as "marathon TV" do a better job of speaking to the progressive nature of the behavior and indicate that the viewer, through action, is controlling the medium as opposed to a "TV marathon." Nevertheless, binge became the buzzword.

Despite the earnest attempts by some media executives "to call the behavior 'marathoning,' since bingeing can have negative connotations," the terms are not synonyms (Stelter, 2013). TV marathon is a deficient descriptor of what viewers are doing for three reasons. (1) It does not have a natural verb form. "Marathoning" is the running of marathons, but English has no verb "to marathon." If viewer control over content is active, then it requires an active verb. (2) Marathon TV does not carry the irony of binge-watching, which better expresses the ambivalent nature of the streaming video era. While marathon runners may sacrifice physical and social well-being to achieve a goal, perceptions of them may be many things—envious, inspired—but not ironic. The sacrifices are too genuine to be mocked. (3) As my findings indicate, TV marathon was a commonly used term during the 20th century. Journalists seeking to differentiate contemporary viewing rituals from those of the network era needed a fresher term. As Marshall McLuhan writes in *Understanding Media* (1964), "Jack Paar mentioned that he once had said to a young friend, 'Why do you kids use "cool" when you mean "hot"? The friend replied, 'Because you folks used up the word "hot" before we came along'" (p. v). The same can be said about "marathon" in relation to television. It is a term constituted and legitimized in the network era. Its use today is as square as the cathode ray console box and its viewers who used the word "square."

From Geek to Chic to Corporate Speak

The history of binge-watching in the press is the story of 20th-century domination of the viewer by the broadcast industry, followed by an erosion of the industry's power through viewer-empowering technology. This led to a paradigm shift in which viewer agency was recognized, celebrated, popularized, and then assimilated into a new hegemonic paradigm: the Streaming Age, the Age of Netflix, or, as Marieke Jenner (2014) calls it, TVIV. The empowered viewer is afforded more control than ever, but journalists spend little time interrogating the mechanisms of that control. Due to professional pressures and sourcing conventions, news articles from June 2012 to June 2016 reinforced a narrative of viewers becoming culturally and technologically liberated from their couch potato past by young, innovative corporations who had slain the idiot box masters. Binge-watching is, ironically enough, an expression of the control won and the out of control act that won it. As an early binge-watcher put it: "Dan Parker readily admits he, too, doesn't have a clue about how much bingeing is going on or whether he's part of a national trend, or the future of television, or a pawn in the plan for world TV domination by a few major players. Nor does he care" (Gay, 2013).

The work of journalists reflects the culture in which their articles circulate. That reflection is not merely of the reader seeking information and entertainment but also of stakeholders seeking the dissemination of certain information about that entertainment. Based on this analysis of 70 years of journalism, the first people to identify as binge-viewers were indeed the tech-savvy cult fans who propagated the term as an inside joke (Bundy, 2003; Oxford 2013). Doing so identified them as informed, subversive geeks who were disrupting network restrictions to improve their viewing experiences. Journalists relied on them as sources during the first decade of the 21st century, when binge-watching wasn't yet mainstream (Werts, 2004). They built upon a narrative of TV revolution, buoyed by DVD technology and the notion of cultural uprising (Newman & Levine, 2012). Soon journalists began reporting on their own experiences as binge-viewers (Choi, 2012; Nussbaum, 2011). Doing so aligned them with savvy superfans and creatives against the monolithic masters of the great wasteland—the broadcast networks.

As broadband internet entered most U.S. homes in the 2010s, the cultural rebels found a hero who promised them freedom to create and consume whatever they wanted, however they wanted. Through the defiant act of binge-watching, viewers could take control of the commercial-driven lowest common denominator that had infested their idiot boxes and transform themselves and the medium into something more than couch potatoes starting at the boob tube. As streaming technology dispersed the term and practice of binge-watching among a wider audience, reporters stopped citing those earlier adopters and increasingly relied on their own professional experiences. With increased adoption and narrative contagion, binge-watching became a buzzword in 2013, and news outlets stepped up to provide explanation of the phenomenon. It's unclear the extent to which the public was demanding information from the press or the press was creating demand in the public. But to fill the pages of newspapers, journalists increasingly turned to authoritative sources who provided "hard data" to bolster assertions and shape the parameters of the phenomenon. That those sources may have been funded by the very streaming companies supplying the technology and services of binge-watching remained outside the sphere of debate. In the press at least, TV's revolutionary narrative became increasingly attributed to Netflix.

This speaks to the ironic nature of binge-watching: through discursive power, a defiant behavior became a monetized experience. That today it is common knowledge that binge-watching, while complicated, can be empowering, certainly compared to what TV once was, is no less true than that Netflix and other streaming companies made that possible. The discourse around binge-watching articulation is rife with hegemony. It was news that viewers were using technology to disrupt powerful media structures and enhance their culture. But the news of how newly powerful media corporations exploited that disruption and co-opted the rebel identity for massive profits was hardly reported during the binge boom. Instead, journalists from 2012 to 2016 credulously shaped these definitional parameters around ideal corporate selling points: viewers endlessly consuming an infinite bounty of uninterrupted content wherever and whenever they want to through technology disrupted the industrial and social controls of broadcast television—in other words, the content, platform, and brand of Netflix.

What's fascinating is how control and limit became interchangeable in this narrative. In the 20th century, viewers had little control over television because the content and flow were limited by the networks. In the 21st century, viewers gleefully lost control because the content and flow became limitless. The moral of the story is that it's better to lose control because of limitless choice than to be controlled by the limitation of choice provided the content is fit for massive consumption rather than fit for the masses to consume (Gladstone, 2017). Journalists, and indeed most of society, viewed that narrative as one of improvement, largely because the content being consumed was being deemed fit for massive consumption (De Keere et al., 2021). But revitalizing the vast wasteland through abundance was not enough to kill the idiot box. Television viewers, those oft-maligned vegetive couch potatoes, needed rebranding too. While journalists provided some deference and humor around viewer rituals and consequences, they rightfully avoided depicting what a binge-viewer was. The advertising campaigns of the powerful, new media companies provided an image and brand capable of decoupling at long last the social shame of television consumers. In Chapter 4, I analyze the commercial rhetoric of the corporate stakeholders who controlled the texts, technologies, and services of binge-watching to uncover how their promotional campaigns influenced our shared understanding of the binge-viewer.

4

From Couch Potato
to Binge-Viewer

"One should only satirize the dead if they wish to live in safety"

[Juvenal, Satire I]

The second episode of the second season of the IFC comedy *Portlandia* opens with one of the first televised articulations of binge-watching. Titled "One Moore Episode," it aired on January 13, 2012. The 10-minute first act begins with the main characters, Claire and Doug, preparing to attend a friend's birthday party when Doug suggests the couple watch an episode of *Battlestar Galactica* on DVD before they leave. Reluctantly, Claire agrees. During the next two and a half minutes, the couple takes part in a depraved, multi-week binge of the cult science fiction series that only ends when they run out of episodes to watch. Not only have Doug and Clair missed the party, but they have also lost their jobs, their health, and their home. In the throes of a post-finale meltdown, they devise a desperate solution. Rather than pull their lives back together, the couple track down *Battlestar* creator Ronald D. Moore and attempt to coerce him into producing more episodes to feed their addiction.

"One Moore Episode" caricatures many of the side effects of "binge-watching" that journalists reported, often tongue in cheek, during the first two decades of the 21st century (see chapters 2 and 3). These included slovenliness, poor hygiene, declining health, and compulsive and addictive behaviors. As a comedy and not a news article, *Portlandia*'s articulation of binge-watching focused on and intensified the side effects to amplify humor—the outcomes appear obviously absurd. But for the humor to work, the audience needed to share an understanding that the consequences of binge-watching, while ridiculous, were not outlandish; they reflected a skewed but imaginable reality.

Claire and Doug are caricatures of a familiar trope—the couch potato. While the trope is a 20th-century construction, *Portlandia*'s writers exploited 21st-century binge-watching technology and culture in a timely reimaging of the couch potato, which is absurd and yet relatable. Neither "binge-watching" nor "binge-viewer" appear in the script, but the behavior is obviously not novel. As my interviewees and journalists confirmed (see chapters 2, 3, and 5), people participated in the activity of binge-watching years before the term was coined, and, like Claire and Doug, did so with DVDs.

Couch potato is a worn trope; the image of a lazy, corpulent TV addict vegetating on a couch has been used in U.S. media since the 1970s (Jenner, 2018; Mingo 1983). What made Claire and Doug different was that while appearing to lose control, the couple focuses on a single TV show, the "planned flow" (Williams, 1990, p. 86) they control through DVD technology rather than a broadcaster's signal. Unlike the couch potato channel surfing through insufferable schlock and commercial breaks, the couple chooses to become immersed in a world of what Doug calls "not just regular science fiction, it's actually good." That *Battlestar* was unexpectedly so engaging and so easily consumable that Claire and Doug were incapable of and/or unwilling to return to "reality" speaks to the timeliness of the joke. In 2012, the narrative that television was evolving into something better was becoming increasingly accepted (Bianculli, 2016; Choi, 2012; Lotz, 2014). And while the narrative was often told as a linear advancement of technologies, texts, and experiences, the identity of television grew more complicated. As I discuss in Chapter 5, contemporary viewers agree that TV is better than it was, but they have difficulty agreeing on what it is. Pinning down the present is complicated. It is far easier to recall idiot boxes and couch potatoes as evidence of TV's evolution into something that while inscrutable is clearly better than that.

The humorous construct in "One Moore Episode" relies on a familiarity with these shared 20th-century TV stereotypes. The irony would fail if Claire and Doug skipped the party to read books, even if they were reading on Kindles. Bookworms are more easily imagined as scholars than as addicts. Our understanding of the "idiot box"—rooted in 20th-century collective memories of the medium and its users—sets the ironic conceit. Claire and Doug's exaggeration of that understanding was in tension with the unexpected reality of television's "evolution" into "significantly more complicated" art that may be worth skipping a party for (Bianculli, 2016, pp. 3–4). This episode shows how in 2012 the couch potato too was evolving (or mutating) into a new trope—the binge-viewer.

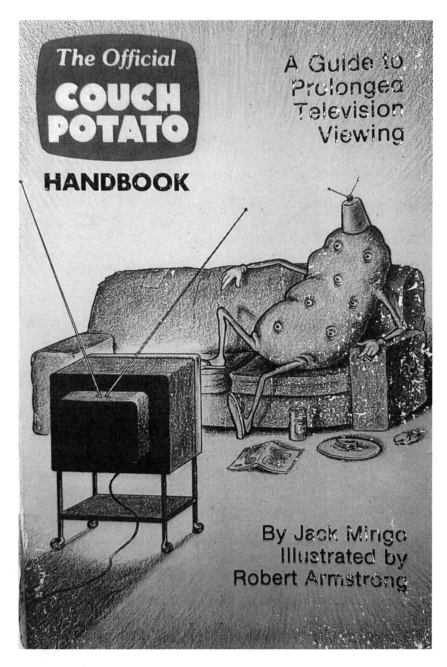

The cover illustration by Robert Armstrong for the 1982 Jack Mingo book *The Official Couch Potato Handbook* parodies the logo of the long-running viewing supplement *TV Guide*.

The writers of "One Moore Episode," like the writers of the vast majority of news stories on the topic, seemed aware of the absurdity of their depicted binge-watching side effects. In the same way that the irony would fail if Claire and Doug were reading books, so too would it fail if television were actually so addictive that it caused viewers to lose their health and homes. If TV were literally a "Medusa which freezes a billion people to stone every night" (Bradbury, 1953, p. 55), Portlandia's skit wouldn't be ironic. At the same time, the episode calls upon our shared memory of 20th-century fears and fantasies about idiot boxes and couch potatoes. Although absurd, Claire and Doug were relatable because they embodied a changing understanding of television and viewer in contrast to our collective memory of them.

The rituals and consequences of binge-watching depicted in "One Moore Episode" became the stereotypical behaviors associated with binge-viewers half-heartedly reported in the press, occasionally depicted online, and even alluded to by viewers but never actually observed in reality. They were the TV

To learn how irony dies, flip to 204 (note 1).[1]

Mr. Hydes—fantastic embodiments of the nerd superfans who coined "binge watch"—alive in all of us if we ever really lost control. The association of those stereotypes with binge-viewers may have been strong, but, as the news reports show, there was an awareness of their hyperbole. At the same time that hyperbole was entwined with a more latent fantasy of viewers who report that binge-watching brings them closer to a story's characters, its writers, and, among those prestige dramas that sit atop the binge-watching hierarchy, its showrunner. These aspirational TV Dr. Jekylls—master storytellers—are alive in all of us too, perhaps, if we could ever take control. While viewers may not aspire to be showrunners, many report feeling connections to and respect for them and their craft. By binge-watching they are taking control of a show's flow and bending it in a way closer to the creator's intent. That belief is found in quotes and commentaries of binge-watching journalism and throughout the audience studies literature (Perks, et al., 2021; Pittman & Sheehan, 2015; Steiner & Xu, 2020). It's why Claire and Doug feel empowered to track down the *Battlestar* creator Ronald D. Moore and think they can help him create more shows.

In this chapter, I deconstruct how Netflix and other media companies used these Dr. Jekyll and Mr. Hyde fantasies to re-brand couch potatoes as connoisseurs of a reimagined art form. On its surface, the two-pronged campaign appears rather traditional: testimonials from experts endorsing the new behavior and public service announcements educating consumers about best practices. However, a closer examination reveals something more perverse. For starters, the two prongs were sending manifestly contradictory messages. The subtly circulated endorsements of binge-watching from showrunners and actors positioned the practice and practitioners as reclaiming control of television (Dr. Jekyll) while the PSAs depicted binge-viewers as deprived addicts (Mr. Hyde).

That contradiction speaks to the bind that companies seeking to profit from binge-watching found themselves in: (1) How do you mass market a behavior that for 60 years had been widely accepted to be mind-numbing, slovenly, and unattractive? (2) How do you make commercials about a commercial-free viewing experience? Traditionally, the strategy with dangerous or addictive products has been to put them in the hands of attractive twenty-somethings engaging in physical activities or to hire healthy and beautiful celebrities to endorse them. Fantasies are pushed forward while the negative realities are hidden. But it's hard to binge-watch while playing beach volleyball. And would anyone care if an athlete endorsed it? To rebrand the couch potato, streaming companies instead took a radically honest and utterly absurd approach: they turned the "side effects" into aspirational fantasies that were promoted in broadcast commercials while subtly using celebrities to emphasize the actual benefits and value through non-commercial channels. In a sense they made Mr. Hyde the face of binge-viewing, while Dr. Jekyll spread public service messages behind-the-scenes. Most bizarre of all, it succeeded.

To unpack how that worked, I begin by sketching a brief history of the public service announcements and 20th-century celebrity endorsements that served as foils for the campaign. Next, I present my analysis of the satirical binge-viewer commercials and sincere spokesperson testimonials to illustrate how Netflix, Hulu, Disney, Amazon, Comcast, Cox Communication, and T-Mobile constructed binge-viewers and framed binge-watching against the memories of 20th-century television. While obviously competitors, the companies shared remarkably similar messaging in their efforts to disassociate themselves and, importantly, their audiences from not just the TV standards of the network era but also its advertising practices. Through my analysis, I expose the contours of a marketing campaign that shaped binge-viewers' evolution through technology, from couch potato to an embodiment of post-industrial consumer ideals: culturally ambivalent, self-aware, and agentic.

If you want to learn more about the theory behind my analysis, turn to 204 (note 2).[2]

If you want to learn more about the methodology and commercial rhetoric selection and sampling for this chapter, turn to 206 (note 3).[3]

Or skip the theory and methods and continue to Informational Television on 106.

Informational Television

In Chapter 1, I outlined how television was the most hated and most adopted 20th-century media technology. While I have described some of the widespread criticism of television that helped construct our understanding of the idiot box and the couch potato, it is important to recognize that not all of its content was considered equally harmful. Shows that were billed as informational rather than entertaining enjoyed a better reputation among critics and regulators (Parker & Dunn, 1972). Educational programming, while not a substitute for traditional book learning, was seen by some as potentially beneficial for audiences (Murphy & Gross, 1966). This more educational and more informational content included public service announcements (PSAs).

Since the middle of the 20th century, these apparently sincere attempts to raise awareness for issues of concern to the general public were aired on the major networks that "donated" airtime as required by the FCC. Like most television of the time, PSAs contained low production values and simplistic stories aimed at a wide audience, but they were understood to be "not produced for a profit" (Lloyd-Kolkin & Tyler, 1991, p. 157). Because of the fears associated with children's use of television, PSAs were seen as an opportunity to enhance the expanding TV diets of young American viewers with more nutritious,

For more information on how communication scholars define PSAs, go to 207 (note 4).[4]

wholesome fare. They are descended from propaganda newsreels of early and middle 20th-century cinema and, later, classroom filmstrips (Gregory, 2004, pp. 18–19).

Filmstrips to PSAs: A Dose of Dull History

As America urbanized in the early 20th century and public school attendance became compulsory, the idea of normalizing education to create workers for the growing nation of immigrants became popular among progressives. Following the Great Depression, however, when "there weren't enough jobs to go around ... the last thing government wanted was an influx of cheap teenage labor competing with workers of voting age" (Gregory, 2004, p. 46). By encouraging students to stay in school, the labor pool was more fixed, and numerous jobs associated with education—teaching, administration, and maintenance—were created. The question of what to teach the swelling ranks of students led to the creation of "life adjustment" curricula—education beyond traditional classroom lessons (Podeschi, 1987, p. 8). While the pluralism of such lessons may have been appealing, teachers had little experience teaching them. One potential solution offered by policymakers and scholars was to utilize video technology in the classroom and beyond (Murphy and Gross, 1966). A popular and economical option was the filmstrip—cheap, mass-produced and able to be shared and replicated across the country. In the years following World War II, the flickering film projector became a fixture in American classrooms. At first silent, with teachers providing voiceovers, the filmstrips allowed for mass messaging of an ever-expanding social curriculum for students. They contained lessons about not just hygiene and safety but also about American values chosen by the Department of Education and other policy influencers.

As the television set became common in 1950s American homes,

This 1958 photograph from Navy Hill School by Adolph B. Rice Studio shows two students in Richmond, Virginia, working with a classroom projector. The technology became a staple of U.S. classrooms during the middle of the 20th century. "The evolutionary filmstrip" by Scott McLeod is licensed under CC BY 2.0

the impetus to reach and teach audiences through it intensified. Cold War pressures made ideological campaigns big business, while local economic interests were also promoted under the guise of education (Gregory, 2004). As with classroom filmstrips, PSAs were born in part from a "noble" motive of helping the citizenry, especially children, though PSAs had a wider if not more captive audience. Public safety messages on the dangers of old refrigerators, strangers, not obeying traffic signs, littering, and forest fires became mainstays of 20th-century broadcast line-ups. Their accompanying catchphrases like "Give a hoot; don't pollute!"; "Stranger danger!"; and "Stop, drop, and roll!" are instantly recallable by Americans who grew up watching them.

On the surface, PSAs appear to serve the public through an announcement of valuable information. However, what PSAs of the 20th century lacked was self-awareness in their messaging. They carried an unacknowledged and unironic paternalism in their constructions, values, and assumptions about the audience. By regulation, the U.S. broadcast airwaves are public, but the economic reality was and is that they are accessible to few. Commercial channels were allowed to use these airwaves, but the networks were required to provide time for content that benefited the public. In step with the social science work on TV at that time, this benefit was reduced to a dialectic of information versus entertainment (Blumler & Katz, 1974) (the seeking of information being an active task compared to the supposed passivity of being entertained). The obvious irony of PSAs is that the messages were meant to serve the public, but they were created by interest groups whose economic and political power allowed them to decide who the public was and what the public needed to learn. That determination was an unspoken announcement of authority over the public—paternalism. Watch this; it's good for you. Why? Because we said so. Any questions (Chen, 2016)?

Encouraging children to eat "square meals" may seem beneficial, but reading the fine print at the end of such ads reveals that American agricultural interest groups were sponsoring the messages. Everyone thinks regular eye exams are a good thing, especially sponsors like the American Optometric Association—an interest group representing American eye doctors. Questioning the motives behind such messages seems oppositional and subversive in the face of what appear to be innocent attempts to help children be healthy. The simplicity of early PSAs reveals an expectation of audience ignorance not just of the manifest message but also of the underlying mechanisms that structure the economics and politics of broadcast television and indeed American society. Through their ham-handed appeals, PSAs constructed the audience as incapable of critical thinking, and, to some extent, rational thought. It's not a stretch to see the buds of couch potatoes sprouting.

What 20th-century PSAs accurately show through their patronizing missives is not that audiences of the time were too ignorant to know better but that they lacked a voice to respond. They were mediated acts of ideological domination—a representation of the unidirectional flow of broadcast TV. In a world with few channels, there was little space on the public airwaves for the public to challenge much of anything. Furthermore, as discussed in Chapter 1, 20th-century TV's advertising revenue model rewarded networks by the quantity of viewers they could capture rather than the quality of their programming. Producers made shows likely to appeal to the broadest possible audiences. Why rock the boat with controversial or outsider voices? Author Charles Sopkin, who in 1967 chronicled his weeklong binge of commercial TV, described the content of the era thus: "The networks really don't want quality. They do *schlock* so much better, anyhow, why should they bother with quality? The audiences don't watch it—at least not in economically feasible numbers" (p. 283).

If 1960s TV was schlock, 1960s PSAs were cheap, medicinal schlock. Commercial TV might have entertained at least, but PSAs nagged the viewers with officious messages and scare tactics from groups who, sometimes overtly, had other interests in mind than the public's well-being. Like the network news anchor taking a break from reading the headlines to light up and extoll the virtue of whichever cigarette brand was sponsoring the show, PSAs felt utterly inauthentic.

In the 1970s, as Americans were clashing over race and gender equality in ways that challenged long-held social strictures, PSAs clung to simplistic messages that reduced the complexity and upheaval of the times into tidy, wholesome bites few could swallow without gagging. Even attempts to diversify the casts of PSAs came across as pandering with token, stereotypical characters inserted with bureaucratic care (Gregory, 2004). Additionally, the cheap production values and poor animation seemed woefully behind the TV technology that was rapidly advancing.

A prime example of this tone deafness was the PSA "Don't Be a Couch Potato" (1988), which uses shaky, fluorescent chalk outline characters affixed to a couch binging on TV and snacks against a black backdrop. A pseudo-rapping voiceover extolls the dangers of mindlessly watching too much TV. The main characters, a boy and a girl, are transformed into potatoes, complete with whirlpool hypnotized eyes, as the song tells the audience to "avoid this dreaded disease" (Lloyd-Kolkin & Tyner, 1991, p. 165). "Leave me alone," raps the boy potato, "just let me

groove with my tube" (p. 165). His sister spud gorges on junk food and
raps, "Got have that. Mama, can I buy that!" while the voiceover croons,
"Watch out for over-eating!" In this we have a cartoon depiction of both
the Marxist and social science criticisms of TV (see Chapter 1) and the
increasing fears of food and entertainment consumption found in 1980s
and 1990s journalism (see Chapter 2) produced in a fashion more likely

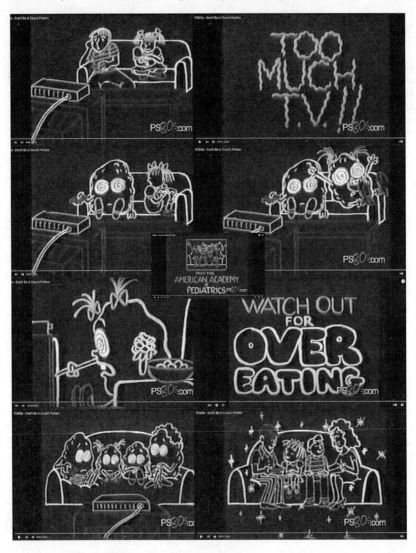

This 1988 PSA from the American Pediatric Society attempts to teach
young children about the dangers of and strategies to avoid becoming a
couch potato. Screenshots from YouTube.

to drive kids to capitalist overconsumption than from it. As the final refrain of "Don't Be a Couch Potato" rings out, the potatoes are suddenly transformed back into a human, nuclear family (the mother and father have unaccountably appeared in the final frame) when they chant "Not me!" while continuing to sit on the couch.

Celebrity PSAs

The spread of cable television in the late 20th century coincided with an increase in celebrity coverage in the media and through this a broadening of the criteria of celebrity status (Schierl, 2007). Increased coverage of famous people on new channels and shows granted fans a new kind of manufactured closeness to media personalities and celebrity lifestyles (Ryan, 2015, pp. 83–84). The private lives of public figures were more accessible on TV than ever before. As the networks were obligated to donate time for use of the public airwaves, celebrities were increasingly called upon to donate their time on the very airwaves that had given them fame. This was of course before social media made being public about your private life a cause célèbre. And celebrity spokespeople were not a new idea—Dick Van Dyke was the star of the "Stop Drop and Roll" campaign—but 1980s spokespeople added an extra layer of irony to the messaging: forced community service. Thanks to Nancy Reagan's public War on Drugs, a new kind of celebrity spokesperson began appearing in PSAs—the reformed user. The irony of a celebrity who was caught using drugs being forced to do a commercial about the consequences of using drugs, instead of suffering the stiffer consequences faced by the general public, to an audience who was increasingly fascinated by, and perhaps aspiring to, the lifestyles of the celebrities who use drugs, is inescapable.

Even as broadcast and cable TV evolved technologically and culturally in the 1990s, PSAs still presented simplistic messaging and scare tactics that overlooked the complicated realities surrounding the issues in question. In 1987, the Partnership for a Drug-Free America released one of the most iconic PSAs of all time. Titled "Frying Pan," the 15-second spot (there is a less known 30-second version) features a single tight shot of a cast iron skillet heating butter on a stove. A stern, male voiceover then addresses the audience: "This is drugs." An egg is cracked into the pan; it begins to fry. "This is your brain on drugs." The egg is burning. "Any questions!" The final line is not a question but a statement that what drugs do to your brain is so obviously harmful that you don't need to think or ask questions but "just say no."

Ten years later, as television was on the cusp of its "Platinum Age"

(Bianculli, 2016), the commercial was remade with little complication added. The new version opens with actress Rachel Leigh Cook in a kitchen holding an egg. "This is your brain," she says laying it gently on the counter and picking up the familiar cast iron frying pan. "And this is your brain after snorting heroin," she says, smashing the egg with the pan. Holding up the pan she then tells the audience, "Wait, it's not over yet." (Cue the complication.) Smashing the pan through a rack of plates she yells, "This is what your family goes through! And your friends...." She smashes several glasses and then a wall clock ("and your money"), a coffee pot ("and your job"), and a pendant light ("and your self-respect, and your future!"). Standing in the destroyed kitchen she says softly, "and your life." She throws the pan on the stove and repeats the rhetorical statement, "Any questions!"

The idea of an unquestionable authority telling you what's in everyone's interest while ignoring individuality and context became the shared understanding of PSAs—simplistic, campy, and paternalistic. Comedy shows of the late 20th century, such as *Saturday Night Live*, took advantage of that irony by satirizing their obvious hypocrisy. *The Simpsons* also loaded many of the early episodes with parodies of school filmstrips and celebrity PSAs. "Hi, I'm Troy McClure" may be as familiar to Gen-Xers as "Just say no!" In a postindustrial, neoliberal society where authority was questioned when rammed down the throat rather than made enticing, and where the individual was increasingly celebrated through technologies of self-branding, the PSA became an easy target for parody. I remember admiring a friend's poster of the "Frying Pan" spot that replaced "Any questions!" with "This is your brain on drugs with a side of bacon."

Contemporary PSAs are beginning to reflect this changing landscape. Twenty years after destroying her kitchen, an older and seemingly more thoughtful Rachel Leigh Cook reprised her role in a new "Frying Pan" PSA. The complications of addiction and the institutional racism of criminal justice are no longer elided in the messaging, which appears not only aware of the change but also reflective of its past paternalism. A 2016 campaign from the Partnership for Drug-Free Kids, formerly the Partnership for a Drug-Free America, addresses the dismissiveness of "Any questions!" with young people (presumably representative of the target audience) "asking a series of poignant questions about prescription drugs, heroin, marijuana and their parents' drug histories" (Chen, 2016). Even the simplicity of the couch potato has been benched. In 2015, Common Sense Media released a series of binge-watching PSAs called "Make Room for #realtime." Rather than preaching about the dangers of TV addiction or using fear tactics, the spots use humor and realistic situations to encourage mindful media consumption.

Nostalgia 2.0

Acknowledgment of past paternalism can be powerful because its honesty appears authentic and allows for a decoupling of the present from an idealized past. Hussain and Lapinski (2017) showed that such nostalgia can be effective in creating negative connotations for cigarette smoking. Unlike the 1970s Milk Council ad, which incorporates a 1950s greaser character to create nostalgia for the idea of square meals, these kinds of ads use nostalgia to differentiate a negative past from a potentially healthier future. Nostalgia is no longer only about an ache for a past we cannot return to but a reminder of how far we have come.

This reconceptualization of nostalgia is central to how Netflix and other media companies rebranded the idiot box and the couch potato. New, high-quality content and technology were features that differentiated streaming 13 hours of *The Sopranos* in 2012 from staring at 13 hours of broadcast programming in 1982. But quality wasn't enough. The viewer was still spending the better part of the day watching TV, an act that for mainstream American audiences in 2012 still carried that idiot box stigma so poorly represented in the "Don't Be a Couch Potato" PSA (1989). Recasting the binge-viewer as distinct from the couch potato would take a more marketable and empowering action, one that newspapers had been reporting on since the early 2000s. That was when journalists began covering a new breed of cord-cutting, DVD-hoarding superfans who were reshaping the way major networks thought about television. This wasn't just about smarter TV shows, something HBO had been marketing for years, but also about viewers using technology to subvert the commercially imposed barriers between them and the shows' creators. It was about viewers improving a show by how they watched and forcing the TV industry to allow creatives to create more freely. Remember Mary McNamara's (2012) definition of binge-watching is an endorsement of content *and* ritual.

To learn about what 21st-century media scholars have uncovered about the power of self-aware PSAs, turn to 207 (note 5).[5]

While niche in 2006, that narrative was out there and beginning to gain traction. But what if those rebel viewers were re-armed with streaming, portable platforms instead of clunky DVDs? And what if new studies showed that the cabal of underground nerds was growing into a majority (say, 73 percent) of Americans? And what if instead of rumors and speculation about them revolutionizing TV, you got the most famous and respected storytellers to do public service messaging affirming the rebels and extolling the powers of binge-watching to disrupt the corrupt broadcast industry? And what if that was supplemented with a series of satirical PSAs exaggerating binge-viewer side effects so absurdly as to other anyone who actually took them seriously? That might be the kind of campaign that would help the public re-evaluate its anti–TV biases and its perception of someone who streams 13 episodes of a prestige drama.

Abetting Dr. Jekyll

TV parasocial relationships—perceived connections people feel between themselves and media characters who don't know them—have been extensively studied since the 1950s (Liebers & Schramm, 2019). In some ways, that sense of viewer-character intimacy is vital for any show to have an audience. Who wants to watch something about people they have no connection with or interest in (Brown, 2015)? Parasocial relationships have been rewarded and exploited across every aspect of commercial television. They are why Winston paid ABC to have Fred Flintstone smoke their cigarettes and why children's PSAs in the 1980s featured characters from the cartoons they followed. While these relationships may have first been observed with viewers and fictional characters (Horton & Wohl, 1956), as celebrity lifestyles became increasingly televised in the 1980s and '90s, the line between parasocial relationships and fandom grew increasingly blurry (Stever, 2009; Spitzberg & Cupach, 2008). Did a viewer feel connected to the actual actor condemning drug use in the PSA or was the connection actually with a character that actor had portrayed? "'Hi, I'm Troy McClure. You might remember me from such public service videos as *Designated Drivers: The Lifesaving Nerds* and *Phony Tornado Alarms Reduce Readiness*. I'm here today to give you the skinny on shoplifting, thereby completing my plea bargain with the good people at Foot Locker of Beverly Hills'" (*The Simpsons*, 1995).

During the 20th century, TV parasocial relationships were almost always between a viewer and a person on the screen, fictional and/or real. But as TV entered its Platinum Age with shows like *The Sopranos* (1999–2007), *The Wire* (2002–2008), and *Mad Men* (2007–2015), viewers began forming parasocial relationships with a new kind "mediated" character, one that was rarely if ever on screen: the showrunner (Bourdaa, Chin, & Lemerichs, 2016). A descendant of the film auteur and the TV executive producer (Newman & Levine, 2012, pp. 38–40), a showrunner is "the person responsible for all creative aspects of the show, and responsible only to the network (and production company, if it's not his production company). The boss. Usually a writer" (Epstein, 2005). People like David Chase (*The Sopranos*), David Simon (*The Wire*), and Matthew Weiner (*Mad Men*) were the creators and controllers of the prestige dramas that are credited with elevating television to the cultural status of film (Bianculli, 2016; Johnson, 2012). And while audiences were certainly drawn to and repelled by characters on these shows, superfans were also inspired by and connected to their creators. This was a vital shift. As I described in Chapter 2, *X-Files* fans spent days online going back and forth about the characters. But individual writers and executive producers or even its creator Chris Carter never developed the kind of followings that Joss Whedon, Shonda Rhimes, or Vince Gilligan would in the 21st century.

As Netflix prepared to launch its $100 million flagship drama *House of Cards* in late 2012, it deployed the show's two creative forces—showrunner Beau Willimon and executive producer-star Kevin Spacey—not only to promote the show but also to inform the public of the value and the benefit of binge-watching. Although Willimon was a relative newcomer, and Spacey was a decade removed from his Hollywood heyday, they carried an artistic authenticity that resonated as buzz around the show's single season drop grew because their messaging was framed as anti-advertising. Their pitch was that commercials were the enemy of the showrunner *and* the viewer and that binge-watching was the solution. Under the guise of traditional TV show publicity, they and others penetrated award ceremonies, late night talk shows, festivals, lectures, and roundtables where their quotes of audience empowerment and a TV (r)evolution spread organically through social and mainstream media channels. As Willimon explained during an April 2013 online Q&A with *Vulture* readers:

> We might have been the first original series to deliver our entire season at once, but people have been binge-watching for years. Netflix helped expand this phenomenon, but viewers were also doing it through DVD box sets, DVR, on-demand, and other streaming services. We simply responded to a trend that was well under way and which is sure to continue. Our show simply gave people the experience they had already grown accustomed to on Netflix—viewer empowerment. People like being able to decide for themselves when, where, and in what quantities they will watch their content. That power is increasing, and all content-providers must either adapt or fall by the wayside [Adalian, 2013].

In a 2013 *New York Times* showrunners roundtable, Willimon spoke about viewers influencing stories while comparing binge-watching to novel reading:

At its core, it's people having a reason to have a conversation about a shared experience, but there's a lot of ways to have a shared experience. That can be live-tweeting. That can be people that have binge-watched a season of something and told their friend, "You have to binge-watch it, so we can talk about it."

When Dickens was writing his novels, and they were serialized once a month, he read all the letters that came in. His novels were actually a real dialogue with his audience. He was writing to entertain them, and he got paid by the word, and he wanted them to be pleased. But he also wanted to make sure that they got the story he was trying to tell [Manly, 2013].

The melding of media, particularly those traditionally associated with higher culture like theater and books, was often invoked in these Netflix surrogate messages. Speaking at the 2013 Edinburgh Festival, Spacey, who'd been performing Shakespeare's *Richard III* in London, explained: "audiences are no longer making distinctions between television and other media, so let's throw the labels out … if we have to call ourselves anything then aren't we all just storytellers?" Aren't we all just storytellers! With that declaration he articulated the fantastic parasocial relationship between viewer and showrunner. The story's creator and the story's consumer are both storytellers, and both have a hand in making the story great. Spacey's theatrical bona fides and masterful oratory—the antithesis of an idiot box spokesperson—made that fantastic union erudite and authentic, even when he added that it was made possible by Netflix:

The success of the Netflix model—releasing the entire season of House of Cards at once and online—has proved one thing: the audience wants the control. They want freedom. If they want to binge then we should let them binge. And through this new form of distribution, I think we have demonstrated that we have learned the lesson the music industry didn't learn: give people what they want, when they want it, in the form they want it in—at a reasonable price.… We get what audiences want—they want quality. We get what the talent wants—artistic freedom. And the only way to protect talent and the quality of our work is for us to be innovative.

Other showrunners spoke to the power that viewers now had to elevate TV culture. In this way they borrowed a page from the journalism of the 2000s that positioned binge-viewers as culture rebels who were disrupting the TV industry. Three years before inking a multimillion-dollar-a-year deal with the streaming giant, showrunner Steve S. DeKnight told the *New York Times* that "the Netflix model allowed [shows] to spend an entire season gradually unpacking the origins of its characters" (Itzkoff, 2015). As I discuss in Chapter 3, the contagious narrative of television's revolution spread through mainstream media, linking technology-empowered viewers with acclaimed writers and actors who both celebrated Netflix for obliterating the network television conventions of the previous 60 years.

Tim Kring, showrunner of NBC's *Heroes*, aired his grievances with the network TV model during a *Hollywood Reporter* interview to promote his new streaming show *Beyond*.

> With Heroes, we were always in trouble.... Every single week I was getting the call that it is going to be canceled. The relationship with the network is often contentious. Confession: You become very comfortable with lying to people, say yes when you mean no, say things are ready when they are not. You are constantly in the state of telling white lies. There's the hammer of the budget and ratings over your head [Anderson, 2016].

He contrasts that with the power of binge-watching for viewer and storyteller and why TV should be more like Netflix:

> I think Netflix is very much on the forefront, or at least took advantage of a trend that was started with serialized dramas like Lost and Heroes. These were shows that were a superior experience when watched one after the other rather than waiting week to week.... It allows for a deep, immersive experience into a story that satisfies our addiction to know the answers to what the show is asking us to be interested in.

Carlton Cuse, showrunner of *Bates Motel* and *Lost*, echoed that network/Netflix distinction. In 2013 he stated that binge-viewers' technological savvy had "allowed for heavily serialized storytelling, which was an anathema to broadcast networks a few years ago, because they thought if somebody fell out of an episode, then they would never get them back. But now there's so many ways for people to watch shows that they recognized that serialized storytelling actually hooks an audience, and they're not as afraid about people missing stuff because they have so many ways of getting caught up" (Manly, 2013).

One of Netflix's more interesting showrunner surrogates was Mitch Hurwitz, creator of *Arrested Development*. Just like *Family Guy* nearly a decade early, Hurwitz's edgy, genre-bending sitcom had been canceled by Fox but was kept alive by its cult of superfans. Unlike *Family Guy*, though, *Arrested Development* wasn't picked back up by Fox but instead resurrected in 2013 by Netflix. The move demonstrated how subscription-based streaming services unfettered both audiences and showrunners from the burdens of commercials. As Jenner (2018) points out, "Mitch Hurwitz, as the auteur figure, was well positioned to speak to the creative process and the concept of binge-watching" (p. 165).

One of Hurwitz's key talking points was the lack of awareness that major networks had for the narrowing of audiences. As he told *The Guardian*, "[broadcast] television is in this crazy place where it's still trying to get this 12m audience but it doesn't exist. Golden Girls had 30m. We were cancelled when we had 8m" (Freeman, 2013). The notion of individualization of one's TV experience and identity (see Chapter 5) has grown in the years since. But in 2013 it was still somewhat radical to imagine creating a show for a small number of niche viewers. For more than half a century, the major TV networks had successfully operated under the model of audience as a unified mass, and the larger they could grow that mass, the higher the ratings and the greater the ad revenue. As with 20th-century PSAs, this approach flattens individual differences and tastes in search of the broadest possible appeal. Hurwitz emphasized that "you can't be indifferent to your audience" (Freeman, 2013). He described how streaming services like Netflix were disrupting traditional understandings of audiences and episodes creating new TV experiences: "Then this new audience came along and they didn't differentiate between the episodes, they just looked at it all as Arrested and loved it." Hurwitz's voice served to not only demonstrate the unity of viewer and creator; his bona fides also meant that fans and media paid attention to his explanations of the phenomenon. Furthermore, the cult following of *Arrested Development*, enflamed by Fox's untimely cancelling, "ensured Hurwitz' presence on the pages of newspapers and magazines that aimed to reach a young adult, middle-class audience interested in 'cult' TV" (Jenner, 2018, p. 165).

Like Willimon, Hurwitz positioned the binge-viewer as a reader with the technology to control how they experience a book. Beneath that overt message is the subtle implication that Netflix binge-viewers are closer to bookworms than those couch potatoes starting at network pablum on their idiot boxes. Spacey (2013) also linked the audience's evolution to the medium's:

> The warp speed of technological advancement—the internet, streaming, multi-platforming—happens to have coincided with the recognition of TV as an art form. So you have this incredible confluence of a medium coming into its own just as the technology for that medium is drastically shifting. Studios and networks who ignore either shift will be left behind. And if they fail to hear these warnings, audiences will evolve faster than they will. They will seek the stories and content providers who give them what they demand—complex, smart stories available whenever they want, on whatever device they want, wherever they want.

Becoming Mr. Hyde

Creating parasocial relationships with critically acclaimed show-runners who authenticated the fantasy that binge-viewers were making

TV high art cognitively distinguished the binge-viewer from the couch potato. However, there remained certain physical realities of extended TV-viewing that couldn't be denied. As journalists began reporting on potential health effects of binge-watching, there was a very real possibility of public backlash. As hard as it may be to believe in a world where binge-watching is normal, in 2012 mass consumption of television was at best a guilty pleasure. Rather than sit by and let evergreen screeds of couch potatoes past sprout, Disney, Netflix, Amazon, Hulu, Comcast, Cox Communication, and T-Mobile got ahead of the story by releasing a series of paternalistic PSAs and cautionary commercials warning viewers about the dangers of binge-watching and TV addiction. Interestingly these began coming out in 2014–2015 after their research had framed the parameters of binge-watching and just before non-industry studies on binge-watching effects began appearing in the press. You may be wondering why some of the largest and most successful companies on earth would voluntarily depict their products as debilitating and their consumers as depraved fiends. This series of ads stands in seeming opposition to the empowered showrunner messaging campaign of the enlightened and evolved viewer. Taken literally, these spots are the advertising equivalent of a fast-food company showing its customers gorging compulsively, growing obese, having heart attacks, and continuing to gorge despite their doctors' warnings.

On their surface, there is nothing appetizing or attractive about how these 20th-century-styled PSAs present binge-viewers. Through cinematography and scripts, they call upon the viewer to remember that authoritarian voice of the idiot box. The promos use mnemonic cues such as camera angles, narrative structures, voiceovers, graphics, sound effects, and language to activate nostalgia for PSAs. These devices serve to heighten the tension and fear of outcomes as if binge-watching were akin to drug addiction and mental disorders. But it is all a perversion of nostalgia.

The verisimilitude employed to recreate the past as a simple time that was overregulated by alarmist digital immigrants transfers the irony onto the 20th-century TV broadcasters, thereby differentiating streaming companies and viewers from that past. The effect unifies those who get the joke against those who don't and organizes them by technological acumen. The multi-layered irony separates first by digital native/digital immigrant status around the understanding of TV technology and second by young/old in terms of perceptions of TV culture. At the same time, the irony is predicated on a collective memory of what 20th-century PSAs looked like and a perception that the simpler time was simpler in a closed-minded way. The binge-viewer is thereby cast as an evolved, sophisticated couch potato because of the technology, services, and content being advertised.

One of the first of these satirical commercials was released by Maker Studios in March 2014, not long after Disney agreed to purchase the company for $500 million (Patel, 2017). "Dangers of Binge Watching: A PSA" (2014) was released online, generating close to half a million views on YouTube alone. The three-minute parody of both 20th-century filmstrips and PSAs provided a blueprint for the 30- to 60-second constructions of binge-viewers that would follow. "Dangers" is set in the sparse TV-lit den of young, couch-bound binge-viewer Brian "who used to be a successful member of society, until last weekend when he discovered seasons 1–5 of *Breaking Bad* on Netflix" (Maker, 2014, p. 18). It opens with his off-camera wife imploring him to stop watching as a middle-aged white host explains his downfall. "Binge TV watching is an epidemic affecting millions of Americans each and every day. No one is immune to the effects," the host's authoritative voice warns.

This blend of a vignette of young people destroying their lives interspliced with an older expert diagnosing physical and emotional effects of an illicit behavior while chastising youthful temptation to it harkens back to the Partnership for a Drug-Free America ads of the 1980s. In "Dangers" those effects are absurd exaggerations of the immersive benefits of binge-watching along with heightened parasocial relationships. As Brian becomes more engrossed his appearance morphs into the characters of the shows he's binge-watching—Walter White (*Breaking Bad*), Ned Stark (*Game of Thrones*), and a guttural zombie (*Walking Dead*). "Once the show has made it to the brain," the hosts warns, "it's usually too late." Campy infographics illustrate the process by which "the characters, plot, and setting" penetrate a mind in a way remarkably similar to what marijuana does to the human brain in the American Medical Association's 1969 PSA "Marijuana." Next the host provides voiceover for the graphics depicting symptoms which "include sleep deprivation, weight gain, and an increased urge to write fan fiction."

Back in the den, Brain's marriage continues disintegrating. He declares that he is a "lesbian" after binging *Orange Is the New Black.* After his wife finds him pontificating about popcorn à la Don Draper (*Mad Men*) while on the couch with another woman, she demands a divorce. The piece ends with the host, spot lit in front of a black-and-white curtain. "Now that you've learned the symptoms and dangers of binge-watching," he tells the audience, "you've been armed with the tools to protect yourself and the people you love from shows like *The Wire*." However, those tools fail the host almost immediately as he loses his own composure and begins gushing over how transcendent *The*

Maker Studios released "Dangers of Binge Watching: A PSA" in March 2014. The three-minute parody of 20th-century film strips and PSAs provided a blueprint for the 30- to 60-second constructions of binge-viewers that would follow.

Wire is. Succumbing to the temptation of binge-watching, he admits that we are now in the "golden age of television, so watch away!"

"Dangers" satirized a variety of nostalgic filmstrips and PSA tropes, cinematography, and narratives, which it could as a three-minute, online-only video. As other media companies began producing shorter, TV-friendly spots of their own, the satire grew more focused. Some satirize the notion that television could be addictive by providing polemic depictions of possible effects, akin to the anti-marijuana propaganda film *Reefer Madness* (1936). Many of the promos featured celebrities who offer mock warnings about the dangers of binge-watching, which come across as even more ridiculous because of their uncanny facsimile to actual celebrity PSAs of the 20th century.

The More You Know About Celebrity PSAs

Netflix's "Binge Responsibly" (2015) campaign contains overt parodies of NBC's "One to Grow On" and "The More You Know" PSAs, which premiered in 1983 and often aired during commercial breaks and at the conclusions of children's programming and sitcoms. They featured celebrities, usually actors from the shows that just aired, facing the camera against a neutral background and speaking directly to the viewers about avoiding drugs, alcohol, or other temptations. Ironically,

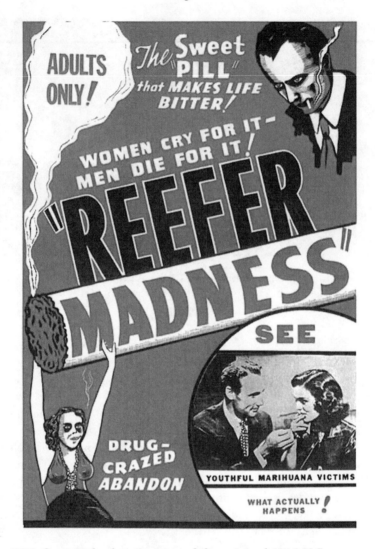

The 1972 theatrical release poster of the original 1936 U.S. propaganda film *Reefer Madness*. The film was originally made as a melodramatic, cautionary tale for parents to learn of the addictive dangers that marijuana posed for children. In the 1970s it was rereleased as a satire.

these PSAs were sometimes part of community service sentences the celebrities had to fulfill to make restitution for crimes committed while under the influence of drugs or alcohol (Cunningham, 2009).

"Binge Responsibly" borrows the cinematic and linguistic structures and musical effects of NBC's 20th-century PSAs to evoke memories of "The More You Know." Actors from the streaming service's

The classic logo from NBC's "The More You Know" PSA campaign. The logo is parodied by Netflix in its "Binge Responsibly" spoof PSA campaign (see next image). Image from gamerscoreblog is licensed under CC BY-SA 2.0

original content look directly at the viewers and warn them about the dangers of binge-watching. Michael Kelly, who played political hatchet man Douglas Stamper in *House of Cards,* advises viewers to "go outside, take a walk, get some fresh air." Taylor Schilling, star of *Orange Is the New Black,* implores viewers to remember a time "before you discovered all these great shows on Netflix.... You used to have a real life, with real friends you could hug." Linda Cardellini of *Bloodline* asks knowing rhetorical questions of viewers about their sleep deprivation and poor hygiene. She speaks in a maternal tone that seeks to relieve the pain that she knows binge-viewers are living with.

The 13 spots were streamed on April 1, 2015, to any viewer who watched more than two episodes in a row on Netflix. Online versions were also released, and many viewers shared them through social media. Musically and cinematically, they also closely mimic NBC's "The More You Know," including a cheerful bell tone at the end of each spot accompanied by a cartoonish "Binge Responsibly" logo with stars scrolling across the screen during the PSA's final seconds. In "The More You Know," the celebrities were not necessarily participating voluntarily or even taking their message seriously, but the assumption was that the audience was ignorant of the motives and receptive to the message. In "Binge Responsibly" viewers were rewarded by awareness of the irony, like an inside joke Easter egg, which they can discover and share in a demonstration of trans-mediated fandom (Jeffries, 2018, p. 297). At the

Netflix ran 13 spoof PSAs on April 1, 2015, for viewers of specific shows after the second episode in a row. The Binge Responsibly campaign was a direct parody of NBC's "The More You Know" (see previous image). Screenshots from YouTube.

same time, those who take it seriously are positioned outside the gag. As a result, the satire minimizes the discomfort or isolation of some viewers and the credulity for actual binge-watching side effects, which, by 2015, some had begun to argue exist (Flayelle, Maurage, & Billieux, 2017; Sung, Kang, & Wee, 2015).

Because of its Easter egg quality, the "Binge Responsibly" campaign went viral through the social media of viewers who saw the ads. Its ironic positioning caught the attention of mainstream media as well, which shared clips of the commercials on TV and mainstream news sites providing Netflix with a stream of additional earned advertising (Luckerson, 2015). It also sparked numerous fan tributes, such as "PSA for Millennials: The 5 Stages of Binge Watching" and "The Dangers of Netflix PSA," which further solidified the exaggerated side effects and consequences for binge-viewers.

Don't Be Like These Addicts!

In an infamous mid–20th-century PSA, a young woman's life spirals into social and psychological disarray because of her slovenly habits—not brushing her hair, forgetting to put away her clothes, and so forth. Such ads create a sense of foreboding for the slippery slopes we all face in our daily choices. But for the grace of God, or making responsible choices, we too will live her shame. The next set of PSA satires follow this form by structuring the plot around the action of a single character or a single couple of deviant addicts. They depicted the experience of moral and psychological breakdowns (a) as a result of a TV binge or (b) in order to facilitate a binge. The 30- to 60-second vignettes are shot mostly with close-ups and medium shots of the bingers consuming mindlessly. They contain little or no voiceover and focus instead on the ridiculous actions of the binge-viewer characters. The sense of deprivation is exaggerated by dreary minor chord background music reminiscent of after-school specials.

In Hulu's "No Commercial Plan—Weepy" (2015), a young, single woman has become so engrossed in an emotional TV show on her tablet that she cries continuously while staring at the screen. Her tears never cease as she wanders about her home attempting normal behavior—eating, receiving a delivery—without taking her tearful eyes off the tablet. In the process she burns through cases of toilet paper and Kleenex, even going so far as to blow dry tears from her face without looking away from the show. Her binge never ends because, as the concluding voiceover explains, "once the emotions start, they don't stop." Such single-minded, histrionic immersion is made possible thanks to Hulu's new commercial-free option.

In the Cox Communication promo "Delivery Guy" (2015) a female-male couple begins to binge-watch a show on their living room couch after the delivery of a pizza. A series of repetitive close and medium shots shows time passing by the repeated pizza deliveries and by the man growing facial hair. As in "One Moore Episode," the couple's descent into compulsive viewing is indicated by their neglect of household cleaning and personal hygiene over the days of their binge: mail begins to pile up outside the front door; their living room grows cluttered with old pizza boxes. The extent of their psychological downfall is also reflected by the returning Delivery Guy character, who remains well-groomed but becomes increasingly concerned about the couple's well-being after each delivery. At first the male viewer tells Delivery Guy that he doesn't want him to spoil the show. As he sinks deeper into the binge, he pleads manically with Delivery Guy to tell him what happens, presumably so he can break free from the show's grip. The minute-long ad ends with Delivery Guy running away from the home as a voiceover

In "Weepy: Introducing Hulu's No Commercials Plan" viewers are warned of the emotional and addictive power of streaming without commercials. "Weepy" song by Tobias Jesso, Jr. Screenshot from tivoads.com.

Cox's "Pizza Delivery Guy" spot captures the depravity a couple goes to when binge-watching a drama. The ad shares similarities with the opening of Portlandia's "One Moore Episode." Screenshots from adland.tv.

proclaims: "With a thousand hours of DVR storage and the best of HBO on demand, Cox is the official sponsor of binge watching."

Xfinity's 2015 spot "Cold" shows a white, female elementary school teacher eating her student's sandwich, after he sneezes on it, in order to make herself sick so she can stay home and binge during Xfinity Watchathon Week. An on-screen graphic reads "COMMON COLD RECOVERY TIME: 1 WEEK." The music remains ominously flat, and the camera angles are similar to "Weepy" and to "Delivery Guy," but the narrative of "Cold" does not center on the effects of a single binge.

Xfinity's 2015 spot "Cold" shows a white, female elementary school teacher eating her student's sandwich, after he sneezes on it, in order to make herself sick so she can stay home and binge during Xfinity Watchathon Week. Screenshots from iSpot.tv.

Instead it focuses on the dangerous and deviant ends "people who love TV" will go to in order to take advantage of Xfinity's week of free, premium, on-demand programming.

These promos mimic addiction PSAs and after-school specials which depict the progression of a single character's downfall into deviance and provide lurid enactments of the morally questionable choices that addicts make to get their fixes. The simplistic cause-and-effect logic is also reminiscent of Ad Council PSAs and school filmstrips of the 1940s through the 1970s, which portray the dangerous outcomes that bad habits, such as slovenliness, can bring upon young Americans. The first two ads feature a delivery person who serves not only as a foil for the absurdity but also as an embodied representation of the on-demand convenience of streaming video culture and post-industrial identity (see Chapter 5). In "Cold" that on-demand identity is demonstrated through displays of X1 menus reflecting on the smiling, though still sniffling, countenance of the teacher laid up in bed and surrounded by tissues.

While othering 20th-century criticism of TV through irony, these commercials make no effort to challenge gender, racial, and sexual stereotypes of that era. All the protagonists are white. "Weepy" hinges on the notion that women are hysterically emotional in content selection and reaction. "Delivery Man" centers on a white, heteronormative couple with the affluence to binge-watch and be served on demand in their suburban home. Although many men today are elementary schoolteachers, the producers of Xfinity's spot chose to stick with the 20th-century gender norm. While proffering a "woke" narrative of binge-viewers, the commercials still rely on gender norms of content selection and stereotypes of domestic gender roles from the outmoded era they are attempting to other.

Rehab Is for Quitters

The final set PSA-skewing spots from 2015 to 2016 offered salvation from the dangerous effects of binge-watching through embracing a company's content or technology. As with life choice PSAs, the dangers are not well contextualized and are fearfully depicted. The solutions are presented as binary choices, as simply achievable as just saying "no," declaring you are not a couch potato, or switching to an unlimited streaming video plan. Any questions?

Amazon Fire TV's "Show Hole" (2015) depicts a young woman's trauma at the end of a 58-hour binge. As the "final, final credits" run, the background music shifts from cheerful to ominous in less than a second. Color washes out of her living room. The voiceover, provided by

Malcolm McDowell (who as Alec in *A Clockwork Orange* [1971] was sub-jected to one of the most memorable forced video binges in cinematic history) proclaims: "You've fallen in the 'Show Hole.'" This fictional malady is an allusion to "k-hole"—a traumatic feeling of dissociation reported by some users of ketamine (Curran & Monaghan, 2001). The distraught woman, alone on a couch, is bathed in gray lighting as the foreboding music closes in on her. To compensate she knits compul-sively as McDowell explains, "The struggle could not be more real. Why even have a TV?" There is a two-second shot of her, still in pajamas, shoveling dirt onto the grave of her half-buried television set. But before all hope is lost, McDowell proclaims, "Then you see it! Amazon Fire TV's vast library of best shows ever!" Instantly the music shifts back to cheerful tones. As the warm lighting returns, the woman's flat affect attempts to smile. "So long, Show Hole," McDowell declares as endless Amazon menus of prestige programming dance across the screen, their glow reflecting off the woman's pale cheeks.

A second "Show Hole" spot continues the theme, with McDowell's voiceover narrating the story of a white, female-male couple watching TV in bed. The scene opens with a shot of the bedroom: the man hold-ing a remote control as the couple stares at an old (pre-streaming) cable TV guide screen. McDowell chastises the man: "You've spent more time looking for a show than watching it. She's over it." We zoom to a

Amazon Fire TV's "Show Hole" (2015) depicts a young woman's trauma at the end of a 58-hour binge. She is miraculous saved from the #ShowHole by "Amazon Fire TV's vast library of best shows ever!" Screenshots from iSpot.tv.

Amazon Fire TV's "Show Hole: TV Ex" depicts the dire dangers couples face when binge-watching through an inferior streaming interface. Before the man is cuckholded by his partner's "TV Ex," he uses the power of Amazon Fire TV's to win her back. Screenshots from iSpot.tv.

close-up of the woman who rolls her eyes disapprovingly and turns over in bed as the music shifts from cheery to dreary. A poof of smoke rolls in the bedroom door, and the color drains from the room.

The couple are suddenly lying in a hellish landscape of smoke and rocks. Their bed splits in half. The husband reaches for his now-sleeping partner as she is pulled, along with the head board, sheets, and blanket, into the off-camera underworld. "Will you TV drift apart?" McDowell asks ominously. "Will she go back to her TV ex?" The husband now stands in the rain outside their bedroom window as a snarky football player lays in bed next to the woman who snuggles against his shoulder pad. "No! You've got Amazon Fire TV." The man breaks the glass and stands triumphantly over his partner and her paramour as a user interface of premium channel shows scrolls powerfully behind him. "It's TV brain knows your TV heart." Cheerful music returns, and the couple lie again in each other's arms laughing with the TV show. "Yes," McDowell concludes, "make up binging is the best! So long, Show Hole!" This commercial was released before "Netflix and chill" became a thing.

Other commercials emphasized the TV addiction narrative but framed it as a solvable problem. T-Mobile's "Binge Watchers Anonymous with Aaron Paul" (2015) incorporates addiction nostalgia and a celebrity guide (who happened to portray a meth addict in the often-binged AMC drama *Breaking Bad*) and plays with the idea of

The three spots of "Binge-Watchers Anonymous with Aaron Paul" feature the *Breaking Bad* star leading a group of would-be binge-watching addicts come to the realization that their TV habits are okay now that T-Mobile has introduced its BINGE ON plan with unlimited streaming. Screenshots from iSpot.tv.

rehabilitation for the overly immersive effects depicted in "Dangers." The three ads of this series are all set in a dark basement at a meeting of "Binge-Watchers Anonymous," a fictional self-help group run by Paul. In the first promo, Paul encourages a man named Jerry to share. He begins to tell his story but Paul interrupts him when it becomes obvious that

Jerry is describing the life of a character from the first season of HBO's *True Detective*. Trying again, Jerry adopts a British accent and describes the Stark family from HBO's *Game of Thrones*. Frustrated, Paul asks him to "tell us about the real Jerry." Jerry takes a deep breath and then he provides the backstory of Walter White, the main character in Paul's show *Breaking Bad*. As the other attendees begin to complain, Paul quiets them and tells Jerry, "Go on; I think I like this one." The screen jumps to a T-Mobile logo with a voiceover introducing T-Mobile's BingeOn, a data plan that allows users to stream unlimited video content.

In the second "Binge-Watchers Anonymous" promo, a woman explains her despair about being on the bus and binge-watching uncontrollably: "I don't even want to think about the overages!" Paul consoles her, saying, "It's okay, now that T-Mobile has gotten rid of overages for streaming video." A surprised attendee asks if it's OK that he "binged an entire season during my kid's piano recital?" Jerry admits that he has done that too. "Yup," Paul assures them before stating, "I think we've made some real progress today." Another attendee who had been binging looks up from his phone and says, "what?"

The third promo features Paul welcoming a woman to the group and encouraging her to pull out her phone to watch. When she asks, "Isn't this Binge-Watchers Anonymous?" Paul explains "it was. Then T-Mobile starting letting people stream all the video they want without the shame of having to pay for extra data." The shame of binge-watching, and perhaps addiction, has neatly been transferred to a question of economics rather than of culture or health.

These widely circulated promos treat the absurd side effects of binge-watching as a reality of modern media culture. They reinterpret those "dangers" to solve actual social, technological, and economic issues that streaming video users may experience—expensive bandwidth, social isolation, and diffuse content. They also play with the nostalgia of one-dimensional addiction and salvation stories endemic to the after-school special and Movie of the Week genres of 20th-century TV. Doing so minimizes the notion that losing control of one's video consumption is something worth addressing, if you can afford to lose control with great content and technology—a narrative also found in the press (De Keere, Thunnissen, & Kuipers, 2021). Actual TV addiction could exist only in our collective memory of 20th-century TV because today we can choose what and how we are addicted. Even the potential career and health risks from "One Moore Episode" are seemingly no longer an issue.

Through their parody of 20th-century authoritarian and campy PSAs, these promos complicate connotations of the word "binge" while branding contemporary TV culture, and associated products and services, as "other than broadcast" television. The producers use the rhetorical devices paromologia and reductio ad absurdum to acknowledge and lampoon potential dangers. They exploit collective memory in their simplified instantiation of 20th-century TV to paint criticism of couch potatoes as passé and overly simplistic for today's self-aware binge-viewer. PSAs and broadcast television represent conformity and simple messaging for a homogenous mass known as *audience*. The binge-viewer, by contrast, is individualistic, complex, and autonomous. It is the same identity constructed by showrunners in the messaging they spread (see "Abetting Dr. Jekyll" on 114).

The rhetorical effects of these commercials are that binge-watching addiction is minimized by reductio ad absurdum, while cultural criticism of television is othered by association with the strawman of 20th-century PSA paternalism. That distinction is reinforced in trusted messaging of showrunners and creatives who promoted the narrative of an evolved viewer and in the newspaper coverage of the binge-watching phenomenon (see Chapter 3). Awareness and acknowledgment of the idiot box and couch potato serve as a paromologia: "We know too much TV might not be good, but maybe it's more complicated than what authority figures preached in the 20th century because we have more choices and resources." The construction then of the binge-viewer is not a direct reflection of commercial depictions but rather a reflection of the actual viewer who gets the joke by believing that 20th-century TV and fears of TV addiction are outmoded and outside of contemporary streaming video consumption.

That distinction between old and new means that binge-viewers distinguish themselves from their couch potato ancestors by their technologically-enabled enlightenment and self-awareness. They can control how they lose control while performing culturally elevating acts endorsed by showrunners and Academy Award winners—their parasocial partners. Despite some occasional poor hygiene, a binge-viewer is savvy, agentic, self-aware, and culturally and technologically evolved. Like Kevin Spacey said in 2013, the audience knows what it wants, and it's not afraid to get lost in a show because, unlike the vast wasteland of 20th-century broadcast television, TV is now so much better. Such a construction creates value for the services and ecosystems of binge-watching via social memory: through mnemonic cues it links the un-woke paternalism of PSAs with the exploitative simplicity of 20th-century TV technology to craft a simplistic instantiation of the past coded in opposition to the complex, ironic present. Obviously, the campaign exploited that simplified past in the furtherance of these media companies' economic ends, but the binge-viewer is portrayed to be in on the joke rather than the butt of it. For the savvy binge-viewer, massive TV consumption becomes a counter-authoritarian act, any criticism of which seems as ludicrous and outmoded as the PSAs. Just ask the world's best storytellers! Don't believe them? Check out what the top TV critics recommend.

Through their two-pronged othering of 20th-century TV, this campaign weaponized the irrationality of TV addiction fears to create a techno-cultural fantasy: we are in the Golden Age of TV; binge-watching isn't the healthiest thing to do, but it sure is cool. This plays against the idiot box identity created by 20th-century stakeholders—parents, corporations, educators, and regulators—preaching the dangers of TV to the masses generally and children specifically (Halpern, 1975). Doing so identifies past technologies as outmoded along with the alarmist fears they carry. The campaign implies this through the commercials and clearly states through their showrunner testimonials that culture and technology have evolved and matured and so too has the viewer: the couch potato is dead; long live the binge-viewer. In form and function, the commercials evoke nostalgia for a "simple" past when PSA producers lacked the self-awareness to see, or at least acknowledge, how ridiculously ironic their messaging was. The strategy reduced the small body of journalism on binge-watching addiction and loneliness into a punchline. It also reinforced the widely-circulated news narrative that TV had evolved through its technology, while celebrities endorsed the cultural cool of doing something your parents told you was bad. When asked if Frank Underwood (Spacey's antihero character in *House of Cards*) binge-watched, creator Beau Willimon said this: "Frank Underwood's all about breaking the rules.... He would applaud it" (Kuperinsky, 2014).

In 1962, Richard Schickel asserted the following in response to the anti–TV hysteria:

> Younger people tend to have a cooler and more realistic attitude toward television than their elders.... These people were born into the communications revolution, they grew up with it, and they show little inclination to regard television with moral and political passions that more properly belong to causes of things rather than their symptoms. In time the attitudes of this generation are bound to become the dominant ones, and when they do, it seems likely that the discussion of television will become more fruitful [p. 469].

That time came in the second decade of the 21st century, if we are to believe journalists' coverage of binge-watching and media companies' construction of binge-viewers. But what about the people doing all that watching? Were they actually evolved? Had they improved TV? Did they follow mainstream media narrative of binge-watching or did they create their own definitions, rituals, and feelings about it? To answer those questions, this story changes direction from an examination of the articulations of binge-watching in the media to an exploration of the actions of contemporary TV viewers. In Chapter 5, I analyze how and why viewers watched TV from 2014 to 2018 and how they felt about the binge-watching phenomenon.

To read more about the implications of this use of nostalgia for memory studies and media, turn to 207 (note 6).[6]

To continue on the journey and learn how viewers defined and practiced binge-watching, go to the next page.

5

Rituals and Motives
of Binge-Viewers in Action

"I can resist anything but temptation"
[Oscar Wilde, 1892]

In Season 11, Episode 13 of *The Simpsons*, "Saddlesore Galactica" (2000), the show opens with the Simpson family attending a state fair. Unimpressed by a military marching band, Homer takes his children to a stage where Canadian rock band Bachman Turner Overdrive is about to perform. Bart asks, "Who are those pleasant old men?" to which Homer replies, "It's BTO—they're Canada's answer to ELP. Their big hit was TCB. That's how we talked in the '70s. We didn't have a moment to spare."

When lead singer Randy Bachman announces to the audience that the band will open with songs from its new album, Homer orders them to play their 1973 hit "Taking Care of Business" (TCB). Bassist Fred Turner implores him, "Sir, we'll get to that..." but Homer interrupts him: "No talkin'! No new crap! 'Takin' Care of Business' now!" The band members shrug in defeat and begin playing "TCB." After the first couple of lines, Homer again interrupts screaming, "Get to the 'workin' overtime part'!" The band again complies with his demand, jumping to the song's chorus, while Homer shimmies to his family's chagrin.

This scene satirizes the on-demand attitude of 21st-century media consumption. Try explaining to anyone under 10 that the show they want to watch isn't "on" right now. When I do my children think I'm lying. How could something/everything not be on Netflix right now? When I tell them that when I was growing up, we had to wait for a show to come on TV because there was no Netflix, they gape. "You mean you only had YouTube?" It goes beyond TV, of course. No longer beholden to broadcast radio or album structures, music fans can control not only what is listened to and when but also the structure and timing of the music itself. Even live concerts can provide audience interactivity with some performers—like the jam-band Phish—relying on social media and fan sourcing to shape playlists and even song arrangements. People in the 1970s may have talked like they didn't have a moment to spare, but in the 2010s, that was how they consumed media.

"Saddlesore Galactica" aired in 2000, when Napster was disrupting the music industry through its peer-to-peer file-sharing interface. This was what Kevin Spacey (2013) was referring to when he said, "we have learned the lesson the music industry didn't learn: give people what they want, when they want it, in the form they want it in—at a reasonable price—and they'll more likely pay for it rather than steal it." If Spotify is any indication, the music industry finally learned its lesson. By the 2020s, internet-enabled consumer control has reshaped the flow of mass media to such an extent that the notion of not being able to access exactly what you want when and how you want it seems a quaint 20th-century inconvenience.

Television viewers enact this control through binge-watching, second screening, time-shifting, remixing shows, and creating and distributing their own content. In previous chapters I have discussed how this has changed the ways journalists and media companies articulated TV watching. In this chapter, I examine how and why viewers interacted with video as the phenomenon became the new normal of TV from 2014 to 2018. Since viewers' actions are central to any discussion of binge-watching, I wanted to find out (a) how viewers conceive and practice it and (b) how their new methods of consumption reshape their relationship with and understanding of television. To do so, I built on the growing body of binge-viewer scholarship at that time to develop questions for a series of interviews that I conducted with TV viewers. My interviews and analyses reveal that the rituals, motives, and feelings of contemporary viewers are built around content control and time management. They also show that how viewers defined and practiced binge-watching mirrored and sometimes deviated from the media coverage.

To learn more about my rationale for interviews and the research process and methodology, turn to 208 (note 1).[1]

Binge-Watching Research Arc

When I began researching binge-watching in 2013, there were only a handful of scholarly articles that mentioned the term (Dillon, 2013; Giuffre, 2013; Phalen & Ducey, 2012). Three years later the National

Communication Association Conference accepted over 20 papers on the topic. In 2017, Boston University hosted a conference specifically for binge-watching scholars. At that conference, Lisa Perks, Matthew Pittman, and I waxed nostalgic about the days when our literature reviews began "Few media scholars are studying binge-watching...." Grant McCracken even crossed the Charles for a keynote speech!

As of December 2022, a growing body of binge-watching scholarship exists, with over 200 articles. Others mention binge-watching in regard to other aspects of media, psychology, advertising, literature, communication, and other fields, some with a greater focus on binge-watching than others. In 2019 an international group of leading binge-watching scholars met to discuss the implications of the phenomenon out of which a collected work edited by Marieke Jenner (2021) devotes an entire section to binge-viewer studies. However, the body of literature using qualitative interviews of viewers from 2014 to 2018 is significantly slimmer and dominated by scholarship that approaches binge-watching like 20th-century TV.

To learn more about the implicit TV biases in that scholarship and my frustrations with it, turn to 209 (note 2).[2]

I began conducting open-ended, semi-structured interviews with viewers in early 2014 and have continued doing so through various protocols to this day (see methodology note). Based on my earlier work, I found six overlapping motives for binge-watching: (1) enhanced viewing experience (EVE), (2) sense of completion (SOC), (3) cultural inclusion (CI), (4) convenience/catching-up (CC), (5) relaxation, and (6) nostalgia (Steiner, 2017; Steiner & Xu, 2020). EVE and SOC were found to be internal motives of gratification that differentiate binge-viewers from linear television viewers. SOC and CC were not practical motives for viewers with little control of their consumption schedule. Similarly, EVE is a motive that exists in contrast to linear viewing; the viewing experience is enhanced by consuming more than one episode per sitting. This aligns with the media narrative and parameters of 2014–2016. We also found that these motives are related to content selection: viewers select programs to binge-watch based on what they are trying to get out of the experience.[3] While uses and gratification studies of 20th-century viewers differentiate information seeking (news) from entertainment seeking (sitcoms), this dialectic is insufficient to explain viewers' choices of complex texts from which the entertainment sought is a function of information gathered. Instead, I argue (Steiner, 2017) that the binge-watching motive-text selection process is predicated on the attentiveness viewers believe a show would require in order for them to enjoy the show:

Interviewees described binge-watching along a continuum of attentive to inattentive, which I coded as the Viewer Attentiveness Spectrum (VAS). More attentive bingeing is a focused study of the text that is both entertaining and educational, often motivated by the need to catch up or feel narratively immersed. Less attentive bingeing is almost always for relaxation, nostalgia, and distraction. The level of attentiveness is a product of the content, but interviewees determined which content they watched based on how attentive they wanted to be.... During more attentive bingeing, the goal is to actively absorb, analyze, and be immersed in the content, which may be narratively complex and emotionally taxing.... The complication is part of the entertainment and the allure to keep watching in high VAS bingeing [p. 151].

Lisa Perks's *Media Marathoning* (2015) uses a hybrid of surveys, one-on-one interviews, book focus groups, and journaling to analyze "marathoners'" experiences with books, films, and TV series from a rhetorical perspective. To capture a more "holistic experience," she maps those findings against a critical examination of the "the structure and content of chosen texts" (pp. xii–xiii). She argues that the sensations of immersion and transportation experienced by marathon readers are enhanced through "marathoning." That position jibes with the binge-watching motives of EVE and SOC (Steiner & Xu, 2020). Perks (2015) argues that the "collective force of these postmodern elements of intertextuality and self-reflexivity blurs the line between reader and text, thus welcoming readers in the story" (p. 181). Or, as an interviewee once told me, binging brings you into the writer's head. The choice to do so is an editorial move by the viewer, which was nearly impossible 25 years ago.

(In the next couple of sections I discuss why advertising and other interruptions are intrusive and the mechanisms of how we can get lost in a story. Although somewhat theoretical, I believe they give context for the user experiences that I gathered during this phase of the project.)

If you want to skip the ads, jump to What Idiot Box? on 144.

And Now a Word from Our Sponsors

When people think about binge-watching, they don't think about commercials or other interruptions, but that doesn't mean they don't happen. Not everyone binges in a commercial-free environment, and even those who do still encounter interruptions to their immersion and control that affect the experience. Moreover, these days we may be more hostile to them than our TV-watching ancestors. Raymond Williams (1990) famously described 20th-century American TV as "extra-ordinarily short units and as it were involuntary sequences, mainly determined by commercials" (p. 74). Breaks in the "action" back then, and still today, not only pay for the shows but shape their watching. Non-broadcast events, such as a play or a football game, are evidently discreet programs when enjoyed in person. When they are televised, they become part of a larger flow of general watching, with interruptions that not only serve to advertise sponsors but also to promote other shows that can be watched. To paraphrase the famous adage of TV executives, they are not in the business of selling shows but of selling audience shares of airtime. Capturing a viewer's attention during and after a program was the primary business of a television network. Thus a 20th-century TV audience's experience was primarily determined by broadcasters' control of content variety and textual and programmatic sequences based on the scarcity of channels and limited airtime: "This phenomenon, of planned flow, is then perhaps the defining characteristic of broadcasting, simultaneously as a technology and as a cultural form" (Williams, 1990, p. 86).

Media streaming and mobile technologies allowed viewers to redirect the flow first, which then forced studios and media companies to create content to remain profitable as a new TV flow (Lotz, 2014). Perks (2015) writes that "insulated flow" has now become viewer-directed and viewer-contained (p. xxii). The growing popularity of second screening—the use of another, usually smaller video technology during TV-watching—and the infinite variety of accessible content make holding a viewer's attention during commercial interruptions more challenging than ever. Nonetheless, binge-watching is never just binge-watching: interruptions and intrusions, like second-screening, may be more viewer-controlled than they were during the network era, but they also may be more frequent and harder to resist.

There remains little qualitatively-oriented research on binge-viewers' perception of time management and flow control with regard to interruptions such as advertising and second screening. Since streaming services like Netflix use a subscription model without traditional commercial breaks, and since they are most commonly associated with binge-watching, there seems to be an assumption in the literature that any interruptions to binge-watching are controlled by the binge-viewer. So has time-shifting and mobility obliterated interruptions. My earlier research (Steiner, 2017) found that viewers still binge-watch through numerous channels, some of which have commercials, and that they encounter other intrusions that they find disruptive during binges (p. 150). Whether streaming service or broadcast network, the business of TV is still predicated on time control and attention. As Netflix CEO

Reed Hastings is fond of saying, "Our biggest competitor is sleep." But binge-viewers' feelings about interruptions are tied to their motives and rituals and therefore also tied to content selection (Pittman & Steiner, 2019). It would follow that certain shows can be enjoyed despite interruptions while others cannot.

Losing Yourself in a Story

You know that feeling when you're watching or reading something that's so good that you forget that you are sitting there watching it? Well, there's actually a word for that: "(tele)presence" (hereafter "presence"). It was first used in 1980 by Martin Minsky to describe technology that allowed subjects to remotely operate robotic devices (Lombard et al., 2000). Over the next decade, the term was expanded to include virtual environments and the subjective sensations of experiences in these environments and other media. According to Draper et al. (1998), "The distinguishing characteristic of experiential telepresence is the mental state involving the suspension of the user's awareness" (p. 356). Put simply, presence is getting lost in a story that is so good you forget it is a story.

Of all the binge-watching motives, viewers describe enhanced viewing experience (EVE) as the most salient differentiator between linear television and streaming video (Steiner & Xu, 2020). This fits not only the press construction of binge-watching improving TV (Chapter 3) but also the commercial narrative of binge-viewers' evolution from couch potatoes (Chapter 4). This motive reflects a viewer's presumption of greater pleasure gained from being able to consume multiple episodes in one sitting and the perceived authenticity of such consumption as an improvement over broadcast TV (Anderson, 2016). EVE is a hybrid motive of entertainment seeking and information seeking, made possible by binge-watching technology and the textual and structural advancements of TV culture and industry (Jenner, 2015; Lotz, 2014). Perks (2015) describes such motivation as a "textual appetite" for both the pleasure of immersion in the story and the use of "cognitive skills" to further the entertainment (pp. 70–71).

To learn more about how presence works in relation to TV go to 211 (note 4).[4]

Viewers have described the pleasure and authenticity behind gaining an "enhanced viewing experience" as a feeling of becoming closer to characters and more immersed in the show's world (Perks, 2015; Petersen, 2016; Steiner, 2017). If each season of a show is a narrative arc, then binge-watching potentially allows viewers to experience that arc without many of the traditional broadcast interruptions. The motivation to seek an enhanced viewing experience through binge-watching is a quest for greater entertainment from and better information about a story. Viewers believe that this heightens a show's realism by bringing them closer to its worlds, characters, and plots (Perks, 2015, p. 63).

The engagement in a more immersive "world" involves viewer activation through an imaginative process of building it. Attentiveness to the process heightens viewer stimulation through discovery, creativity, and growth (Anderson & Kirkorian, 2006). Perks (2015) compares this to "ludic media systems" (p. 4). The concept of ludic media comes from video game design and speaks to a player's experience through interactive engagement and immersion in the story. Lindley (2005) uses structural semiotics to model ludic media and locate connections between game design and user experience in relation to narrative. When the player has a perception of being an "active participant within the ludic world" there may be greater engagement through interactivity with the narrative (Layers of Encoding Within Ludic Systems, para. 3). Perks (2015) extrapolates that connection between engagement and interactivity to binge-watching TV texts that demand greater attentiveness (VAS+) to enjoy. The narrative features of such texts—"long-form story arcs (Mittell), endless deferment (Hills), world building (Jenkins), overflow (Brooker), and textual excess (Gwenllian-Jones)"—she argues "are what inspire active audience engagement and immersion" (p. 4).

Based on this, the EVE motive can be seen as a choice to be cognitively active within a ludic space that rewards the viewer with feelings of presence through cognitive activity. Degradation of presence results from distracting and unrelated materials that obstruct the viewer's attentive world building. As Lindley (2005) argues, disjunctive game flow and editing that interferes with a narrative function is "a break from immersion" (Narrative, para. 6). If this were extrapolated to TV, would intrusive interruptions outside the viewer's control create similar interference during more attentive binge-watching?

Schweidel and Moe (2016) assert that binge-viewers become "immersed in an alternate reality ... and advertisements shown during these sessions can be seen as unwelcome reminders of the viewer's true reality" (p. 3). As Logan (2013) argues, advertising is an intrusion that interrupts a viewer's proximity to the content. This indicates that binge-viewers' experiences with interruptions may be related to the telepresence dimensions of transportation, engagement, and social/perceptual realism. But fundamentally any motives and experiences of binge-watching are tied to viewer rituals. Action is an intrinsic prerequisite to understanding any outcomes.

What Idiot Box?

The first thing I should report is that people have been very eager to discuss how they watch TV with me. This led to snowball sampling: interviewees told friends about my project, and I would engage these friends in informal conversations. When I've conducted interviews in public places, random people who overheard me would sometimes offer their takes on binge-watching. It's clear after more than seven years of interviews that people consider television-watching a safe and fun topic to discuss with a stranger. The popularity and novelty of streaming technologies and the shared belief that TV had rapidly improved over the past decade contributed to their enthusiasm and candor. But I also gleaned, over the course of these discussions, that people consider their viewing choices to be a form of self-expression that they can discuss without fear of being too personally revealing. They described their rituals and content choices like costumes that gave them TV identities, in which they expressed who they are in relation to other viewers' TV identities (see Chapter 6). This is not to say that all interviewees felt copacetic about their relationship with television; in fact, some expressed shame and regret about the amount they watched. But whether proud, ashamed, or both (and most were both), they all appeared, to varying degrees, excited about the opportunity to discuss television. Several thanked me at the end of interviews, noting that they had "never thought so deeply" about an activity that takes up so many hours of their lives.

Defining Action

As early as 2016, binge-watching was how nearly all the interviewees consumed television. These interviews, even more so than earlier ones I've conducted, confirm Netflix's claim that "binge-watching is the new normal" (PRNewsire, 2013). The only exception was a 69-year-old retired professor who didn't own a television. "Nope, I don't watch TV," he said, though he did "borrow movies from the library" and watched online videos, both on his computer. A 35-year-old banker reported that she didn't "have time to binge," though her descriptions of viewing rituals were similar to the criteria that she and other interviewees used to define binge-watching (see below). All the interviewees claimed some awareness of what binge-watching was, but they differed in their definitions. Several thought that some official definition might exist. Because they knew I was studying contemporary TV viewers, some asked me what the "official definition" is. To avoid influencing their interviews, I responded to such questions honestly by explaining that there are differing opinions about the behavior and that their opinions were as valid as anyone else's.

An interesting difference between how the media articulate binge-watching (see Chapters 2–4) and how "ordinary people" do it is that interviewees often binge-watch multiple shows concurrently; that is, they don't wait to complete one show before starting another one. "I have some shows that I'm watching by myself," a 39-year-old financial planner told me, "and others that I watch with my wife." Depending on their preferences, motives, and schedules, viewers will strategically select and consume multiple shows over varying periods of time, while considering all or part of that consumption to be binge-watching. This behavior is akin to people who read multiple books concurrently. Viewers describe controlling how they feel through what they are watching: "Every time I finish a new show, I need to go back and re-watch something I've seen before. I get emotional about the TV shows so I can't jump into a new one right away because I'm not over the old one. So I re-watch a bunch of stuff after every time I finish a new show just to calm myself down before I start another new show. So that's what I binge-watch consistently." So while there are specific motives for choosing a show at any given time, viewers revealed that their choice is often made in context of whatever else they may be watching concurrently. The act of choosing a particular viewing experience is based on the relationship between different shows that the viewer knits together over time. This indicates that the viewing experience goes beyond discreet shows to function as a holistic entertainment identity.

Another difference in the interviews compared to the media coverage of binge-watching was the length of time or number of episodes deemed necessary to constitute "a binge." No interviewees disputed that watching an entire series from start to finish meant "binging a show," but their parameters of "a binge" differed. A 19-year-old server asserted, "if you watch a full season in one day you are definitely binge-watching; that's the definition." He also felt that "a binge" meant the same thing, watching an entire season in one sitting. Another interviewee disagreed. She believed that a binge could start after only "two episodes." Many interviewees offered definitions based on total episodes, ranging from two to five depending on the type of show and its length. "If we're talking *Parks and Rec*, that's what, like 22 minutes an episode. You watch three and it's only an hour.... Yeah, for shorter ones I'd say four or five." For some interviewees, "a binge" was measured by time alone—"at least three or four hours"—as the primary criterion, even if the last episode wasn't finished.

Bingeable Content

Viewers' content choices for binge-watching in some ways matched the hierarchy described by some journalists (see Chapter 3). Prestige dramas were often the first shows that viewers associated with the practice. Netflix content and that of other streaming services like Hulu and Amazon fit more easily into viewers' understanding of binge-watching. Sitcoms and reality TV were considered less "binge-worthy," while movies and live TV were seldom mentioned in the context of binge-watching. A few interviewees pushed back against the mainstream content hierarchy of 2016, stating that any video could be binged: "As long as I'm watching a lot, isn't that a binge?" When I pressed interviewees about whether live broadcast television could be binged, most felt it could. "I'd call a *Law and Order* marathon a binge," a 25-year-old social worker claimed, "but it's easier to just stream it."

Viewers did not mention sporting events as appropriate content for binge-watching. "I love college basketball; I just don't think watching March Madness is binge-watching," a 26-year-old server stated. Since he had defined binge-watching as the consistent viewing of a single narrative over a long period of time, I asked him if the multi-week NCAA basketball tournament could fall under his definition. He responded with "I think maybe there's classic binge-watching on Netflix and then there's like general binge-watching; that's just a lot of TV.... So yeah, so March Madness or the playoffs or something could be general binging." His notion of general binging came up in other interviews as "a binge" in opposition to traditional "binge-watching." While no one considered live broadcasts of news or events to be binge-watchable content, they sometimes referred to longer than usual periods of time watching them as binges. For instance, one young viewer called watching the 2016 presidential election night coverage "a depressing binge."

General Binges versus Binge-Watching

It is remarkable that a term most people had never used in 2011—binge—had a "traditional" and a "new" connotation only five years later. It presaged what researchers began calling for in 2019—a binge-watching typology (Perks et al., 2021). The possibility of general TV binges, as the mass consumption of any video, may be related to the current ubiquity and flexibility of the term's use in media after 2016. It also may be related to earlier uses of TV marathon and TV binge from the 20th century (see Chapter 2). But its use stretches "binge-able" content beyond some users' comfort levels. For instance, several younger interviewees believed that YouTube content was binge-able: "I can watch for hours.... Sometimes I start with something I'm interested in like this fashion vlogger I follow. That will lead me to other stuff I wasn't expecting, and it will turn into a binge." By contrast a 55-year-old lawyer said, "I consider watching YouTube to be surfing the web. You can watch a video, but you are not watching TV because you click on things and you move around." When I asked if YouTube could be binged, she told me flatly: "Yes, if you mean an internet binge.... As I understand it, binge-watching refers to television-watching. So if you are clicking and checking email or whatever, you're doing other things in addition to watching.... They are not the same thing."

These descriptions speak to the challenges of differentiating between a single binge and binge-watching (which interviewees sometimes used interchangeably) by content alone. The former was used to describe a single large time period of consumption of TV. Interviewees described the latter in terms of consistent completion of one or more seasons of non-live content in multiple sittings, the length of which they controlled. A 61-year-old theater director felt that he had binge-watched *Game of Thrones* by watching two seasons in about a month. When I asked him how many he watched in a sitting he said, "One. I generally did not watch two in a row.... I'd watch one a night for a few weeks or something, and I would miss some nights; it was never that regular." A 44-year-old literacy instructor described how control and completion shaped her understanding: "I don't have time to watch more than an episode or two a day. So, I watch what I watch when I can.... More than two episodes is too much for me, but I'm still binge-watching the show.... I keep watching until it's over, but that can take me a few weeks or a whole summer." Another interviewee compared this to reading. "As long as I'm consistently watching that show, then yeah, it's binge-watching." She only had time to watch short spurts, but she perceived a season as a complete unit that she was finishing "like a book," on her own schedule. Her definition of binge-watching was about controlling the narrative flow and closure at her convenience rather than the slower broadcaster-controlled flow she had grown up with.

Viewers' Definition

Based on these interviews, the defining action of "binge-watching" is the purposeful and consistent viewing of certain types of video (see "Bingeable Content") over whatever period of time an individual deems necessary to achieve a desired outcome (usually understanding, sometimes enjoyment) on their terms even if the desired outcome is not achieved or changes. Fundamental to that action is (1) viewer-controlled flow and (2) time management. Binge-watching, however, often involves video consumption binges. The defining action of "a binge" is the viewing of more minutes or episodes of video content than the viewer feels is "normal." The scope of normal is unique to each viewer and related to individual experience with and perceptions of TV. Furthermore, binges could be part of a viewer's binge-watching rituals, but they could also include content that viewers perceive as outside the scope of binge-watching (e.g., live sports). Most importantly, binges often involve either a loss of control of time management or an adjustment to the priorities and planning around the video consumption, depending on the flow of the show and the perceived attentiveness required to gain a desired outcome.

Tech Rituals

Interviewees described a wide range of technologies and viewing channels through which they watched. The media hardware included TV sets, smart TVs, computers (both desktop and laptop), video game systems, DVD players, tablets, and smart phones. The viewing delivery systems included cable/broadcast networks, streaming services, on-demand outlets, internet sites, and social media platforms. A 36-year-old technology entrepreneur had been getting most of his TV through streaming services, but he had "recently got a digital antenna for live stuff." Viewers who grew up using the internet were less likely to subscribe to a cable television provider, particularly those still in school. Many of the older viewers I spoke with had cable TV subscriptions, though some were considering cutting the cord too. "If Comcast hadn't added Netflix, I would have dumped cable TV," a 35-year-old sous chef told me. "But Comcast is smart. The deals for just high-speed internet are priced just high enough that you're better off bundling" (the deals offered by MVPDs for subscribing to multiple services including internet and cable TV). "It's annoying, because you can stream football now," another interviewee complained, "but there are lags ... and buffering sucks." Since 2018 this has become less of an issue.

Younger viewers reported greater comfort and usage of streaming and pirated services to watch shows "illegally" through torrent sites. None of those who did so expressed concerns about violating copyright laws, though one joked that the authorities might come after him "when this gets published." I assured him that all interviews were anonymous, though it was clear he was not really concerned. "Everybody does [it]," a 21-year-old psychology student told me. If my interviewees are a representative sample of U.S. viewers, then that is not the case. However, it does appear that younger viewers are more likely to be aware of and use pirate services than older viewers. The reason for this difference in ritual seems to be a product of Gen Y to Zers growing up in an internet-connected media world of free on-demand information, being more familiar with torrent technology, and having less money than older professionals who can afford and are used to paying subscription fees for media services. The theater director, a "divorced father," said he "find[s] that it serves me and the kids to have cable.... I'm not going to waste my time trying figure out how to set it up or what to do when the internet slows down." His interview took place in 2016, before Disney+. When I followed up in late 2021, he stated that he had stuck with cable, but that the "polarities have reversed since [he] became addicted to *The Closer, Major Crimes,* and *The Good Wife.*"

Interviewees who paid for cable often preferred binge-watching through streaming services and DVRs over MVPD on-demand services. "I still use on-demand, but if I DVRed the show I'll watch it there first." DVR viewing appealed to interviewees because of their perception that doing so afforded greater control and time management: "Sometimes on-demand has commercials, and, I don't know, it's just easier on DVR." This interviewee described how Comcast's X1 interface made his collection of DVRed content like his own streaming library. "Whenever I've moved, I'd always make a list of the shows I've saved in case I lose them or the box gets messed up.... I have my bank of shows I need to watch.... Comcast gives you so much space now." The non-binge-watching interviewee preferred DVDs, which he rented from the library. The theater director collected DVDs of movies but used on-demand for the television shows he and his kids liked because he was less comfortable with streaming technology and did not have a smart TV.

Netflix was the most popular streaming service among this group of interviewees and earlier ones I've spoken with, though Hulu was favored by those seeking access to newer shows. Hulu and Amazon were mentioned more by this group than in my earlier research, which reflects how non–Netflix services gained market share in the streaming space from 2016 to 2018. Of course, I conducted these interviews before the launch of Apple TV+ and Peacock, among others. The major draw of Hulu for viewers in 2016–2018 was the immediate access and control of recently broadcast content: "I can watch *SNL* the next day." Even though Hulu began offering original content in 2011, it wasn't until the success of its award-winning sci-fi *Handmaid's Tale* (2017–) that its reputation as a creator of quality TV was established. Viewers who entered the Hulu ecosystem to watch a recently broadcast show, like *SNL*, often stayed to watch other content, resulting in binges that were less intentional at first but potentially satisfying. This speaks to the fluid nature of viewer motives in streaming TV ecosystems. "They have every episode of *Seinfeld* and no commercials!" exclaimed a Hulu-using interviewee who was a toddler in the early 1990s when the NBC sitcom dominated Thursday night television. In 2021, *Seinfeld* moved from Hulu to Netflix in a deal reported to be "north of $500 million" (Chow, 2021). Not bad for a "show about nothing." (See Chapter 6.)

Where streaming occurs and what devices are used to stream depend on the viewer's comfort level with technology and perceived social norms. Younger viewers raised around ubiquitous cell phone penetration tended to use mobile technologies more readily and interchangeably for watching. Those who came of age when television was only available on a TV set tended to prefer larger screens, though their more affluent financial and residential situations may also play a role in the preference. Non-millennials I spoke with also used laptops and tablets for streaming shows, but phones were rarely mentioned as a primary technology choice. The 69-year-old non-binger described liking how the laptop got warm on his chest when he watched movies in bed. The literacy instructor told me, "I don't have a smart TV in my living room … so, yes, for Amazon shows I do have to use a computer. It's not the best…. I will probably end up buying a smart TV." The financial planner who grew up in the 1980s with "TVs and VCRs in every room" described himself as an "avid binger." He used a laptop "sometimes when I travel for work" but he preferred "watching on my couch at home."

Another age/technology differential that I found is that younger viewers reported often using headphones to watch TV on computers and mobile devices while older viewers did not. A 25-year-old social worker preferred wearing headphones for binge-watching: "If there's construction happening outside my place, or I'm on a bus or something, or if my roommates have friends over and they're pregaming or something like that, I'll put headphones in just because it's easier than trying to intensely focus." I noted that two older interviewees expressed surprise when I asked them about wearing headphones. It was not for ignorance of how headphones connected to devices, but rather that wearing them was uncomfortable, inappropriate, and/or deleterious to the sound quality. "Headphones bother my ears," the non-binger said. This choice may also be a product of lifestyle and comfort with wearing headphones to watch video. In the 20th century, headphones were almost exclusively an audio technology. Viewers might have used headphones while watching an airplane movie, but that was a rare exception. Sony's Walkman was orders of magnitude more successful than the company's portable TV, Watchman. No older viewers reported binge-watching on mobile phones in public places, and they were also less likely to share smaller apartments or dorms with roommates. "I'll watch in bed with my laptop if my husband is watching something else downstairs.... I just wouldn't use headphones.... I don't know why, the sound maybe, I just don't." Whether alone or in public, younger viewers reported more comfort with the viewing ritual of putting on headphones to block out the external world.

Binge-Viewer Rituals (Time and Place)

According to my interviews, most binge-watching takes place at home, in the evenings of workdays and on weekends: "I don't have time to watch the shows when they air, so I usually, on the weekends, dedicate several hours to binge-watching my TV shows." When describing these rituals, interviewees often used the possessive pronouns "my" and "mine" in reference to the content. A 32-year-old consultant, who works from home, told me that binge-watching was part of her workday: "I use my downtime to watch my shows.... I set my own schedule, so I can." Most other interviewees chose prolonged periods of downtime outside of workplaces to binge-watch. The sous chef often worked late—"I'm usually not home before midnight"—and spent the few hours he had before falling asleep "watching my shows." The director stated, "I have this sort of fiber shake I'm supposed to drink every night, and I would sit down and watch an episode while I drank that."

Interviewees also reported using holidays and vacations to binge entire series, particularly popular shows they were forced to skip because of other commitments such as work or school. "I don't understand why Netflix can't release *House of Cards* during Christmas," complained one interviewee who had to wait several months to "watch properly." Long weekends were described as ideal times to "stay in and binge." One interviewee told me that for her "staycations really mean bingecations." Another interviewee admitted to taking sick days in order to complete a season of the Showtime spy drama *Homeland*.

While on the one hand viewers seemed to celebrate the freedom of being able to control the content flow, they also acknowledged the power of the content to control them and their schedules. To combat their temptation to keep watching, they managed their time by saving the more "addictive shows" (see "Bingeable Content") for times when long binges wouldn't interfere with their responsibilities. "*Sopranos* scares me," a busy 23-year-old medical assistant told me. "Not the show, but finding time to watch it all."

Social Rituals

Interviewees reported that long binges are often solitary (for non-live content), while binge-watching can sometimes be a shared experience with friends and spouses. There is some overlap, such as couples going on a weekend binge, but typically the longer the binge, the fewer the people who participate in it. Different tastes, motives, schedules, and stamina result in shorter group binges compared to solitary ones. In-person binge-watching groups seldom exceed two people (for non-live content). Not surprisingly, the smaller the screen, the fewer the binge-viewers. "How long can two people share an iPad?" one interviewee pointed out. Headphones also make for solitary binges; however, some viewers who share the watching experience with others through social media feel that they are not watching alone even when they watch alone:

> I have a close group of about five or six guy friends and we text all day; we're like on a thread on WhatsApp.... I grew up with them and we have similar interests.... Then you have six minds on a thread together and we all go back and forth about what we like.... There was this show called *Vinyl* two of us really liked it, and some of them are really into music, and I really liked it along with another guy, but the other four hated it and really bashed us for it.

Several interviewees described binge-watching as a way to have quality time with their significant others: "There are some shows that I watch by myself, but we like to share other shows together.... For a while, *Friday Night Lights* was our thing. We looked forward to it." The ritual of sitting down together after work and sharing a story often involved food but never degenerated into the satirical excesses depicted in advertising constructions of binge-viewers or "One Moore Episode" (see Chapter 4). Binge-watching usually started conversations about a show that continued outside the actual watching rituals and also led to planned events to jointly immerse in higher-Viewer Attentiveness Spectrum (VAS+)

shows or "veg out" with lower-VAS shows. It also created shared themes and characters that the social bingers referred to in other conversations and which drove the planning of new binge-watching. One interviewee explained how she enjoyed the comfort of "date-night" binge-watching: "We have our shows … and we don't have to get dressed or go out.… I really look forward to it at the end of the week.… It's not that I'm antisocial, well, I guess I am a little.… It's nice to just curl up."

The control and access of streaming technology enhances the immersive experience of sharing a story in ways that going to a movie or a play cannot. But that heightened control comes with new perils for binge-watching couples. One of my early interviewees described the ritual of binge-watching *Lost* with his wife as being based on cooperation and trust (Steiner, 2017). Neither had seen the show before, and their nightly routine involved cooking dinner together and watching "two or maybe three episodes. But on weekends we really binged." Choosing when to stop sometimes involved negotiation. "It's so addictive, and if I wanted to watch more and she didn't we might fight.… I mean not really, but it was hard." Their ritual was predicated on uncovering the mysteries of the show's world together, and there was an understanding that watching ahead was "cheating." However, when his wife left town, the temptation to "cheat" became too much for him. When she returned, they picked up the show where they had left off, but the ritual had been violated: "I kept trying to pretend like I didn't know what would happen, but I couldn't do it." He eventually admitted to his infidelity and after some time was forgiven—"she still jokes that I cheated on her."

Sleep-Watching

Another ritual of contemporary TV-watching tied literally to technology is sleep-watching. Four viewers, all 32 or younger, reported binge-watching video on their phones in order to relax in bed at night. "I'll stream Netflix on my phone just to fall asleep." No one reported doing this with laptops. These larger and perhaps more fragile devices were removed from bed before their viewers fell asleep. "It's not so warm that I conk out!" laughed the non-binger, referring to his warm laptop. The size and weight of cell phones are more conducive to sleep-watching, but they are not without their discomforts. "Sometimes I wake up and the headphones [wires] are choking me," one interviewee admitted. These interviews took place before wireless headphone technology was as mainstream as it became in the 2020s.

Sleep-watching on a phone was understood by these interviewees as different from falling asleep with a television playing. They explained that smaller screens and headphones made it feel more intimate and "less bright." The personalization and privacy they described seemed more akin to falling asleep while reading a book. "Having the TV on is noisy," one said. "It's not relaxing." The control of content, brightness, and sound made this ritual soothing for some younger viewers. Older viewers seemed surprised when I brought up the ritual. "People really do that? I don't understand how you could fall asleep staring at [a] phone." Interestingly, that viewer had fallen asleep with the TV on. "I don't do it regularly, though," she said. "Sure, a few times I've dozed off on the couch... Whatever, it wasn't a good sleep."

Speed-Watching

Intentionally accelerating a show's delivery speed is a new TV ritual that I had not encountered in my earlier interviews. While similar to time-shifting, this ritual involves restructuring a show's flow beyond the skipping of commercials that VCR users celebrated in the 1980s (see Chapter 2). These days, some viewers actually speed up the show's central text, either fast-forwarding through select parts or using apps that can play entire episodes at faster rates without losing sound, though the dialogue pitch "becomes like *Alvin and the Chipmunks*." The practice may have started with audio podcasts, but viewers were beginning to experiment with using it for binge-watching in 2016. I coded this ritual as speed-watching. The five viewers who had speed-watched did not do so often. It instead was more of a boost to their regular viewing rituals only worth doing to catch up on currently airing shows and achieve a sense of completion often to attain cultural inclusion.

One interviewee remarked on how speed-watching had altered his relationship with professional football. Because of his busy schedule, he DVRed NFL (National Football League) games that he couldn't watch live and watched them more quickly later. Although he grew up with season tickets and considers himself a football fan, he reported struggling to enjoy live football the way he "used to." It now felt too slow. When he watched the recordings, not only did he fast-forward through commercials but he also fast-forwarded through instant replays and "boring parts" of the game. And there are lots of "boring parts." According to a *Wall Street Journal* study, an average three-hour NFL broadcast only contains "10 minutes and 43 seconds of actual playing time" compared to 17 minutes of replays while a whopping 75 minutes "or about 60% of the total air time, excluding commercials, is spent on shots of players huddling, standing at the line of scrimmage or just generally milling about between snaps" (Biderman, 2010). Because he had so little free time, this interviewee chose to spend it on what he felt were the most important parts of the game. He was motivated to find out the result of each play as quickly as possible and then skip to the next play: "When you DVR a football game you can get through it in an hour or less depending.... It's a different experience, but I get through it." He described the difference as less "rich" than the way he had grown up watching football. "I'm watching the play, I'm not watching the game," he explained with measured regret. "I'm getting a certain aspect of enjoyment out of it. I balance what I'm not getting by the other things I can do [with the time I saved]."

He also described how this new ritual had cost him socially and culturally. Because he no longer watched plays before the ball was snapped, he had not heard Denver Broncos quarterback Peyton Manning's signature cadence at the line of scrimmage during the 2015–2016 seasons. "He would call out audibles, 'Omaha, Omaha!' but I never heard it." Other people did hear it, and Manning's "Omaha!" became a meme that spread across social media with numerous popular cultural parodies. "I guess I kind of ignored [the meme] because I didn't know what it meant." When his friends who watched games at regular speed referenced "Omaha, Omaha," outside of football contexts, the interviewee had no idea what they were talking about: "I don't know if I even have the sound on sometimes. That's what I mean about it not being as rich an experience." But he added that "life is about time." Perhaps that's the cost of "Takin' Care of Business" in today's on-demand media world.

A 23-year-old graduate student, who proudly identified as a binge-viewer, speed-watched streaming content in a similar selective fashion. She was a fan of Korean dramas but reported struggling to keep up with "all the great stuff" that's now available. To save time she fast-forwarded through repetitive parts of shows and scenes where she anticipated little dialogue: "I can tell from the music cues and the camera angles if they're going to kiss or something ... that's usually when I will skip ahead." Her familiarity with the genre's format and structure allowed her to make the editorial choice of speeding through sections that she deemed to be less additive to her experience: "I don't do it for most dialogue, though, except stupid stuff ... like if they're repeating something or it's really obvious." She watched unexpected or "important" segments at regular speed because she believed they contained important information and entertaining surprises. This is a demonstration of the Viewer Attentive Spectrum, but instead of selecting shows to watch based on how much attention was necessary to enjoy them, she was selecting scenes based on it (Pittman & Steiner, 2019; Steiner, 2017). When she felt that watching a segment would not enhance her understanding or her pleasure, she chose to change the show's flow. As with the football fan, her speed-watching rituals helped her manage time while gaining some pleasure from the show and feeling cultural inclusion with her friends and family who watch. But her older sister, whom she sometimes watched with, "won't let me [speed-watch]." Unlike the football fan, though, she did not report experiential, cultural, or social costs other than her growing preference to not "watch with [her sister] as much anymore."

While these two interviewees were using "conventional" technology to speed-watch—their remote controls—others occasionally utilized apps to accelerate their consumption on digital players. In 2015 Google Chrome released a patch for video players that allowed viewers to toggle the display speed from 1× to 3× in increments of .1×. Today it is a part of most video interfaces. One undergraduate student had heard about similar apps for speeding up the audio for textbooks on tape. He said that he led a busy life, explaining, "I'm always working or in class or going to work or studying. There's not enough time." When he discovered the patch, he decided to use it for catching up on a show that his friends were talking about: "*Game of Thrones* Season 6 was coming out at the end of last semester. When I got done with finals, I just binge-watched the first five seasons at about 1.3 to 1.5 speed." This meant he devoured around 50 hours of George R.R. Martin's fantasy drama through HBO GO in under a week. "It takes some getting used to," he admitted sheepishly, "but I saved 12 hours." After that he decided to watch Season 6 at regular speed. "It didn't work at first," he said, and "everything felt slow." He also reported not remembering a lot of the earlier seasons. "I'm not sure if I ruined the show," he laughed. "In some ways, it was better my way."

Motive-Ritual-Content-Attentiveness Process

My interviewees described motives that aligned with contemporary binge-watching research (Castro, et al., 2021; Perks, et al., 2021). One exception was the Nostalgia Motive, which they cited more frequently than in my previous studies. Re-binging a show to experience the feeling of the story again was reported across genres, but because the story is no longer new, nostalgia-motivated binges typically require lower attentiveness (VAS-) to the show regardless of content and involved relaxation and distraction. Several interviewees claimed nostalgic re-binging helped them to "decompress" after work; as one interviewee explained, "I know what's going to happen, so I don't have to pay attention to every word." She cited *Buffy the Vampire Slayer* as her "go-to" re-binge because "it takes me back to high school" when her life was less hectic. Familiar low-VAS shows were the content of choice for sleep-watchers. "I couldn't do that with a new show," one noted. "I'm falling asleep now to *The Office*," said the interviewee who was almost choked by his headphones. As viewers fell asleep, they reportedly looked at the screen less and eventually only listened to the audio on their headphones. Because they were so familiar with the shows they can "sort of remember what's happening in the scene ... or maybe I'm imagining what happened. Sometimes I can't remember, and I'll have to check. But other times ... especially if I'm so tired, I can just let it go and remember what I want as I fall asleep." No sleep viewers reported being able to remember if what they were watching found its way into their dreams. "I can't really remember my dreams much, to be honest, but it wouldn't surprise me."

Speed-bingers were typically motivated by cultural inclusion, sense of completion, and catching up—viewers wanted to be up to date on a show or an event so that they could participate in real or virtual discourses about it. As the young man who plowed through five seasons of *Game of Thrones* demonstrated, speed-bingers are willing to alter the quality of the content in order to be able to join the cultural discourse of fellow fans. This extrinsic motivation differs from that of binge-viewers seeking an enhanced/immersive viewing experience—this group actually watches more slowly by rewinding and replaying scenes. The primary pleasure for speed-watchers, at least initially, is in the perceived movement from outsider to insider (cultural inclusion) through consumptive completion (sense of completion).

Interviewees confirmed that they binge-watched certain shows more attentively than others. They described shows that they binge-watched less attentively as "background noise" and "something to have on." Often the binging involved multitasking: "I do laundry, cook." Shows binge-watched less attentively included sitcoms with single-episode plots like *Family Guy* and *30 Rock*, police procedurals like *CSI: Crime Scene Investigation* and *House,* and reality shows with formulaic structures and frequent recaps like *The Bachelorette* and *Real Housewives.* One undergraduate binged reality TV on Sundays: "I usually do that if I'm hungover." Less attentive binging took place any time viewers wanted to "relax and just have something on." The motives reported for less attentive binge-watching aligned with the motivations of relaxation and nostalgia.

Viewers cited dramas with season-long plot arcs, innovative

storytelling, and complex characters and plots, such as *Orange Is the New Black*, *Mr. Robot,* and *A Game of Thrones*, as the types of shows requiring more attentiveness (VAS+) to enjoy. These aligned with my earlier findings on content and the Viewing Attentive Spectrum (Steiner, 2017) and fit Perks's (2015) description of ludic media that encourages interaction and heightens the immersive experience (p. 4). Interviewees described these binges as "intense," "deep," "heavy," "draining," "more real," "the best way to watch," and "getting closer to the writer." The literacy instructor compared it to the "world-building" she experiences when reading "good books," while the consultant compared it to taking an "expensive dream vacation." The quest for information and entertainment came across in their descriptions of this enhanced viewing experience, and it was driven by their feelings of transportation and immersion in the story.

Most interviewees noted some connection between their viewing attentiveness (VAS) and the show's complexity. Some reserved shows that required more attentive binging for long weekends and vacations when they had the time to complete an entire season in a single sitting. This allowed them to immerse themselves in the characters' world and enjoy the plot as a unified arc. A 29-year-old MFA student described how she watched a whole season of *Orange Is the New Black*: "I binge-watched it. Hard. It came out, and I woke up at like 7:00 a.m., and I just watched it all the way through. I couldn't—I didn't want to stop." She was motivated by a desire to be transported to the world of Litchfield Penitentiary and be immersed in the lives of the women incarcerated there as the story evolved over 13 hours.

Interviewees were also aware that differences in a show's required attentiveness affected their experience and enjoyment of that show. "There's a lot more nuance," a 42-year-old bartender explained of higher attentiveness shows (VAS+). "A lot more character development, subtle things that are happening. If you're not paying attention, when something changes later, you don't know why it changed. You're lost, and you have to rewind." This speaks to the connection of information-seeking and entertainment-seeking. In a sitcom, such details are usually less relevant to a viewer's entertainment experience. "I feel like with comedy, it's kind of low brow. It's usually a little bit more accessible, easier to understand," a 37-year-old writer pointed out. He went on to say that "you can often pick up a comedy halfway through an episode and still figure out what's happening, still laugh. That's more of challenge with a show like *Breaking Bad*. If you miss the first 15 minutes you better start over."

Although structure, genre, and complexity—frequently described in terms of weight—often determined how attentively viewers binged, viewers made their show selections with some sense of that determination. "I think the heavier a show, just in plotline and everything like that, I get more into it," the psychology student explained. "I'm not as productive in other things. I dedicate all of my time that I have to watching that show. Versus if I'm watching a lighter-hearted show, I'm not dedicating all of my time to watching the show." At the same time, she chose to watch "lighter" shows to take a break from immersion after "heavier" shows before returning to them. This corroborates Anderson and Kirkorian's (2006) finding that attentiveness intensifies stimulation (p. 35).

Comments like these indicate that viewer motives may predict their initial attentiveness and level of immersion. That is to say, if a viewer seeks relaxation and distraction, they are more likely to select a show that allows for inattentive pleasure. If a viewer seeks engagement, transportation, and immersion, then they are more likely to select a show that demands attentiveness to enjoy. An exception to this is when a viewer's motive is nostalgia. Viewers report re-binging a variety of shows for the familiarity it brings them. When it comes to the nostalgia motive, a viewer's familiarity with the show trumps its complexity as the determinant of attentiveness. "I've watched *Breaking Bad* so many times," an interviewee explained, "I don't need to look at the screen."

Ad Reception and Interaction

When asked what they thought of advertising, interviewees expressed hostility: "Irritating, annoying, pain in the ass. Wish I could circumvent it. It frustrates me that it's not only watching TV, but now if you want to watch something on YouTube, you've got to watch advertisements there." When commercials could not be skipped, viewers often ignored them or avoided them. "I usually don't watch them," one said. "That's my something-break. Like smoke break or eat break or bathroom break, whatever." A 31-year-old counselor said, "I kind of zone out or play on my phone for 30 seconds while the ads are playing on the TV or something like that, rather than pay much attention to them." Others reported using ads as an opportunity to check social media or text friends. "I generally will pay as little attention as humanly possible. I'll go online ... anything I can do to kind of ignore them basically." In line with the Netflix narrative, several interviewees indicated that traditional commercial breaks are antithetical to binge-watching. A few also implicitly distinguished Netflix from TV, even if they watched Netflix on a TV set. When I asked the bartender to describe how he binged, he replied, "Mostly on television. I do occasionally stream *Bob's Burgers* on Netflix." Later in the interview he told me that he streams Netflix to his living room TV through a video game console. As I have discussed in chapters 2 and 3, journalists have created a strong association between Netflix and binge-watching, while the company has marketed itself as being other than TV. For viewers, the lack of commercial breaks on Netflix has created an understanding that binge-watching exists or is at its best outside the traditional interruptions of broadcast TV.

Interruptions and Control

All the interviewees initially associated interruptions to flow with traditional commercial breaks rather than the more common interruptions from their second screens, such as mobile phones, which they later admitted to experiencing. While viewers dislike all intrusions during binges, they reported a spectrum of displeasure that corresponded to how immersed they were in the show and their perceived control over the intrusion. For higher-attentiveness shows (VAS+) viewers sometimes turned off or silenced their phones and favored channels that didn't have commercial breaks. Such rituals were less common during lower-VAS viewing. "If I'm grading papers, I'm barely watching anyway," one viewer said of her multi-tasking during evening binges of sitcoms she'd seen before. But as attentiveness and immersion increase, so does hostility to intrusions. "I'm usually pretty calm, but it does annoy me that they do it right when something important happens and you can't skip," the sous chef said of trying to binge-watch *The Americans* through AMC's on-demand service. "And I hate that there are more and more toward the end of the episode." The uncontrollable intrusion of ads was too great for one undergraduate who gave up on *This Is Us* because of commercials. The MFA student who binge-watched an entire season of *Orange Is the New Black* in one day said that if the Netflix show had had commercial interruptions "I would not have finished it in a day.... I may have quit." "It kills the experience," the tech entrepreneur stated. He went on to say that he'd "wait a few months until it's out on Netflix." Viewers like these chose not to immerse themselves in complex worlds where intrusive messages from sponsors may invade at any time and exile them. In presence language, such viewers seek a feeling of transportation and engagement (ISPR, 2000) that is enhanced through binge-watching. The social/perceptual realism of the world they have been transported to and engaged with increases immersiveness but it is broken by interruptions that exile them from that world. While eating or bathroom breaks may also interrupt flow, they are the choice of the viewer, not of the broadcaster. So are social media use and outside communication that viewers can control.

If You Don't Notice an Interruption...

Interviewees familiar with product placement expressed a preference for it over traditional commercial breaks. "I think it's kind of a smart way to advertise," the literacy instructor acknowledged. "Instead of just playing the commercial. People usually hate commercials so if you placed a product during the show ... you know you might notice it but it's still less annoying." For some, the novelty made it a more compelling form of advertising. "One of those shows that I absolutely adore is *30 Rock*," the counselor said: "And they are very self-referential about product placement, to the point where it is really obvious what they are doing, but they are sort of poking fun at it.... I have never really seen it done that way in another show."

Interviewees reported appreciation for product placement during higher attentiveness (VAS+) shows, provided the placement made sense within the show's context. "Like in *Breaking Bad*," a 28-year-old "super fan" of the AMC drug drama explained, "Walt's car was that Pontiac crossover, the Aztec or something.... It was obvious that they were paying to have it there. But so what? People drive cars; they need to get places. Some drive Pontiacs.... That advertising didn't bother me.... It fit." This was not the case for AMC's zombie apocalypse drama *The Walking Dead*:

> [In] Earlier episodes they always have the same car, this Hyundai [Tucson] crossover. It's like a rounder version of Walt's car.... Anyway, there are way, way too many appearances, and it never seems to breakdown or even get dirty, which you'd kind of expect, right, in that world?... It was always waiting for them to escape, and I mean come on, it's not a Humvee, I don't think it even has four-wheel drive.... It just didn't make sense, which is probably why they got rid of it [in 2015].

Such distracting product placement hailed the viewer's attention away from the story and toward the business that pays for it. Doing so interfered with the world's social/perceptual realism, thereby exiling the viewer from the story.

Social/perceptual realism may be less important to viewers of lower-attentiveness shows (VAS-). Take, for example, the counselor's experience with an episode of the ABC sitcom *Modern Family*:

> I remember there was a very specific scene where one of the characters is talking about his car. He mentions that they got a new car because they were trying to adopt a second child, so they needed a bigger car and this car

was a bigger size than the one that they had previously. He talked about how there was so much more room for this or that or the other, and it was pretty obvious that it was product placement too. It didn't really sort of take you out of the narrative.... I don't necessarily see that as breaking the fourth wall to sell me something.

The expectation of advertising on network programming means that the social realism of the world can stand intrusions without losing as much integrity as a streaming show. This aligns with the narrative Netflix promoted and the fear journalists initially had for its pricing model (Choi, 2012). In this case the viewer (a) expected interruptions to immersion and (b) selected a show that can provide enjoyment with less attentiveness. We'll see how Netflix survives with ads.

Additive Interruptions?

Two of the interviewees reported encountering non-intrusive advertising other than product placement that they felt enhanced the shows they were watching—*Atlanta* and *Mr. Robot*. Both sets of commercials "interrupted" their attentive viewing at first, but both interviewees expressed appreciation for the commercials' "depth" and "creativity." The advertisements were structured like traditional commercials, but their tone and content fit the shows they were interrupting to the point where viewers could not tell whether they were "real," part of the show, or both. While not identical, this type of commercial has similarities with native advertising in journalism—the practice of packaging ads as news articles and embedding them on the page among real stories (Artemas et al., 2018). It also shares similarities with showrunners promoting binge-watching benefits under the guise of discussing their new Netflix show. While some critics have decried native advertising as deceptive (Roland, 2015), the interviewees who encountered these televised versions reported being thrilled by the novelty and innovation.

A 26-year-old server watched the *Atlanta* episode "Black American Network" (1.7) on DVR and almost skipped the commercials because he was so used to fast-forwarding during breaks. But then.... "I was like, 'what?' Back-up." The six "sponsors" in these ads appeared to be pushing real products—beer, cars, iced tea—but they were in fact satirical spoofs written by *Atlanta* showrunner Donald Glover: "It's an inside joke for us.... I loved it!" He explained that viewers who encountered these ads would have to be familiar with Glover's subversive humor and perspectives on race and popular culture in America to get the joke. Fans on the inside were rewarded, making the ads an enhancer of the viewing experience. If this sounds familiar, you probably read Chapter 4.

Mr. Robot 2.6 "eps2.4_m4ster-slave.aes" expanded the satire beyond the commercials creating a 15-minute opening act aping 1990s sitcoms and television. "[Showrunner Sam] Esmail is always pushing the limits," said this fan of the U.S. cyber-drama. He described how Esmail regularly inserts fake commercials from the show's hacker collective—Fsociety—before breaks "as if they had taken over the network." But what impressed him was that "m4ster-slave.aes" used period-appropriate ads and TV graphics "to keep the 1990s feel real.... If you grew up in the 90s you remember those cheesy sit-coms and USA *Up All Night.*" He also felt that the realism of the time-traveling opening act was enhanced by the audio-visual details, such as 1990s USA logos, theme music, sitcom cinematography, and opening credit font selections, which typically indicate a show's vintage. When an actual Bud Lite commercial from 1990 appeared during a "real commercial break," the interviewee was "blown away! The show literally took over the commercial." The promotional re-release, which Budweiser provided and paid for, intensified his feelings of transportation and social realism rather than intruding on his immersive experience. I asked him if he would fast-forward through the ad if he re-binged the season, and he said, "Why? It's part of the show."

Viewer-Controlled Interruptions

The interruptions most commonly reported by interviewees were those they controlled. Second screening happens for viewers almost without thinking—though the term is less familiar: "Half the time I'm on my phone and my laptop.... Is there [a] third screening?" Viewers engaging in higher attentiveness (VAS+) shows take steps to prevent outside intrusions on their phones, though they still occasionally look at them. That conforms with McCracken's (2013) and others' celebration of binge-watching as an island of focus in an ADD (attention deficit disorder) world. During lower-VAS experiences, a viewer may pay more attention to their second screen than to the television screen.

Live TV, particularly big media events with large audiences, are well suited to social media second screening. "I was on Twitter the whole time," said one undergraduate about watching the 2016 election coverage. Using social media during the Super Bowl and the Oscars not only serves as a distraction from a broadcaster's planned flow but creates additive discourses about the events. For higher attentiveness binge-watching (VAS+), social media is avoided during the viewing, though viewers report discussing their shows with like-minded fans after. This is part of the cultural inclusion motive. However, these viewers may also second-screen during viewing if that interruption enhances their understanding. "I will pause to look stuff up," the financial planner told me. "Like in *Westworld* there were all these different theories about, you've seen it, right? Yeah, so about who's a robot and who isn't. But it's hard to keep track of all the different timelines and who might be who.... I'm pausing, rewinding, checking names and places—you have to!" The choice to intrude may have disrupted his flow, but the information gathered during that disruption ultimately enhanced his viewing experience.

Synergistic Loop

The action of binge-watching involves technology, rituals, texts, and motives which together create an experience that shapes how the behavior is understood by viewers. For organizational and analytic purposes, I have divided these findings using those categories. Doing so is artificial and a consequence of using language to capture actions. A more precise way to understand binge-watching in action is as this synergistic loop:

Viewers' experiences and understandings of TV in specific circumstances shape (1) their motives for binge-watching which guide (2) their content selections based on their momentary understanding of those motives, in relation to the time they are willing to spend to fulfill the motives, in relationship to concurrent viewing content. Viewers' perception of the video content—familiarity with that show specifically and with its genre, structure, and available technology generally—creates a predetermined estimate of how attentively they need to watch, the control they can exert over the flow, and the amount of time they need or want to devote to it, and how that relates to their overall TV identity. This is a dynamic process. Once viewing begins, motives may shift, the content may defy expectations, time passes, interruptions intrude, moods change, and motives update, as does interpretation of their TV identity, which shifts choices for the next show based on their updated experiences and understanding of TV in a new circumstance.

Based on my analysis of the interviews the following process emerged: viewers seeking an enhanced viewing experience (EVE) often choose shows they believe demand greater attentiveness (VAS+). As a result, they will create rituals that allow them to allocate what they believe to be adequate attentiveness and time to enhance their viewing experience. Whether because of synergy or circularity, viewers report that content demanding greater attentiveness often results in feelings of greater immersion. The more immersed viewers report feeling in a show, the more hostility they report feeling toward interruptions, in relation to their perception of the interruption's intrusiveness and their ability to control the flow and manage their time.

Shaping Your Binge-Viewer Identity

While lacking in the personalized and infinite variety of *Rick and Morty*'s "Interdimensional Cable," most 21st-century television comes in a multitude of styles and genres available through a variety of technological platforms that afford viewers innovative ways to "read" its texts (Fiske, 1987, p. 14). A viewer's choice to speed-watch may be the final hurdle in the convergence of book reading and TV watching. Earlier, completion time was variable for the former and fixed for the latter. Today it seems you can be a speed-reader and a speed-watcher. This carries with it the cultural baggage of the couch potato/bookworm dialectic as well as industrial/textual disruptions for TV producers and viewers (Ellingsen, 2014). We still see this legacy in the ambivalent feelings viewers have about watching TV, despite the re-branding campaign. While the mix of pride and shame remains, this group of interviewees seemed prouder and more excited about TV than in my earlier research. Nonetheless, binge-watching is complicated.

It remains an ambivalent expression of abundance, enacted by viewers through a negotiation of control. While binge-watching implies a loss of control through binges of TV, it also implies a choice of how, when, and why control is lost. As I found in my years of speaking with them, viewers binge-watch in a variety of ways with a variety of content for a variety of reasons. When they seek relaxation and distraction, they tend to select shows that require less attentiveness (VAS-). When they seek an enhanced viewing experience, they tend to select shows that demand higher attentiveness (VAS+). The enhancement over traditional broadcast TV is an experience of increased presence—what viewers describe as being so into a show that they forget they are watching a show. But it is also about the proximity they feel to the show's creators and ownership they feel over its interpretation (Hills, 2018). Enhanced parasocial relationships are emotionally moving and yet heavy.

Binge-watching can create powerful feelings of transportation, engagement, and immersion through a "more real" mediated world. But the action of binge-watching is also a powerful expression of viewer control over a medium that for more than half a century afforded limited agency. At the same time it is an extremely lucrative phenomenon for the powerful companies that gained control of the medium by promoting that narrative. That negotiation of control is television. Today's viewer rituals like speed-watching demonstrate the reclamation of time and flow. Furthermore, the texts and the technology of our contemporary Platinum Age are designed to reinforce the sensation of personalized viewer access to any and all experiences. As the terminology and practices of binge-watching mainstreamed, in congress with other internet-driven media behaviors, they created an expectation of free and unfettered viewer control over the pursuit of entertainment and information. That expectation allows for feelings of ownership of content. The act of choosing content and the rituals of consuming it weave viewer identity into the fabric of the media. A viewer's drive to be closer to a story is manifestly about understanding it and latently about being understood by it. While viewer-showrunner communication may be facilitated by social media, it is the technology and editorial control exercised by binge-viewers that materializes their feelings of identity and understanding on the screen. They are changing the stories to suit their needs and to fit their schedules down to the second. They demand, "No talkin'! No new crap! 'Takin' Care of Business' now!" (*The Simpsons*, "Saddlesore Galactica," 2000), and the band appears to comply.

While viewers mostly tolerate low subscription fees and gladly relinquish their personal data (the real cash cow), they are hostile to interruptions of their control of flow. Hearing and seeing that hostility, particularly to commercials, from interviewees reminded me of an orchestra conductor stopping a show and staring down the audience where a phone had just rung. Intrusions on these immersive mediated experiences disrupt viewers' cognitive sensations of presence while threatening their relational control of the storytelling and thus their closeness to the storyteller. As a result, they express not only hostility toward the interrupter but also hostility at the media technology and the channels that allow for intrusions that they, as viewers, cannot control. Advertising has always intruded on the shows we watch, but in the 20th century it was an accepted aspect of a broadcaster's planned flow. Viewers couldn't choose when, where, what, or how they watched television. It was free, and the experience was worth every penny. Today viewers have become so used to personalized control and variety that the only thing they often have to wait for is enough free time to binge it all properly. Or so the story of Peak TV goes.

Binge-viewers feel that intrusions are antithetical to their experiential expectations. Netflix and other streaming services don't own the copyright on that sentiment. Intrusions not only disrupt immersion, but they also challenge viewers' perceived control of that immersion. To paraphrase an interviewee, binge-watching is like taking an expensive vacation, and commercials are like getting urgent emails from your boss throughout the trip. Not only do they interrupt your pleasure and remind you that the vacation is fleeting, but they also force you to attend to the very reality you had gone on vacation to forget. For many people, the idea of a vacation hinges on an escape of control and even identity. If one works and can save enough to take a vacation, one's expectation is that one's identity during that time shifts from worker to vacationer. The vacationer identity materializes in different clothing and behavior. It is disjunctive to be wearing a bathing suit and sunblock while being forced to don to your work persona (at least it was pre-pandemic). Doing so is a reminder of work's control over you. As some news anchors segueing to commercial breaks joke, "we have to pay the bills," but must paying the bills be intrusive? These findings indicate viewers prefer appropriate product placement and native advertising. To stretch the vacation metaphor further, they are like your boss sending you free drinks and surprise upgrades to your hotel. While these may remind you of work, you tolerate them if they are enhancing the vacation experience and not challenging your control of time. This is in part why Netflix's Binge Responsibly PSAs were such a single-use-only hit: even though the spots interrupted binge-watching, they enhanced the viewing experience.

Advertising, particularly when it is obvious and intrusive, interrupts the focused continuity and narrative immersion that viewers associate with binge-watching. It obstructs the pursuit of entertainment and information. Viewers recognize that they have more choice and control over their experience, as they demonstrate through their motive-based show selections. When they lose control of the experience, especially during more attentive binges with unexpected commercials that are unrelated to the show, they express hostility because their identity is being threatened. That power to choose their identity is at the heart of why so many viewers believe that binge-watching killed the idiot box. Any interruption is a reminder that their control is limited and fleeting.

At the same time, there is a creepy and pernicious side to native advertising. Traditional commercial breaks draw a clear line between show and sponsor. Blending content and advertising may improve the viewer experience while subtly reclaiming viewer control. It can also lead to slippery questions about show and sponsor boundaries. Viewers who binge-watch higher attentiveness shows (VAS+) may pay a great deal of attention to ads if they forward the plot or enhance the immersion of the show, as with *Mr. Robot*. Such ads could use insider knowledge and humor to foster loyalty with fans who hold parasocial relationships with the show-runner, as in the case of *Atlanta*. This is a delicate proposition to be sure: native advertising is only as native as it appears and only native if the natives approve. Today the natives are restless. If binge-watching allowed television to shed its 20th-century reputation as the idiot box, and allowed viewers to shed their reputation as couch potatoes, perhaps it will allow advertisers to shed their reputation as show intruders. Tune in to my next book to learn the outcomes of that!

Reader's Authority

Binge-watching has overflowed the media's definitional boundaries and reshaped how viewers use and understand television. If most media today are social and most phones are smart, perhaps it is time to consider reclassifying binge-watching as simply "watching" and name the small percentage of TV outside of it as "legacy viewing," "appointment TV," or "linear watching." Doing so recognizes the ubiquity and normalcy of binge-watching and the fundamental distinction of viewer-authorized flow versus broadcaster-controlled flow. That sounds admittedly optimistic, but at their best, binge-viewers are part of a storytelling process and have authority of their TV identities. The cancelling of Kevin Spacey aside, "aren't we all just storytellers?" (Bradshaw, 2021; Spacey, 2013). Whether they are reflecting the media coverage or the media coverage is reflecting them, the fantasy of authorship drove this phenomenon. Binge-watching streamed, in high-definition clarity, that author and reader are bound and beholden to each other in the circuit of televised communication. Viewer rituals for consumption allow them to move and be moved by moving the content. That movement allows them to journey anywhere and to get lost without losing themselves unless they want to. Above all, there is a fantasy that viewers now set the terms (because no one reads the actual terms and conditions). Sometimes those terms involve a journey to a faraway place, a new world of the viewers' making. Other times they may just want to go someplace familiar, a place that they've been that reminds them of who they once were when they last visited, a place they can close their eyes and re-remember as they begin to dream. In Chapter 6, I examine my own journey through this project as a binge-viewer studying binge-watching, and I explore how my own TV rituals and motives and media identity interact with my research.

6

Reflection and Postmortem of the Idiot Box and the Couch Potato

"In autobiography, as in all literature, what actually happened is less important than what the author can manage to persuade his audience to believe"
[Salman Rushdie, 1981]

"We all got roles to play. What's your role?"
[*The Wire*, 2003]

Really Nothing

Episode 155 of *Seinfeld* is one of the few in which Jerry is not at the center of the plot. Instead, "Muffin Tops" revolves around his friends'—Elaine, George, and Kramer—struggles with the creative experience, authenticity, and identity. In the A-plotline, George, Jerry's feckless pal who is loosely based on *Seinfeld* co-creator Larry David, steals the clothes from a tourist's suitcase he was supposed to be watching. George then takes on the role of an out-of-towner after being rescued from pushy New Yorkers by Mary Anne, a friendly guide from the New York City Tourist Board. Thinking that she is attracted to tourists, George tells her that he is visiting from Little Rock, Arkansas, where he works as a hen supervisor at Tyler Chicken.

In the B-line Elaine, a former publishing assistant at Pendant, attends a book signing for the autobiography of her new boss J. Peterman—a character based on real-life fashion cataloger John Peterman. In an earlier episode, we had learned that Elaine ghostwrote Peterman's book *No Placket Required*. Because she was running out of ideas, though, Elaine fabricated the manuscript with life stories she stole from

169

Kramer, Jerry's zany neighbor whose character was based on Kenny Kramer, a former real-life neighbor of Larry David. When Kramer discovers that he is "part of the pop culture now," he rushes off to help Peterman sign books. At the signing, Elaine bumps into Mr. Lippman, her former boss at Pendant, who now works for Pundit, the publisher of Peterman's "autobiography." Nonplussed by her writing, Lippman asks Elaine, "Why is it that every halfwit and sitcom star has his own book out now?" (At the time Kathleen Tracy was working on the first biography of Seinfeld, *The Entire Domain*.) While Kramer haggles with Peterman over who the *real* J. Peterman is, Elaine gets approached by a woman who asks her why she's been decapitating muffins at the snack table. Elaine tells the woman and Lippman that she only eats the tops of muffins and throws away the stumps. "It's the best part, really ... it's where the muffin sort of breaks free from the pan and does its own thing. That's a million-dollar idea right there," she opines. "Just sell the tops." Their conversation is interrupted when clerks forcibly remove Kramer from the bookstore.

As George's lie mushrooms—he now dresses in the tourist's clothes, stays in a hotel room, and visits New York City attractions—he discovers that the tourist identity may be fleeting. Although Mary Anne says she likes spending time with him, she knows that he will soon have to return to Little Rock and his "three-legged dog Willy." When George tells her that he is considering a move to New York, Mary Anne laughs: "George, this city would eat you alive!"

Across town, Elaine discovers that Lippman has opened a bakery called "Top of the Muffin to You!" She confronts Lippman—who, as her boss, had chastised her liberal use of exclamation points—arguing that selling muffin tops was her idea. He explains, "Elaine, these ideas are all in the air." She retorts, "When that air is coming out of this face, it is my air and my idea." (Ironically, *Seinfeld*'s writers may have stolen the idea for "Muffin Tops." In a 2016 podcast, Joe Rogan claimed that comedian Kevin James had been doing "the muffin bit for years" and that James had performed it for NBC executives during a pitch meeting.)

Meanwhile, Kramer decides to capitalize on Peterman's stolen identity with a school bus experience called "The Real Peterman Reality Tour." He tells Jerry and George, "People want to know the stories behind the stories." Jerry disagrees: "No one wants to go on a three-hour tour of a totally unknown person's life." Kramer defends his idea's validity saying that tourists pay only $37.50 and they even get a bite-sized 3 Musketeers, "just like the real Peterman eats." When George asks him if Peterman really eats them, Kramer says, "no, I eat them.... I'm the real Peterman." George then attempts to clarify this identity complex:

"I think I understand this. J. Peterman is real. His biography is not. Now, you Kramer are real. But your life is Peterman's. Now the bus tour, which is real, takes you to places that, while they are real, they are not real in sense that they did not *really* happen to the *real* Peterman, which is you." Satisfied, Kramer asks Jerry if he now understands. Jerry replies, "Yeah. $37.50 for a Three Musketeers."

Seinfeld has famously been called a show about nothing. In fact, *nothing* was what it had in common with mainstream 20th-century television. *Seinfeld* was self-aware, experiential comedy. It resisted sitcom conventions of formulaic plots where good-hearted stock characters learn lessons. Instead, *Seinfeld* focused on the mundane rituals of four anti-social New Yorkers. While episodes were filled with snappy quips and physical humor, the appeal for many fans was that they and the writers were in on a joke that was critiquing the standards and practices of network television and American society. *Seinfeld* was subversive and self-referential with stories that blurred reality and fiction. One of the hidden jokes in "Muffin Tops" was that the real-life Kramer, Kenny, had actually started his own "reality" bus tour a year before the 1997 episode aired. To paraphrase George, Larry David had created a character based on a real person who became so popular that the real person believed he had become a part of popular culture. In response that real person started selling experience tours, which, while real, took tourists to places that the fictional character frequented on the show. A year later the fictional character parodied the real person's "reality tour" in an episode where his identity was stolen by the ghostwriter of an autobiography of a fictional character who was based on a real person. Understand?

Seinfeld often played with reflexive meta-narratives in ways no television show had. The most famous example is a multi-season story arc in which Jerry and George, again based on the show's creators Seinfeld and David, try to pitch the fictional NBC run by ruthless executives and witless sycophants the pilot for *Jerry*, "a show about nothing." *Seinfeld* and *Jerry* were nearly identical, except fictional NBC cancelled *Jerry* after just one episode. Through its self-aware critique of the power structures of television, *Seinfeld* knocked down the fourth wall and invited viewers inside its world of nothingness. The sprawling storylines and complex, loathsome characters afforded a rich terrain for fans to dig through and re-imagine as their own. Iconic characters such as the Soup Nazi have been birthed into consumer brands, while the show's catchphrases such as "Yadda, yadda, yadda" have been adopted into English vernacular. It may be the only television show to inspire a religious holiday—Festivus (December 23)—complete with rituals (airing of grievances and feats of strength), iconography (the unadorned aluminum pole), and thousands of devoted celebrants (O'Keefe, 2005). For many people *Seinfeld* is not just a show that entertained them but an indication of their identity. It is an immersive experience with a participatory culture that extends beyond each 23-minute episode.

David Bianculli (2016) chose *The Sopranos* as the first show of TV's Platinum Age, but he described *Seinfeld*, which ran from 1989 to 1998, as "an evolutionary quantum leap" (p. 333). While improving technologies and texts were steps (and sometimes leaps), TV's journey from vast wasteland to Platinum Age was also a narrative of evolving identities—the viewer's and the medium's. The narrative gained traction after the turn of the last century along with another story of evolutionary progress: the shift in first-world economies from service to experience (Pine & Gilmore, 1999). In this chapter, I use both stories as a backdrop for the synthesis of my research on binge-watching. I explore how changes in the articulations and actions of TV watching reflected perceptions of TV's transition from industrial control to viewer experience. Finally, I turn the critical lens on myself to interrogate how my identity influences my experience with television and this project holistically. Like *Seinfeld*, I hope to knock down the fourth wall through reflexive narrative and invite readers into the stories behind this story. Doing so is a transparent proffer of verisimilitude that hopefully affords you a more immersive and informed experience.

Birthday Cake and the Experiential Economy

Pine and Gilmore (1999) argue that the entire history of economic progress can be understood through birthday cake. Yes, birthday cake. In the 19th century, when America was largely an agrarian economy, the celebratory confection was made from scratch with commodities grown on local farms. In the 20th century, the economy industrialized and the population urbanized; some parents saved the time it took to acquire and bake commodities by spending more money to buy box cakes, like Betty Crocker, with premixed ingredients. As the economy shifted from industrial to service, parents began spending more money to buy their children's cakes from supermarkets. By the turn of the last century, "parents neither make the birthday cake nor even throw the party. Instead, they spend $100 or more to 'outsource' the entire event to Chuck E. Cheese's ... or some other business that stages a memorable event for the kids—and often throws in the cake for free" (Pine & Gilmore, 1999, p. 97).

Each stage of this progression offered different cultural and economic values, and consumers' choices of those values were an expression of their identities. But unlike in previous times, today's experience economy has an expectation of variety and consumer control baked into it—the on-demand attitude. A homemade cake is "natural" but takes longer to produce than a store-bought one. Today's busy parents may believe that their time is better spent experiencing something else, or they may cherish the experience of baking because it feels authentic. In the 2020s, it may actually be more expensive to procure "natural" ingredients for the time-consuming activity of scratch baking, which potentially positions the agrarian-style cake as an expression of affluence (like urban chicken coops). A store-bought cake and a party at home can be less expensive than going to Chuck E. Cheese, but parents might also believe that a party at home offers a better experience for everyone than Chuck E.'s epileptic, animatronic mayhem. Parents who identify (or aspire to identify) themselves and their children as educated may throw a museum birthday party. Critics of consumerism may choose a public park for their party or not have a party at all. Parents with fond memories of Betty Crocker may want to share the box cake experience with their children.

In this way the experience we choose when celebrating a child's birthday is one that we identify with and one that identifies us. The tangible difference between now and then is in the perception of experiential choice and identity malleability. Whatever the entertainment ritual, consumers today enter the marketplace with an on-demand expectation of control balanced against their management of time and resources. It was just as impossible to go to Chuck E. Cheese in 1960 as it was to binge-watch Netflix. In 2023, consumer experience and identity feel more fluid because of the perception of choice.

Experiencing TV Identity

Television has followed a similar economic and cultural trajectory, though it never really enjoyed the same agrarian roots of birthday cakes.[1] Instead, TV came of age in post-war America as an industrialized mass medium, sometimes sponsored by Betty Crocker (2016). A key benefit of industrialized products is that they are standardized, which allows for lower cost, uniform fabrication and mass distribution through commercial channels. Twentieth-century critics maligned those standards in mass media (see Chapter 1). As an expression of identity, broadcast TV-watching was considered a cheap, processed substitute for "authentic" cultural consumption (Postman, 1985). Twentieth-century journalism reflected this identity of commercial TV as passive, lowbrow art. The passivity of watching programming produced for the masses was derided, particularly when it was consumed massively (see Chapter 2). Early journalists minimized viewers' cultural roles by omission, focusing instead on the controllers of broadcast flows—TV I (Jenner, 2014). When viewers were included, their identities were homogenized into stereotypical groups—gullible children, sports fan husbands, nagging homemakers, key demographics—or the amorphous "audience." Journalists' omission of unique viewer identity also reflected the technology and texts that typified TV's idiot box identity— fuzzy reception, two-dimensional characters, and formulaic stories, what *Seinfeld* mocked.

As the unwitting, powerless audience was supposedly sucked deeper into the vast wasteland, journalism reflected and perhaps exacerbated the fears of other ideological state apparatus agents—educational authorities, religious leaders, and government regulators (Althusser, 1970). The word choices and news frames of 20th-century articulations of TV binges reveal a paternalistic attitude toward a lemming-like audience. This was the brainwashing of mindless masses through mass consumptions of mindlessness that critics railed against (Horkheimer & Adorno, 1977). *New York Times* radio editor Jack Gould (1948) offered this early admonition of the impending doom:

> The American household is on the threshold of a revolution. The wife scarcely knows where the kitchen is, let alone her place in it. Junior scorns the late-afternoon sunlight for the glamour of the darkened living room. Father's briefcase lies unopened in the foyer. The reason is television.... Superficially, video may seem no more sinister than mah jongg or gin rummy, a trifling example of paralysis in the parlor. Indeed television's host of experts have maintained a meaningful silence on the impending crisis. However, it is no longer possible to conceal that our way of life since Lincoln and Jackson is more than just in danger. It has gone [p. 1].

At times, mid–20th-century journalists verged on catechistic language when they chastised the sloth and gluttony of the American audience and the greed of TV networks that exploited lust and wrath to create envy for their sponsors' prideful products. Even as television moved from broadcast industry to cable service, 1980s and 1990s journalism continued to describe passive audiences as "at risk" and reported on protective solutions for weaker groups such as children (see Chapter 2).

That paternalistic hyperbole would become the fodder of streaming media companies seeking to differentiate themselves from traditional TV in the 2010s. They used PSAs as a mnemonic totem of network era authority while associating non-streaming TV with low-quality industrial standards. The Partnership for a Drug-Free America's "Frying Pan" (1987) was self-unaware and treated the audience as incapable of questioning authority. By satirizing such 20th-century warnings on TV, the commercials in Chapter 4 offered this meta-narrative: streaming services were self-aware and aligned with self-aware viewers who demanded better television. That narrative was endorsed by TV creatives who declared binge-watching to be the liberative ritual for couch potato evolution. Together they stood in opposition to the broadcast and cable networks that still hid behind the authority of their static fourth walls.

Binge-watching journalism from the 2000s cited tech-savvy superfans and described their rituals as edgy and subversive. A few years later the narrative was co-opted by Netflix and other streaming media companies. Their mock PSAs helped mainstream the binge-viewer trope through subversive nostalgia and showrunner endorsements. They used the couch potato identity as a foil to illustrate viewers moving from an outmoded television industry and service to an immersive entertainment experience. The story aligns with the economic progression narrative that differentiates functional services from interactive experiences that are "inherently personal, existing only in the mind of an individual who has been engaged on an emotional, physical, intellectual, or even spiritual level" (Pine & Gilmore, 1998, p. 99). Through binge-watching, television becomes an individualized experience of emotional, intellectual, and spiritual (and perhaps someday physical) connection between author and reader that reimagines their relationship.

That transition of identity is at the heart of binge-watching. Interviewees and journalists reported that streaming companies successfully positioned themselves as the catalysts for couch potatoes to shed the networks' bondage and emerge as "liberated" binge-viewers. While the molting might not have been so clean cut, the underlying narrative is now embedded in our collective understanding of television's (medium and viewer) evolution. Broadcast TV was an industry; cable TV was a service; streaming video was an experience that met a viewer's demand for variety and control in his or her unique enactment of identity. Binge-watching became the ritual that enabled the transition through viewers' supposed demand for experiences of better quality and variety. Journalists in the first decade of the 21st century wrote about how the TV industry was improving in response to technology and a few early adopters. In the second decade, they reported how binge-viewers and streaming video companies were changing the identity of TV. The marketing campaigns of those companies highlighted the enhanced technology and texts, but it was through their absurd, satirical depictions and authentic celebrity endorsements of binge-viewer rituals that the companies identified themselves as enablers of user experience rather than mere providers of a uniform service.

Exploiting Self-Awareness

It is impossible to know how a mid–20th-century advertising agency would have promoted a company like Netflix. However, the climactic scene of the first episode of AMC's *Mad Men* offers an analogous situation. Sterling Cooper, the fictional 1960s ad agency that anchors the show, is struggling over how to sell cigarettes for its client Lucky Strike in the wake of new regulations against promoting tobacco as healthy. A young account executive suggests the following paromologia: "Why don't we simply say, 'So what if cigarettes are dangerous? You're a man. The world is dangerous. Smoke your cigarette.'" The Lucky Strike president is shocked: "What the hell are you talking about? Why not just write 'cancer' on the package? Are you insane?" This antithetical notion of acknowledging consumer awareness and agency is oddly reminiscent of PSAs from that era (see Chapter 4). Authority need not be explained to an audience that cannot question it. What could be gained by breaking the fourth wall with self-awareness and realistic complication? If Netflix profits from binge-watching, then, from an industrial or service economy perspective, it should create advertising that depicts binge-viewers in an attractive fashion. Announcing that it's addictive would be "insane!"

And yet binge-watching was pitched and reported to be a complicated behavior of the experience economy. Streaming video companies weren't promoting oral hygiene to sell mouthwash as Listerine did in the 20th century (Marchand, 1985, pp. 18–20). Instead, binge-viewers were constructed with an ambivalent identity: While they were consuming voraciously, they were simultaneously playing a counterhegemonic role in opposition to traditional couch potatoes under the thumb of powerful TV networks. On the screen they appeared to be addicts, but in "reality" they were self-aware and demanded real recognition and real control. Journalists and other authorities had forged the idiot box narrative in the second half of the last century, and they spent the early part of this one gleefully tearing it down. Advertisers may not have played a direct role in popularizing the identity of TV viewers as couch potatoes, but they exploited that identity to construct binge-viewers by contrast for the benefit of streaming companies. While the upshot positioned network TV as halitosis and Netflix as mouthwash, such an obvious, preachy narrative would have turned off self-aware binge-viewers. "Netflix: The Cure for the Common Show" sounds like something Sterling Cooper may have pitched.

Interviewees reported that a major value of binge-watching through streaming services was the ability to avoid commercial interruptions. At the same time these advertised constructions of binge-viewers were often commercial interruptions! Rather than hide this conflicted identity, advertisers embraced it; the commercials thus appeared self-aware. They acknowledged the hypocrisy of a commercial promoting a commercial-free experience with rituals that promoted freedom as addiction. The self-aware parody gave the binge-viewer caricature a verisimilitude in line with the complicated nature of post-network television. That social realism, while manifestly absurd, staged the binge-watching experience as more authentic and immersive, aspects which viewers and journalists reported as motivations for binging. As with a popular NBC sitcom making fun of the very network that airs it, the mock PSAs let the viewer in on the joke, thereby sharing the subversive experience with them. The press and the public liked that story so much that they made it their own, even though it had been their own before Netflix co-opted it. Now it seems so real that it's easy to forget the mediation: the history is approaching maximum presence, no longer art but reality (ISPR, 2000, p. 5).

Immersive Authority

The commercials and the official sources cited by journalists were part of public relations campaigns that shaped the action and articulation of binge-watching in the mainstream media. Such articulations—in newspapers and commercials—may be less relevant for Gen Y and Z consumers who grew up in the experience economy. Today's media companies and studios also offer immersive world-building experiences to cultivate their fan bases beyond 20th-century media sources. They use online, interactive platforms to provide "fans with the means to participate in the active construction and (re)affirmation of the characters and their intersectional identities" (DeCarvalho & Cox, 2016, p. 507). The goal may still be for people to subscribe to their services or buy their content and technology, but it's marketed as a holistic experience of identity. Doing so promotes the narrative of the viewers as authors. While few interviewees in this research aspired to be showrunners, nearly all had some desire to be the authors of their binge-watching

experiences and their TV identities. Interviewees described their relationships with shows and video technology beyond mere services. A bus
service can take you from point A to point B. A bus tour may have the
same place of embarkation and terminus, but it potentially provides rid-
ers with a memorable three-hour experience and perhaps a Three Mus-
keteers bar. That experience is why customers were willing to pay 15
times the price for Kramer's Reality Tour as they would for an MTA bus
ticket. For binge-viewers, their rituals create personal identity on whatever emotional, intellectual, or spiritual level they choose.

Binge-viewers' distinctions between service and experience are
about identity control in balance with their management of time and
resources. The football fan I interviewed who chose to speed-watch
games believed he was cheapening his NFL experience (see Chapter 5).
He was using his DVR to move from play to play, snap to down, at the
expense of the rich football viewing that he had cherished as a younger
fan. Essentially, he was using technology to transform a bus tour into a
bus ride—focusing only on point A to point B. But the choice to create
a less rich experience was his, not the broadcaster's. Like a parent who
has a birthday cake delivered, he speed-watched because he could not
spare the time to watch football "naturally." He was aware of the costs,
and he controlled the flow. He identified as a professional adult who was
still a young fan at heart, but one who prioritized other experiences and
responsibilities.

What and how a viewer watches are expressions of identity control. But as my interviews revealed, one's TV identity exists not only
in the show being binge-watched but across the variety of shows, technologies, and motives being managed. It is also shaped by external
perceptions of cultural values, which roughly align with the journalistic hierarchy of binge-worthiness (see Chapter 3). A person reporting regret about spending a Sunday binging a reality program is in part
reflecting cultural standards about such texts. That regret, though, is
balanced in the enactment of personal motives like relaxation: "Today
I'm going to be a bum." Similarly, a person's pride about spending a Sunday binge-watching a critically acclaimed drama is shaped by perceptions of internal rewards and external recognition. Viewers want to "get
inside the writer's head" because that proximity is believed to make the
story more "authentic." They perceive the search for authenticity as a
worthwhile activity—discovering a story's "true" meaning. Reality TV
shows are often reported to be "shallow." Their values are considered
"cheap" because the superficial thrills can be obtained without spending much attention. The "truth" behind them is perceived to be simple and obvious (and thus less authentic), which costs less to cognitively

obtain. However, they do have value for viewers with other motives than enhanced viewing experience (EVE). It's a lot harder to relax or multitask while binging HBO's reality-bending sci-fi *Westworld* than it is by glancing at reruns of ABC's entrepreneurial reality show *Shark Tank*. A viewer cannot experience nostalgia for a show they haven't seen before. But shows requiring differing attentiveness can be used together to create a larger experience. As I reported in Chapter 5, some interviewees watched shows requiring less attentiveness (VAS-) to "decompress" in between more intense viewing or to balance their emotional experience. Together the variety of television experienced can be used to perform a shifting array of identity.

But it can take more work to get inside someone else's head when his or her story is complex. Complexity can be appealing because it appears authentic and perhaps because it costs more cognitively (like an agrarian cake). The choice to understand also reflects perceptions of external values and internal rewards. An enhanced viewing experience provides a better understanding of a TV world with the potential for a better understanding of one's self in the world. When a viewer seeks relaxation there is an implication of inattentiveness to the cultivation of one's TV identity—other activities are determined to be more pressing. A viewer binge-watching attentively does not want to see herself as being cheap, obvious, or simple. The action of immersing one's self in a complex world is a deeper experience with an aspirational reward of self-enhancement and socio-cultural standing. When viewers determine that the reward justifies the effort and time, they report interruptions as inhibitive to their creative process. Within an on-demand, experiential economy the loss of control of flow is an affront to identity creation.

Rebranding the Idiot Box

According to Sarah Banet-Weiser (2012) "brands are about *culture* as much as they are about economics" (p. 4). This is certainly the case for fashion but also the merchandise of fandom (Serazio, 2019, p. 14). If we are to believe that binge-watching killed the idiot box, then television was rebranded as a means of expression through the agency of binge-watching. Television has always been a struggle for control over an entertainment experience, but the brand of TV was culturally renegotiated during the 21st century. The process flowed from product to consumer and from consumer to product—both of whose identities are now fluid. The binge-viewer is branded as an agent controlling their TV by binge-watching it. The TV set is no longer an idiot box but a person-alized hub of cultural exchange. The programming is a co-production of studios and fandoms. This story is never just happy or sad but an evocative experience that viewers embrace as the protagonists in a life-style fashioned on demand, tailored to their tastes, and "real" in its self-conscious indulgence.

Through this perspective, the television set is moving beyond its technological materiality and its 20th-century idiot box identity. The technologies that allow for the action of binge-watching facilitate the cultural identity of the binge-viewer (Banet-Weiser, p. 4). This con-vergence of culture and technology foments ambiguity of "how these components (content, device, and context) interact with each other" in contrast to the cleaner significations of 20th-century TV (Cour-tois et al., 2013, p. 422). So too the advertising of and on it. The agentic 21st-century viewer also problematizes long-accepted notions of media flow and critical studies methodologies that focus on either audience culture or the political economy of broadcast systems (Banet-Weiser, 2012). And yet the binge-viewer identity is a co-production of com-mercial rhetoric, strategically constructed and satirically packaged to control the viewer's time and money. That new media companies par-tially reveal their strategy appears at first glance enlightening, and the diversity of content appears empowering to the viewer. Such ges-tures promote trust, particularly when presented in opposition to the cold dominance of the 20th-century television industry. That offering of trust, variety, and "freedom" may also help conceal the companies' less palatable aims, such as the aggregation, manipulation, and distri-bution of customers' personal data (Turow, 2017). If the business of net-work era television was selling a quantity of the audience, the business of streaming-era television is about capturing the quality of individual identity.

Identity Journey

Identity involves more than what and how we are experiencing. While immersive binge-watching may allow some to imagine them-selves in new ways, identity is always tethered to some past. Television's identity is no different. The idiot box and the couch potato may have passed, but our understanding of TV today is tied to them through col-lective memories. We can detect them in the articulations of contem-porary journalists guiltily and gleefully describing (and endorsing) their binge-watching indulgences and the disruption of commercial networks. We can uncover their exploitation in the commercial rhetoric of new media companies. We can feel them in the ambivalent rituals and effects of binge-viewers. Identification acts as a destination, but identity is a journey. The point of embarkation and terminus are reimagined with each act of identification and the experience of movement from past to future identities. We appreciate the journey by gaining knowledge of progress. Acknowledging context enhances the experience. That goes for this project too. As Johanna Uotinen (2010) writes, "research should be based on conscious and reflected situating at a certain place and position, from which I look and do research. The produced knowledge is thus contextualized" (p. 164).

> To read more about my theoretical justifications for this choice turn to 211 (note 2).[2]

Reflexive Narrative

My Backstory

I loved Edward Packard's *Choose Your Own Adventure* book series when I was growing up. The primitive ludic media, written in the second person, allowed me to feel the illusion of control over my reading experience. Of course, *Choose Your Own Adventure* books don't really allow you to choose your own adventure. They are more akin to mazes, with (usually) one path readers could follow to "win" and many paths leading them to "lose." Nonetheless, the popular 1980s series afforded me an illusion of choice and control over the fate of whichever of the 184 stories I selected.

I am still a little ashamed to admit that these were the only books I actively sought out as a young boy. My medium of choice, as you may have guessed, was television. This was not because I grew up in a house without books—in fact, quite the opposite. My parents were both literature professors, and our home was filled, quite literally, from floor to ceiling with books of all different shapes, genres, and languages. If I close my eyes, I can still see the multi-colored patterns of spines packed tight on the bookshelves of every room—a wide, red Michelin guidebook, the crackled black of Umberto Eco's *Name of the Rose*, several taupe tomes of *Russian Formalism*, and a purple zigzag along *The Colors of Rhetoric*. They surrounded me in every room. Despite the privilege of growing up in a library, I was always drawn to the flickering screen of our lone, cable-less, 25-inch RCA, much to my parents' chagrin. "Read a book!" they would beg. "Why?" I would reply. "You read the books." It's not that I was against books, but that was their thing. TV was mine.

Every Saturday morning I would watch cartoons from seven until after noon, flipping through the six or seven channels available in the Philadelphia area during the mid–1980s. I hated the lack of variety, but I made do. The broadcast flow grew to be a part of my daily after-school ritual, and my parents could reliably call upon me to know what shows would be on when. It was easier back then. Of course, it was also a lot more frustrating. I remember feeling outraged when I discovered, after rigorous testing, that the networks coordinated their commercial breaks so that no matter which station you were on you got an ad. It seemed so unfair, so illegal somehow. I actually wondered if anyone knew about their vast conspiracy, or if I was the only person wise to it. But I also remember the parasocial relationships I formed with the characters—Arnold and Mr. Drummond, Scarecrow and Mrs. King, Luke and Bo, Michael and KITT, B.A., and others. Their stories became our stories, and I didn't care if my parents thought they were "mindless."

When we got our first VCR, I was in heaven. Finally some control! Of course my parents couldn't figure out how to set it up, so I had to do it for them. To this day, when they call me to figure out some aspect of streaming video or on-demand, I jokingly ask them, "How many PhDs does it take to program a VCR?" That primitive technology gave me a feeling of expertise, and it became my tool for empowering my entertainment experience. I burned through mountains of VHS tapes recording my favorite shows and watching and re-watching them at my convenience. They filled the shelves under the TV and a small one on the bottom shelf of the nearest bookcase that I had annexed.

But my voracious TV consumption and lack of reading began to concern my parents. After I had gone on a binge of professional wrestling that I'd recorded and kept re-watching, my father, a Tolstoy expert, decided to intervene, presumably for his son's cultural benefit. He called me a "couch potato" and an "American barbarian." Then he locked me in my room and wouldn't let me out until I had read Gogol's book *The Nose*. I was eight at the time. When I emerged tearfully some hours later, he asked me what I thought. I told him I thought the story was stupid; "the guy's nose falls off, so what?"

"Don't you think it's funny?" he asked.

"No, his nose ends up in someone else's house. I don't get it."

"But you have to understand the meta-narratives...."

"Why is that funny?"

"Meta-narratives make it funny."

"Meta-narratives are stupid!"

I didn't know what meta-narratives were, and I didn't hate books.

It was just that I found forced entertainment less entertaining than the voluntary variety. Watching TV was my choice, and because of that, I could experience it my way. I wanted to choose how I was entertained and my choice was television. I identified with it, and it identified me. Now, you can certainly make the case that professional wrestling allowed me to be a passive consumer of culture, that such simplistic stories fostered a non-critical interpretation of media. But I didn't feel that way. I recognized that the good guy usually won and that the matches seemed formulaically scripted, but the backstories behind the characters were funny and the sprawling world of the WWF (World Wrestling Foundation) with its never-ending sagas and intrigue felt so much more immersive than Gogol. My interpretation could evolve over time and I could choose which aspects to identify with. Like with *Choose Your Own Adventure,* I felt the illusion of control and the freedom to be immersed at my own pleasure.

While writing this book (my dissertation originally), I had been thinking quite a bit about how the ideas of immersion contribute to the authenticity of a text. Immersion seemed to be everywhere in my data. As I went through the iterative process of qualitative analysis, I began wondering how that sensation of immersion could be expressed in this project. I lacked the courage and perhaps also the talent to successfully compose a *Choose Your Own Adventure* dissertation, but I thought maybe if I could adapt it for wider audiences, I could incorporate some elements of choice. Genre conventions frame and bind the words a PhD candidate can use. And while to be successful any work of literature must be different enough from previous works engage the reader, it must also be similar enough to previous works to be recognizable to the reader.

Although a *Choose Your Own Adventure* dissertation was too radical for me, I believed my inclusion of narrative in this work to be valuable to readers and this genre. Perhaps it could be where my muffin breaks free from the pan. The idea of breaking the fourth wall to bring a reader closer can provide a richer experience through evocative narrative. Appealing to scholarly readers' feelings is delicate but potentially potent. I certainly don't want to throw away my stump. But the self-awareness of my move indicates an openness for the pursuit of the "real story," which as scholars we aspire to pursue. But as the marketing campaigns I analyzed in Chapter 4 show, it can also be exploited to create a sense of trust between author and reader. The narrative must not feel manipulative and it must also contribute to the goals of the research project. To be successful, such a move "should be personal and research-like, evocative and analytic, descriptive and theoretical at the same time" (Uotinen, 2010, p. 165). Now, as I convert this to a book for audiences wider than my wonderful dissertation committee, I feel more comfortable giving readers the choice of how they experience this story.

If you would like to learn more about how this muffin was made, turn to 212 (note 3).[3]

If more meta-narrative is not your thing, continue to "Reflexive Binge."

Reflexive Binge

When binge-watching came up in my interviews, I usually asked participants when they first heard the term. Most didn't remember a specific time, but I do. My first encounter with the word binge-watching was in the December 2011 issue of *Wired Magazine* (Choi, 2012) but I knew I had been doing it for years. I remember the feeling reading those words in the kitchen of my walk-up in the Art Museum Area. It was like "Yes! That's what you call it." And I could tell, right away, that Choi wasn't talking about channel surfing or watching CNN all day; she meant something more than 20th-century TV.

While interviewees had difficulty remembering the first time they heard the term, many could recall early binge-watching experiences they had had. Like a lot of them, my first time was with DVDs. Coincidentally enough, Bianculli's first show of the *Platinum Age* (2016) was the text for what I believe was my first "traditional" binge-watching experience: *The Sopranos* in August of 2002. Though it premiered in 1999, I had resisted the HBO crime drama because it sounded over-hyped, and I didn't have HBO in college. But, in the summer of 2002, I had some downtime and decided, upon my mother's recommendation ("It's like Shakespeare on TV!"), to give *The Sopranos* a try.

My mother had never recommended television to me before. She had on occasion surreptitiously stuffed my bookshelves with books of the Western canon, and she had on multiple occasions sonorously decried my affinity for American popular culture. So this recommendation came as quite a surprise. With the fourth season scheduled to air in September 2002, I rented (from our local video store, where I had worked as a teenager) the DVDs of seasons 1–4, if I remember correctly. After the first episode, which I watched with my mother, I was hooked. Children of addicts often blame their parents, but I'm confident I would have become a binge-viewer regardless. At least this way I started with "quality" product under adult supervision.

Only a few days later I was slinking out of the video store again in search of more *Sopranos*. Season 2 would have to be a letdown, a sophomore slump. But no, the show just kept getting better! I ended up watching all 39 episodes from seasons 1, 2, and 3 over an obscenely short period of time. Like my interviewees, it is difficult for me to recall the exact amounts of real time it took to get through the show in part because my mind was more in synch with *Sopranos* time. And it was the tail end of summer vacation. It was just me, our old 32-inch Sony, and a hardworking Magnavox DVD player, which only let me jump from scene to scene or from chapter to chapter. Because I was on vacation, my viewing patterns were inconsistent. There was at least one night when I stayed up watching, got a few hours of sleep, and then woke up and immediately wanted to return to David Chase's North Jersey story. I was binge-watching, even though I didn't know that word yet. Had an interviewer studying the topic asked me why I was watching that way, I would have said that the show was too good to stop. As soon as an episode ended, I wanted more, and, unlike with broadcast TV, I could have more—as much more as I wanted. What I was doing felt like a better way to watch TV. And I also finally understood what all the hype had been about. I wanted to return to those many conversations I'd ignored or been left out of and throw in my two cents. That motivation was tangible though less manifest. I was in the story with Tony and Dr. Melfi, but under that immersive experience I knew that as soon as I had caught up, I could join the conversation and even start one of my own! I had never seen a TV show like *The Sopranos* before. It really was like Shakespeare, and I was mesmerized.

As the final credits ran on Season 3, I felt distraught. What was I going to do? I didn't want to wait until the September 15 premiere of Season 4 to re-enter that world. So I chose not to. I started binge-watching the first three seasons again. Sometime around then my mother told me I was watching too much television. Looking down at my disheveled appearance, I feared she was right, and I felt guilty, ashamed and lethargic, but I didn't stop. The show was too good, and it was my summer break, or had the semester already started?

Since then, I have watched the complete series from beginning to end (the last episode aired in June 2007) five times and dipped into seasons many more times. Over the next 10 years I used a combination of DVDs, DVRs, and on-demand options to consume a canon of great and not-so-great shows from around the world. I can't recall my first Netflix streaming experience, but I can vividly recall binging *House of Cards* Season 1 over a couple days and over a variety of platforms including my phone and laptop. Like my interviewees and indeed much of the world, binge-watching is how I watch TV, but I am aware of its seductive allure—it is an experience with which I am constantly negotiating control. As a binge-viewer studying binge-watching, I can be analytical about my own rituals and motives, though if the story's good enough I might forget for a few delicious moments. I do realize, though, how they, along with my history, influence how I perceive the phenomenon. That influence can create biases for me and add insight. I used my experiences to enhance my textual analyses, interview questions, and rapport with interviewees. For instance, if an interviewee brought up characters from *The Sopranos* or aspects of other shows that affected their rituals, I didn't pretend that I hadn't heard of them. The best interviews are personal conversations, not clipboard surveys. The TV texts I used in this book to set scenes or describe aspects of binge-watching come from my own experience watching them, as did many of the articles and commercials I analyzed. They were the media that caught my attention, like Choi's (2012) article did when I picked up my roommate's copy of *Wired* in December 2011 and read binge-watch for the first time. They shaped how I perceived and interpreted television's identity.

As I mentioned, one reason why interviewees binge-watched was their perceived improvement in narrative immersion. Most preferred the streaming, full-season release model to the once-per-week model of broadcast television. "This is how a show should be watched," stated one viewer, who felt consuming a complete narrative arc brought her closer to the showrunners. This perceived authenticity of the viewing experience was a common justification for viewers selecting higher attentiveness shows (VAS+), a justification I share with them. Binging a whole show or season affords an experience of getting "inside the writer's head."

But why do people want to feel immersed in someone else? Why do we want to be transported to a new place? Where did this need to inhabit an imagined world come from? Psychiatrists studying "TV addiction" in the 1950s lamented the medium's "hypnotic and seductive action on its audience" (Meerloo, 1954, p. 290). They wrote that viewers cannot handle "real" issues in their lives and therefore use TV to escape. This still forms the theoretical basis of contemporary behavioral health studies of binge-watching. But do viewers want to escape? And what was I as a binge-viewer trying to escape from? Who did I want to be? This led me back to reflexivity. I began to think about what kind of character I am, and what role I was playing in this project.

Unpacking My Binge Backpack

After some self-reflection I feel that the character I most often perform is a stranger/chameleon hybrid. It allows me to play many supporting roles temporarily and no lead roles (other than it) permanently. I like to believe I can enter any scene and feel welcomed despite being an outsider. I take pleasure in fitting in from without. Oddly, it is the role I feel most comfortable playing. I say oddly because on the surface it resists suture—I can never *really belong* anywhere because I can really belong *anywhere*. I can never have a stable identity because I am constantly moving and reflecting other passing identities. For me closure is boring, and I bristle under its fixation. I prefer to be open and find connections between people and things that few expect. This may explain in part why my analysis of the interviews led me to the finding that viewers' TV identities exist across multiple shows and that they are malleable. While this was what they reported, it was also what caught my attention as relevant for this project.

My attraction to the stranger/chameleon role is a product of my background. I have always felt different and often been an outsider who had to reflect what was around me to be welcome. I have a name that no one pronounces correctly the first time, or the second, or third. I am the first person in my family born in America. My mother was born in Canada and my father was born in Czechoslovakia. My skin is whitish, and I grew up in West Philadelphia where most people had darker skin. To fit in I had to learn codes of language and affect that were foreign to my parents. As a young boy, I embraced hip-hop culture of the 1980s. At the time it was largely ignored by white America, but my black neighbors found my attempts to rap and break dance endearing.

But Philadelphia wasn't my only home. During the summer I lived in Osečany, a hilltop village in central Bohemia where no one spoke English, including my Russian grandmother who cared for me and my sister. Most of the villagers had never been on an airplane or met an American. To fit in I learned Czech, albeit with a Russian accent that I picked up from my grandmother. That additional difference ingratiated me with the local proletariats who took my Russian lilt as evidence of the strength of their political identity. Lenin must have been on to something if even Americans speak with Russian accents!

During the school year I attended a Quaker school on the Mainline where most students' parents were doctors or lawyers. My parents were professors; we lived in the city. Most of my friends had cable television in their homes. We didn't. My father called TV "the idiot box." Most of my schoolmates were Jewish, and although half my family died in the Holocaust, I was not Jewish like they were. We never attended synagogue services, celebrated the High Holidays, or ate deli. My parents had ideologically scrubbed all trace of Judaism from our home, a move that may have saved my forebears during World War II. And yet

here we were, living in America, free from persecution, able to light can-
dles and spin dreidels to our hearts' content, and what did we do? Bupkis! Worse than bupkis, we were actively rejecting the very rites they
had died for. Such shame, such guilt!

Troublesome Terminology

But was it shame and guilt that attracted me to a topic marginalized
by high culture academics? Binge-watching was considered shameful
because of historic connotations of the words "binge" and "TV watching." The binge-viewers I spoke with didn't just feel guilty or ashamed;
it was more complicated. Despite the word's current ubiquity, its meaning is still being negotiated in and through the media. Its connotations
carry an ambivalence that belies its popularity. Are binge-viewers trying to escape themselves, as 20th-century psychiatrists argued (Meerloo, 1954), or trying to learn and empathize? Is binge-watching healthy,
dangerous, manipulative, empowering, or all of the above? In the articulations I selected from those 10,000-plus articles, the behavior is mostly
described as a positive advancement for viewers (Stelter, 2013). Subver-
sively, so too is the identity of binge-viewers constructed by the Jekyll
and Hyde marketing. The campaigns position the freedom and convenience of streaming video against the passivity and authoritarian rigid-
ity of a broadcast TV model that forced viewers to wait a week to find
out what happens next. Dirges lamenting the cliffhanger's demise and
how to break the habit can be found, but journalists were more likely to
joke about the hygiene viewers have traded for the freedom and splendor
of TV's new Golden Age (Harlow, 2012). Mainstream media contorted
the word "binge" by its framing of binge-watching. It is a subversive use
of a signifier to ironically exaggerate the signified.

The subversiveness of binge-watching is a direct link to the word's
origins in the chatrooms of self-conscious TV nerds debating *The
X-Files*. But I have personal motives for binge-watching too, which
should be disclosed. In my childhood home, watching television was an
act of defiance. I always loved watching, but identifying myself as a TV
viewer went beyond the pleasure of any one show. My mother and father
studied written texts—literature and language. For them television was
the idiot box, in name and function. For me it was an expression of my
individuality in opposition to their authority. In some ways I have been
fighting for TV's legitimacy all my life, because its legitimacy is an indication of my own.

I believe such recognition is important to your understanding of this research. It reveals the potential for bias in my interpretations that you should be aware of. For me, having awareness of that bias potential made me more critical of my analysis and interpretations of the data I collected. During the process of writing this book I frequently would question my interpretations, framing, and word choices, particularly when describing 20th-century articulations of TV. Was TV really the idiot box that my evidence suggested or was I seeing those constructions through the lens of a TV apologist? Was it paternalism or my own father that I was hearing? At times I may have been overly corrective by forcing the inclusion of those few voices that called TV benign. Though I stand by my findings, I leave it to you as reader-author to decide if I went far enough.

Escaping the Madeleine

Although my self-reflection acted as a constant and at times cumbersome check on my research process, it also allowed me to discover other aspects of myself that I believe enriched this work. While hunting binge-watching's journalistic origins (Chapter 2), I made an interesting discovery. The first appearance of the term I found (I discovered Wickstrom [1986] during a secondary search) was from an August 28, 1988, *Toronto Star* review of the Vancouver Fringe Festival. On that day, John Masters used "cultural binge viewing" (p. 4) to describe experiencing multiple theatrical performances in a single day. My initial thought upon discovery was whether it could be considered a legitimate articulation, since Masters was talking about plays, not TV shows. Theater binging-viewing seemed more high culture to me than TV binge-watching. How would academics, like my parents, perceive my work if I was studying audiences who binged plays instead of shows? As I read his 601-word review, though, a memory popped into my consciousness. No, a shudder didn't run through my whole body, as the vicissitudes of life became indifferent to me like they did for Proust. But a story of my actual first binge did begin to reform in my mind. That memory allowed me to see connections between immersion and experiential identity that I believe are at the heart of binge-watching.

Presence of Mind

I was nine when my parents divorced. Soon after my mother moved my sister and me to London. I attended an all-boys prep school with uniforms and corporal punishment quite different from my previous Quaker school experience. I was bullied by my peers and my masters because of my American accent, so I, the adaptable chameleon, began speaking with a British accent. This changed my status from being different to being acceptably different. Nonetheless I remained an outsider.

My mother, always the English professor, decided that the best way to ingratiate me was to take me to the theater. On weekends we would visit the Barbican to take in performances of the Royal Shakespeare Company (RSC). My favorites were history plays; I liked the battles. Encouraged by my interest in "high culture" and "history," my mother decided to try something revolutionary. One rainy spring weekend she took me to see *The Plantagenets Trilogy: Henry VI, The Rise of Edward IV, Richard III*. This RSC production combined *Henry VI* parts I, II, III and *Richard III* into a nine-hour Wars of the Roses marathon.

Bringing a 10-year-old to any play, let alone nine hours of Shakespeare, is risky. And I was a pretty hyperactive kid. They say TV'll do that (Healy, 2004). But it turned out to be one of the best experiences of my young life. From the opening scene I was hooked, immersed, and transported to 15th-century England. I wanted to be in this world and the plays brought me there. I was mesmerized by Richard III, not the soft-spoken Henry VI, played by a young Ralph Fiennes. But most of all I wanted to save young Edward V. Something about the boy-king who was locked away with his brother in the Tower of London spoke to me. I wanted to be him, but to escape. Of course, I knew he never would. History had spoiled the ending. And yet I hoped he would somehow, in this adaptation, break free and rule England. I knew, though, as the minutes ticked away toward the final curtain, that he would not escape. I was the one who would be released from the Barbican, but I didn't want to go. I wanted to remain immersed in that story. As the Lancasters and Yorks battled and plotted and battled, I became a part of something so exciting and engaging that I forgot I was sitting in a theater watching a stage, and, in some way, that I was me. I felt presence. But alas, the play carried me, measure for measure, against my authorial will, toward its climatic finale, when Richard begged "a horse, a horse" to escape his fate on Bosworth Field. I would have gladly given him one if only to keep the house lights from turning on again and to silence the standing ovation that would end my immersion.

On that day in London, over 30 years ago, I experienced what some binge-viewers have called "Unseasonal Affective Disorder: Post-Binge Malaise." This post-binge-watching blues is the "malady of our time," according to a snarky *New York Times* article: "'It leaves you with a feeling of emptiness.... You feel kind of ridiculous, but it's a sense of abandonment'" (Schneier, 2015). I knew, though, that that sensation was only "news" because the *New York Times* still considered binging theater to be higher brow than binging TV. Had they been with me that day in London, they would have known the feeling existed across media. Those lingering values that classify one medium as highbrow and one as low are being challenged by today's convergent media environment. A person can speed-read and speed-watch on the same screen. To paraphrase one interviewee, would a person today feel more guilty about spending a weekend binge-watching *Mad Men* than she would binge-reading *50 Shades of Grey*? It depends on who you ask, and who's asking.

But it also depends on how and why you do it. In the summer of 2017, my mother and I attempted to relive our Barbican experience on TV. We binge-watched PBS's show *The Hollow Crown: The Wars of the Roses*, a six-hour adaptation of those same plays. It did not work. Perhaps my nostalgia had idealized the plays, or the production was worse than in London, or my trying to observe myself and take notes on the experience ruined the immersion. A lot can change in three decades— the approximate length of the actual War of the Roses (1455–1485). But my takeaway was that Shakespeare belongs on a stage. I am so used to seeing crisp, high- definition, CGI (computer-generated imagery) warfare on TV screens that the pantomimed battles intermingled with beautiful verse destroyed the social realism. In a theater you overlook this discontinuity; you fill in the gaps by focusing on the language. But is the journey from text-centric to video-centric communication making us dumber and lower brow? I don't believe it's as simple as that. The convergence of media is confounding distinctions of taste and thereby enlivening discourse about how we account for our values. Soon enough, virtual reality (or some other immersive, sensory technology) will allow a 10-year-old boy to binge a nine-hour RSC performance in his living room. Will his distressed parents call him a couch potato or a cultural snob? Only time will tell....

Celebrating Ambivalence

The desire to be immersed and transported is not simply good or bad—it's complicated. Notions of high versus low culture attempt to simplify this by saying that a play or a book is worthier immersion. But this is a play of the powerful. Prescribing value to one mode or text of culture over another may be unavoidable, but it should always be questioned. What makes the feelings of presence different in binge-reading or binge-theatergoing is as important as why we perceive the experience as more valuable than binge-watching TV. Furthermore, we must question the choice of the word *escape* and the chooser. People, like those I interviewed for this project, describe their relationship with binge-watching ambivalently. They are okay with that, and so am I.

In terms of methodology, the hours of open-ended conversation I've had with viewers, allowed me to feel their experiences and understand their motives. Interviewing itself may be a form of escape and so much more. Reading through pages of fuzzy newsprint transported me to the world of 20th-century journalism with its sexist language and paternalistic social structures (and utterly bizarre ads!). I wouldn't want to live then, but it was eye-opening to experience that world through the pages of a medium that I respect. So too was trying to figure out what was going on inside the heads of advertisers who used showrunners to celebrate binge-viewers and PSAs to satirize them. My search for these more "authentic" stories was interesting and challenging not just for what I learned about binge-watching but what I learned about the people behind it and myself. That process is at the root of what C.W. Mills called the "sociological imagination" (p. 351), a perspective that allows the observer to occupy multiple subject positions simultaneously, to enter someone else's experience and feel it as your own. Reflexivity thus richens and empowers the research process through its shared enactment. My desire to be immersed in the stories of others is why I enjoy binge-watching and how I study binge-watching.

Epilogue

Performing Identity

When I returned to America at age 12, I was harangued because of my British accent. Once again, I adapted how I spoke to fit my situation. As soon as I did, it became much easier to make friends. I became fascinated by the power of being able to change how people identified with me by adjusting my language and appearance. Writing this now, I see connections to my choice to analyze textual articulations of journalists writing about binge-watching. Their words and frames shaped TV's understanding. As a teenager I had experienced how framing and word choice influence definitions and interpretations. I began to experiment with different costumes, roles, and expectations, taking pleasure in the confounding of stereotypes. I began to dress in various extreme styles to provoke reactions and then would undermine the perceived sartorial identity with opposing language and affect. One day I wore hip-hop fashion to a baseball game but addressed anyone I met in a proper British accent.

In high school I became the only "white" member of the Black Student Forum (BSF). This vexed some members (and non-members) who felt I didn't belong. My appearance and language were a costume that could be seen through. Because I couldn't change my skin color, I deduced that the only way I could gain acceptance would be to acknowledge my whiteness while demonstrating curiosity for and copious knowledge of ("urban") black culture. Building on my love for hip-hop, I developed an encyclopedic knowledge of early gangsta rap music. For adolescents, cultural authenticity is often a product of cyphers to communicate taboo topics. In the early 1990s, rappers were characterized by authority agents as public enemies—the surest way to entice teenage boys to imitation. If you could rap, you got respect. By acknowledging my outsider status while demonstrating insider knowledge, my friends in the BSF accepted me as an exceptional white person, though never by the president Phillip Goff (2014), who was a few grades ahead of me. He's now a renowned psychologist specializing in latent racial bias. I was still an outsider but one with a privileged position. Perhaps this influenced my desire to study a "low culture," outsider topic in the academy.

What I began to learn as I matured was that people are comforted by similarity and intrigued by difference. The art of playing my character was to assess the mood in any scene and adjust the way I spoke and what I spoke about to fit the space between those impulses. I began to hone my role as a stranger-chameleon by being different enough to be exciting but not so different that I couldn't be understood. This may explain why, while attempting reflexive narrative, I am putting it at the end of this book and basing my findings on evidence gathered by more accepted research methods. Is that offset by the ethos of knocking down the fourth wall and/or is the move a transparent paromologia? It's complicated.

Although I cannot imagine living otherwise, the stranger-chameleon is often a lonely and tiring role to play. I find myself at home when I am away: meeting new people and finding connections between us. I can say "cheers" in more than 10 languages. But where do you go after the play ends? What does a chameleon see in the mirror? I imagine it must be easier to be either/or—to know who you are in a stable, thoughtless way. I often find myself longing for the suture of clearer identification. But playing such a role feels inauthentic to me and probably impossible for anyone to embody.

At the same time I acknowledge that most people would identify me as a white, cisgendered, American male. Even though I like to play with identity, I am not blind. And it would be inauthentic for me not to recognize that those external identifications afford me the privilege of the roles I play. Doors open for me that wouldn't for other stranger-chameleons. It is perhaps the subconscious guilt of that privilege that drives me to seek outsider status and undermine assumptions of identity. The sutures I seem to seek are traumatic. I blame my parents and I thank them. My project is an acceptably performed defiance. What could be a better way to challenge parental authority while winning parental acceptance than by using the rules of their game to legitimate a cultural form they decried? To make them accept TV-watching as culturally relevant because I earned a PhD studying it? To adapt my dissertation to the book you now hold? But what do I really want them or you to accept? Is it more than a performance? I binge-watch because I don't want the play to end. I study binge-watching through these methods because the process transports me into the world of others. It allows me to feel their experiences and explicate them with greater clarity and verisimilitude. It allows me to remain present in my analysis through feelings of presence.

Presence and binge-watching are terms of play, this play. My exploration of them is a quest to affix understanding to media experience that is ongoing. By doing so I am arresting their action. I am suturing their meaning and perhaps my wounds. These are the binds of discourse that I struggle with in writing this book. Still I battle that battle against position, in hopes that my words might dance through meaning and my meaning dance through words. A play is terminal, but the play must go on.

So what of my role in this play? I may try to be a methodological chameleon by analyzing outsider culture, but am I really choosing my own adventure, or am I simply finding my way through a maze? My father's eyes grew myopic writing his dissertation, and I fear I will soon be wearing glasses. In the spring of 2018 he taught for the final semester of his career. That May I defended the dissertation that would become this book. In the fall of 2018 I taught my first class as an assistant professor. What choice do we really have in the roles we play or the life we experience? Is identity ever real or just a story based on other stories? Has binge-watching killed the idiot box? I don't know, but that is my perception as far as I can see and as near as I can tell.

Final Thoughts: Limitations and Boundaries

I appreciate that the exploratory approach to this research project may be less action-oriented than the critical traditions of much of the theory upon which it builds. This is a valid criticism. In post–Trump America, taking an ambivalent position can seem an act of aggression. Irony itself has been stripped back to its least subtle reality. And so, to write about binge-watching, the subversive act of mediated pleasure, popularized during those seemingly complex and halcyon pre–November 9 days, now feels somewhat empty and bourgeois given the existential drama of the real world. What do binge-watching rituals and TV history matter when a global pandemic rages and the U.S. democracy collapses? I admit it radiates tin-eared privilege.

Much like my focus on American-based viewers and Western media, my explanation, if not excuse, is a lack of resources for the situation. There is only so much time to write a book. Let me be clear though: I am not arguing that U.S. viewers are all viewers and that they have been emancipated from corporate industrial structures that function overtly for profit. Or that heteronormativity and racial inequality are no longer issues to dissect in the content (Belcher, 2016; DeCarvalho

& Cox, 2016). Far from it. I would be critically derelict if I ignored the irony that American viewers' expression of freedom in the whatever, whenever, wherever on-demand TV narrative is to consume as much as possible. But I feel that the situation is complicated and nuanced. And while issues in the world today have been riven to a point of binary opposition, where truth and lie and right and wrong are quite clearly black and white, the world is often and will be a lot more complicated. The capacity and complexity of ambivalence will return again.

Chapter Notes

Chapter 1

1. Scholars of culture, particularly Marxist theorists of the Frankfurt School, further asserted that the ever-growing consumption of television was contributing to the "masses" losing their critical abilities to distinguish authentic beauty from mass-produced pop culture. This threatened their power as purveyors of taste. Moreover, they argued that the variety of programming available was a farce promoted by networks to create a false sense of choice for viewers (Horkheimer & Adorno, 1977). The feared outcome was a nation of "dupes" brainwashed into consumer ideology by formulaic Americanized culture that could be thoughtlessly consumed (Storey, 2012, p. 64). The dangers of TV went beyond culture and economics. Marcuse (1968) argued that "prescribed attitudes and habits" in mass entertainment created a "'false consciousness' for audiences" that stymied the impulse for political change (pp. 26–27). Television thus became a terminal vessel for a range of social fears in the rapidly shifting identity of Cold War America.

Return to the Cultural Boogeyman story on 5.

2. While television was framing the wars and elections of the 1960s, cultural theorists of that era began challenging traditional demarcations of high and low culture through Marxism (Storey, 2012). Unlike earlier critics, however, this new generation of scholars at the Centre for Contemporary Cultural Studies in Birmingham and elsewhere argued that social class played an important role in shaping the distinctions of culture. By choosing to explore diverse, subordinated, and non-traditional voices and media, they legitimized the academic study of popular and folk culture in a multiplicity of forms. During that time, the "cultural sphere [was] divided into two hermetically separate regions" (Bennett, 2009, p. 82): Film, television, and popular literature (media) were studied through the theoretical lens of structuralism, while lived events (rituals and customs) of the working class were studied through "culturalism" (p. 84). According to Bennett, the former sought patterns in the content as evidence of the ruling class's domination of the masses through mechanized subservience. Conversely, the latter scoured popular culture for "romantic" and "authentic" expressions of subordinated voices shouting proudly against the tempest of domination. Bennett proposed merging the two through Gramscian hegemony in order to "disqualif[y] the bipolar alternatives of structuralism and culturalism" (p. 83). Such a move acknowledged the complexity of a viewer's power to negotiate meaning and the nuances of the economic and political structures behind television, both culturally and technologically. Doing so opened the possibility of examining the role of audience agency and the value of popular culture (Bennett, 2009; Fiske, 1989; Hall 1980; Jenkins, 2006; Williams, 1973).

Return to "Resisting and Consuming the Masses" on 8.

3. Building on the work of the Birmingham School, cultural theorists of that time worked to rebrand popular media as a challenge to the status quo (Bobo, 1995; Weedon, 2009). Radway (2009) encouraged negotiation and renegotiation of "the relationship between audiences and texts" (p. 199), while Bobo (1995) challenged the top-down power dynamics and unidirectional flows associated with media structures and social science methods of the 20th century. This new wave of cultural communication scholars argued that a person's choice to watch soap operas (Ang, 1985; Geraghty, 1991) or read romance novels (Radway, 2009) could be interpreted as a renegotiation of the boundaries of identity against existing power dynamics. As Stacey (1994) pointed out, "consumption may signify an assertion of self in opposition to the self-sacrifice associated with marriage and motherhood" (p. 238). Hegemony then becomes discursively processual and not necessarily determined by previously constructed identities and structures (Torfing, 1999, pp. 194–196). Through this lens, the choosing of a popular text could be seen as the playing of a counter-hegemonic role. A TV viewer's agency was enacted by her consumption of media texts rather than determined or controlled by the textual structures or the political and economic forces behind them. Thus, the action of viewing was celebrated because of its power to redress the cultural value of texts and the ideologies that classify them.

While this reimagining of the viewer was empowering for the study of popular culture, it was neither totalizing nor mainstream. A person's choice to watch *Kate & Allie* or *Hill Street Blues* was important to understanding mediated culture because it could be counter-hegemonic but also because it could reify hegemony. Hall (1990) adroitly noted the limitations of audience agency within discourse. Building on semiotics, he argued that "distinction must be made between the encoding of media texts by producers and the decoding by consumers" (Kellner, 2001, p. 3). His discursive circuit model of television stressed the active negotiation of

encoding and decoding from production to reception. It gave voice to the audience without ignoring the structures that attempt to control it. The encoding producers, he argued, have greater access to sources of information and resources for transmission than viewers. Despite the asymmetry, viewers can express some power in the discourse through their decoding of the messages. He theorized that within the circuit viewers could have three potential codes: "dominant hegemonic," "negotiated," and "oppositional" (Hall, 1990, pp. 100–103). His choice of terms delimited audience agency in the meaning-making process of popular culture, which he characterized as "an arena of consent and resistance. It is partly where hegemony arises, and where it is secured" (Storey, 1996, p. 3), and therefore it was a place for (limited) antagonism through subordinate decoding.

At the same time, Hall (1990) predicted that "a new and exciting phase in so-called audience research, of quite a new kind, may be opening up. At either end of the communicative chain the use of the semiotic paradigm promises to dispel the lingering behaviourism [*sic*] which has dogged mass-media research for so long, especially in its approach to content" (p. 94). This new phase of audience research blossomed in the theoretical frameworks of feminist cultural theory of the 1980s and 1990s and allowed for scholarship that empowered audience resistance to the ideological forces of popular culture through its very consumption.

Ien Ang (1991) further challenged the mass media perspective of homogenized audiences and what Carey (1989) called "transmission models of communication." She argued that "the ordinary viewers' perspective is almost always ignored" in the study of television (Ang, 1991, p. 2). Ang contended that this "institutional perspective" treated "'television audience' as a definite category whose conceptual status need not be problematized" (p. 2). Whether in industry or scholarship, the use of the term *mass media* carries certain implications. For quantitative audience studies the implication of *mass* is often a large group composed of individual responses that can be controlled and modeled to create operational value. Outliers are ignored; deviation is standardized. Such treatment lends itself to the social-science orientations and behaviorist methods favoring the homogenization of popular culture texts and the aggregation of the audience as a mass subject of study. It creates what Martin Burber (1937) calls an "I–It" (p. 16) relationship between researcher and subject. A social scientist's pursuit of objectivity is, therefore, an intentionally anti-social action that assimilates individual humanity into artificial conditions of variable dependence. As Raymond Williams (1989) observed, "there are in fact no masses, but only ways of seeing people as masses" (p. 11). While I believe his observation pithily obliterated the preference for, if not the value of, studying the audience as a mass, institutional norms from network era transmission models persisted.

> *Return to TV's multi-channel transition in the 1990s on 8.*

4. Media and communication scholars' differing approaches to studying television stem from the field's breadth with roots in both science and humanities. This lingering dialectic is evident in the varied approaches to binge-watching research. James Carey (1989) divides the communication field into two alternative perspectives: "a transmission view of communication and a ritual view of communication" (p. 12). Although he stresses that these serve to organize scholarship descriptively through metaphor, he notes distinctions that demonstrate how philosophical orientations affect the interpretations of audience reception of media texts. Scholars of the transmission view study communication "as a process whereby messages are transmitted and distributed in space for the control of distance and people" (p. 12), and, he asserts, they treat the research of communication as science. Alternatively, ritual view scholars study communication as "the representation of shared beliefs," and they treat research as a critical interpretation of culture (p. 15).

The Source-Message-Receiver-Channel (SMRC) model (Weaver, 1968) exemplifies transmission view research. In it, the audience is conceptualized as receivers at the end of an electrical transmission that absorbs the sender's information in a uniform fashion. Knowing the history, culture, or identity of individual receivers is irrelevant in the SMRC model because the audience, en masse, has been objectified. Conversely, Bobo's (1988) examination of the ways black women create meaning through their reading of *The Color Purple* "to empower themselves and their social group" (p. 365) exemplifies the ritual view. The audience's identity is vital to the process—they give the text meaning.

Brennen (2013) connects Carey's alternative perspectives to methodology, stating that his metaphors "illustrate fundamental differences between qualitative and quantitative research" (p. 13). Based on their ontological and epistemological orientations, scholars with the transmission view are likely to objectify the audience in order to employ quantitative methods to measure the effects of media on them (p. 15). These methods include observational experimentation, surveys, structured questionnaires, and content analysis to gather data that can be numerically reduced for interpretation with statistical analyses. Their research projects will employ deductive reasoning, building a testable hypothesis before gathering data (McCombs & Shaw, 1972). Often their goal is to demonstrate causality or, more often, correlation between variables "within a value-free environment" (Brennen, 2013, p. 3).

Brennen links Carey's ritual view to researchers using qualitative methods. Their idealist ontologies and rational/constructivist/social constructionism epistemologies value the subjectivity of the individual viewer and the researcher. Methodologically, they stress flexibility (Charmaz, 2014), openness and malleability (Hesse-Biber & Leavy, 2011), and reflexivity (Emerson, Fretz, & Shaw, 2011). Unlike in quantitative laboratory experiments, qualitative researchers do not start by stating a hypothesis they hope to confirm, but rather by gathering data from texts, sites, and people.

This is often referred to as a grounded theory approach; grounded theory is a "general methodology," rooted in the Symbolic Interactionalism (Blumler, 1972) assumption that "interpretation and action [is] a reciprocal process" (Charmaz, 2014, p. 262). It was formalized by Barney Glaser and Anselm Strauss in the 1960s "for developing theory that is grounded in data systematically gathered and analyzed" (Strauss & Corbin, 1994, p. 273). Kathy Charmaz (2014) describes its methods as consisting of "systematic, yet flexible guidelines for collection and analyzing qualitative data to construct theories from the data themselves." This is an inductive/abductive process, of building explanations for phenomena from the ground up, using "iterative strategies of going back and forth between data and analysis" (p. 1). As a process, the researcher first gathers data through qualitative methods, such as interviewing and ethnography. Those data allow the researcher to develop theories out of them, while they continue to gather data and adapt and refine the developing theories to reflect them. Barney Glaser's (1996) characterization of grounded theory as "a sociology of gerunds" speaks to the dynamic nature of the process. This characterization opens the researcher to the motion of culture. Their tools for gathering data include, but are not limited to, "ethnography or field research, interview, oral history, autoethnography, focus group interview, case study, discourse analysis, grounded theory, textual analysis, visual or audiovisual analysis, evaluation, historical comparative method, ethnodrama, and narrative inquiry" (Hesse-Biber & Leavy, 2011, p. 5). The goal of these methods of data collection and analysis is to see the world of research participants from the inside rather than studying them from above (Charmaz, 2014, p. 24). Unlike randomized audience surveys employed in larger-scale quantitative studies, qualitative methods like textual analysis and in-depth interviews allow for the collection of rich, thick descriptions of specific groups at specific times.

A scholar's choice to use qualitative research indicates a belief in the value of "social inquiry that focuses on the way people interpret and make sense of their experiences and the world in which they live" (Holloway, Wheeler, & Allen, 2002, p. 3). The philosophical assumptions of the nature of existence and knowledge indicate that the qualitative researcher believes social worlds are constructed by individuals and/or groups and that those groups have some power in those constructions (Littlejohn & Foss, 2002, p. 27). Furthermore, a researcher's focus on different ways of interpreting experiences and texts, indicates a belief in the subjectivity of authors and readers as individual and/or social constructors who perceive the world uniquely. I see myself as studying binge-watching from within, rather than from above. Therefore, it is necessary for me to reveal my own orientations and how they have played out in this project.

Ultimately, I orient myself as philosophically ambivalent and context dependent about methods. This approach allows me to be both procedurally pragmatic while simultaneously aware of the ideology behind the choices I make when proceeding through research. Methods are tools politicized through work. There are times when quantitative and qualitative methods can be useful, but the practical move of determining utility is bound by my perspectives as the researcher. Therefore, my choice of a particular method for a particular project is ideologically practical. It is bound to my unique perspectives, which are at constant play with my experiences, identity, and my interpretation of the situational phenomena and the society, politics, and economies around me. When I select the tool that I feel is appropriate for a research project I am discursively creating an identity as a researcher in a time and place, but I am bound by external forces shaping my positionality. This is a process that I fix through my articulation of method, but it is also always subjected to the constant rearticulation of myself and others.

Because of my more idealistic ontology, I tend to prefer research questions that are open to the subjectivity of interpretation and criticism, rather than empiricism. While projects that measure frequency and correlation can be illustrative of certain communication phenomena (e.g., the frequency of "binge-watch" in newspaper headlines), I believe that they can also be limiting in the understanding of emotional, sociolinguistic, and relational aspects of human interactions and culture. I find that questions of how and why can be more fully articulated through stories than with statistics. If the goal of social science research is to build theory that provides insight and understanding of experiential society and its mediation, then it feels more appropriate to construct those theories out of the thick descriptions gained through personal interpretation and conversation about the complexities of a phenomenon like binge-watching (Emerson, Fretz, & Shaw, 2011; Geertz, 1973). Attempting to reduce that experience for the predictability of narrow abstractions rarely appeals to me as a writer and scholar. Nor does it make practical sense, in this project, for analyzing how folks understand and experience TV. Language is limiting enough.

My perspective of existence in process significantly conflicts with experiments attempting to analyze it by artificially arresting the process to measure operationalized relations in a vacuum. Television is changing through the actions and articulations of individuals and groups. Therefore, in this project I chose qualitative methods and employed the dynamic approach of grounded theory. I feel it is more valuable to learn about a few people's experience in depth than many in breadth, particularly for questions that attempt to understand the structures of people's feelings within their whole way of life. Any act of writing is an abstraction, and the use of qualitative methods does not preclude the researcher from this bind. As Burke (2005) asserts, "Change is structured and structures change" (p. 2). This play on the motion of language speaks to my sense of the significant action of communication.

Return to the main story by going to "Executing This Project" on 15.

5. Semantically, the complication may be found in the term's fluidity between

Burkeian master tropes from the industrial metonym of reduction in the 20th century to the postindustrial irony of dialectic in the 20th century (Burke, 1945).

Chapter 2

1. What constitutes "the public" is complicated and subjective. Furthermore, how and to what extent influence is exerted depends on the cultures, languages, politics, and economics of the groups and individuals who encounter news stories. The purpose of this chapter is not to debate whom press coverage reaches or how much that reach affects opinions. Instead I work under the assumption that journalists contribute to public discourse about ideas, particularly ideas about technological innovation and its public adoption (Beal & Bohlen, 1956). This assumption is based on the fact that journalism, through its publication, enters the public discourse through mass channels that can reach many members of the public quickly. Journalists are privileged to have access to those channels, and their "routines of newsgathering produce 'certified news'— information that seems valid" (Sigal, 1999, p. 234) for their readers who have less access. Because of their authoritative position within the discursive circuit of information and their professional role as producers of news, journalists have the power to call attention to the significance of objects (Hall, 1980). While what makes the news *news* is that it is new (Park, 1940), there are infinite new things at any given moment. Historically, but still today, journalists have been the selectors of which *new* is news (Hall et al., 1978). Because humans are curious, and new things often need explanation, the words journalists use to articulate a phenomenon like binge-watching, influence how readers understand it. Though readers can decode a news story any number of ways, the act of selecting a particular story typically indicates an interest in gaining information, in some capacity, about that topic (Hall, 1980). As Patterson and Seib (2005) point out, "information is as much a consequence of inquiry

as a cause of it.... It is the media's job to put it there. There is no other source that can routinely provide it" (pp. 190–191).

Return to "What Journalists Can Tell Us About Binge-Watching" on 22.

2. To map the journalistic history and definitions of binge-watching I began with a cross-database search of all newspaper articles at Temple University Library (including results beyond Temple's collection) from January 1, 1930, to December 31, 2016, containing the following terms: "binge watch" OR "binge watching" OR "binge view" OR "binge viewing" OR "TV binge" OR "binge TV" OR "television binge" OR "binge television" OR "binge viewer" OR "binge watcher" OR "binging" NEAR "TV" OR "binging" NEAR "TV" OR "binging" NEAR "television" OR "binging" NEAR "television." This search yielded 10,290 results. (Alas, databases update and shift, so this and other numbers may vary; they represent the totals found when I searched (2017–2018, 2020), and should remain approximately accurate). A secondary search of the following terms with matching dates and exclusions: "TV marathon" OR "marathon TV" OR "marathon television" OR "TV marathoning" OR "television marathon" OR "marathon television" OR "television marathoning" yielded 1,802 results.

For accuracy I checked these findings against two archival news databases, NexisUni and ProQuest, which roughly corroborated those numbers. Finding and keeping track of overlaps, particularly for older entries, was time-consuming and frustrating. I used Excel sheets and RefWorks citation tools to store the various categories and lists. While Temple Library search technically uses ProQuest in its cross-database queries I found early articles on ProQuest that were absent in the Temple search. At the same time ProQuest lacked early archives of some magazines like *Variety*. While Temple Library turned up issues with mentions of my keywords, in certain cases (i.e., *Variety*), the library had no online copies. In such cases I scoured the internet to acquire the documents,

backdooring through paywalls when necessary.

Return to "Methodology aka How the Sausage Gets Made" on 25.

Chapter 3

1. Even being forced to wait a week to find dramatic resolution has been largely vanquished, though some streaming services—HBO Max, Apple TV+—exploit the wait to prolong fan engagement.

2. Shaw and McCombs (1977) argue that news coverage patterns influence the salience of issues on the public agenda and at the same time public demand for understanding issues influences news coverage patterns.

3. To investigate journalists' descriptions, accounts, and sourcing during that period I further filtered this set of 9,989 articles for those where the behavior appeared to be the primary focus by limiting the search to articles that had these keywords in the title. This shrank the group down to 664. I conducted a textual analysis of these articles, which yielded three frames of binge-watching articulation—ephemeral (articulations through evocation of mood and attitude, first-person accounts), clinical (articulations with declarative statements, traditional news-reporting conventions), and review (critiques of content) (Burke, 1966, p. 44).

From them I coded four definitional aspects (parameters, content, rituals, and consequences/significance). Noting patterns in sources and official statistics cited by journalists, I also performed a series of comparative content analyses on the 664 articles and 10,000-plus articles (from my master dataset) using the keywords through ProQuest. This helped me understand the flow of news coverage and determine the trends and frequencies (periods of heavier or lighter publication of articles) with which different aspects of the stories and sources were mentioned from 2012 to 2016. Building on Pierce-Grove's (2017) analysis of press definitions, I examined the descriptions and accounts of the journalists as well as their sources used to shape definitions and implications of binge-watching, particularly "official sources"—insider/expert quotes and research (polls/surveys/studies). Doing so provided context for understanding the "constellation of narratives" (Shiller, 2019, p. 86) that drove binge-watching contagion and the cultural and economic value for the variety of stakeholders. Collectively those criteria and sub-categories helped organize a vast quantity of journalism into a story about what binge-watching is, and how and why it came to be understood as the disruptive phenomenon that reshaped our understanding of television.

Return to "Initial Frames and Categories" by flipping to 70.

4. Here's a breakdown of the definitional analysis categories:

Language

If you think of these defining news stories on binge-watching as a meal, the language is the food served. Philosopher Kenneth Burke (1966) describes two approaches to understanding language, which were essential to my analysis. First is the "scientistic" approach, which he describes classifying what something is by what it is not. The approach "begins with questions of naming, or definition" (p. 44). What's the recipe—ingredients and preparation? He characterizes the "dramatistic" approach as "derivative; and its essential function may be treated as attitudinal or hortatory: attitudinal as with expressions of complaint, fear, gratitude, and such; hortatory as with commands or requests" (p. 44). How does the meal smell and taste? The scientistic approach allows for a definition of binge-watching based on an examination of reported parameters—length of viewing, content, demographics/penetration. Essentially, follow this recipe and you'll get binge-watching. The dramatistic approach explains how we should understand binge-watching based on ephemeral description, voice, and the frequency and pitch of tones used to express attitude in those

articles—what does it look like to binge-watch and how does it feel. The dramatistic approach can also account for the irony in coding the tone: "Even if any given terminology is a reflection of reality, by its very nature as a terminology it must be a selection of reality; and to this extent it must function also as a deflection of reality" (p. 45).

Framing

If the language of journalism, its words and tone, is the food in a meal, journalistic framing is the meal's presentation. Patterson and Seib (2005) argue that "the power of the press to a large degree issues from its ability to frame events. Framing is the process by which journalists give interpretation or definition to an event or development in order to provide an explanation or judgment about it" (p. 193). Gamson and Modigliani (1987) note that the language of news is presented in packages that are recognizable to the public. New topics rely on "culturally available idea elements and symbols" (p. 376) to explain them. The language and symbols come together as packages that are recognizable. At the heart of the package is a frame—"a story line that provides meaning to an unfolding strip of events" (p. 376). Without imposing this meaning, a "news story would be a buzzing jumble of facts" (Patterson & Seib, 2005, p. 193)—a steaming bowlful of jambalaya served sans bowl on your laptop. The frame may be hidden, but it is indicated by "signature elements" (Gamson & Modigliani, 1987, p. 376). Frames are akin to thematic tropes and comparisons to history that journalists use to provide context to readers for difficult to understand news stories (Berkowitz, 2010). "By measuring the relative frequency of signature elements over time," Gamson and Modigliani (1987) suggest that "we can trace the ebb and flow of different packages" (p. 376). This can be used definitionally to interrogate which rituals and content types are most normative of journalists' articulations of binge-watching.

Sourcing

If the language is the food and the framing is the presentation, the sourcing is the ingredients and where they come from—organic farm or factory biproduct. Sociologist Herbert Gans (1999) describes "news as information which is transmitted from sources to audiences, with journalists—who are both employees of bureaucratic commercial organizations and members of a profession—summarizing, refining, and altering what becomes available to them through sources" (p. 237). Journalists' professional roles and sourcing practices, therefore, need to be considered in the analysis of binge-watching's ascendance from irrelevance to ubiquity. Since journalists do not create definitions out of thin air, my analysis also examined whom they relied on as sources for the definitional parameters and sociocultural consequences of binge-watching, and when and how frequently those sources are cited across articles in relation to other sources. This is critical, because journalists have a great deal of influence to shape public understanding, and as a result of that privileged position as information vectors, they must be skeptical of information and sources of information that they include. Examining the sources in these articles sheds light on who influenced the parameters and values of binge-watching's definition.

Return to "Initial Frames and Categories" by flipping back to 70.

5. Although 222 of the 5,728 newspaper articles from 2015 to 2016 reference "lonely" OR "loneliness" OR "isolation," less than half (95) mention the UT Austin survey by name. Much like with the industry-sponsored research, journalists tended to drop sources all together or link to other newspapers where the data had appeared, as the results became accepted.

Chapter 4

1. The irony captures television's liminal identity in 2012 (Hong & Kierkegaard, 2013, p. 35), caught between its similarity and difference within our collective understanding of it (Derrida, 1978). In 2012, TV was becoming something unexpectedly more than we knew it to be (Choi, 2011). This was a "hauntological" moment for the medium (Derrida, 1994, p. 241): a temporal disjunction of identity found in the mnemonic dissonance of viewers who were forced to question whether what they remembered TV to be was what TV was now. At the same time though, the humorous construct centered on the couch potato trope and was still medium dependent. The joke would fail if they skipped the party to read books, even if they were reading on Kindles. Our collective understand of the "idiot box" as both mind-numbing and potentially addictive allows for the irony to function in its exaggeration of our social memory from that time when TV rotted brains and the unexpected reality that TV was potentially good enough to choose over a friend's birthday party or a good night's sleep. The trope of the couch potato was exploited in this script but it is also being reimaged as new 21st-century trope: the binge-viewer. As the joke would fail if Claire and Doug were reading books, so too would it fail if television were actually so addictive that it caused viewers to lose their health and homes, and yet it wasn't unimaginable. The irony exists in a narrow and liminal space of being and not being between similarity and difference of expectation (Derrida, 1978)—what Soren Kierkegaard called "the quintessential space of irony (Adams, 2009, p. 393). It functions by using the collective belief as a foil, while acknowledging that the technology and texts of television now allow for binge-watching. Portlandia's binge-viewers embodied an attempt to rationalize the changing nature of television through its contrast against the past television.

Thus by explanation irony dies.

Please return to "One Moore Episode" on 104.

2. In Chapter 3 I explored how journalistic articulations of binge-watching

are reshaping our understanding of television. The news media is but one stakeholder in the discourse on binge-watching. Generally speaking, their financial motives are to sell news-papers and pageviews rather than to rebrand TV and viewers. Media com-panies, content producers, and inter-net providers on the other hand, have a direct and clear motive for promot-ing binge-watching. As one star points out in *Entertainment Weekly's* (2014) mock PSA, "The more you binge-watch, the more we binge-make." The medi-ation of industrial stakeholders is, therefore, a rich and valid area for investigation of the social construction of binge-watching and binge-viewer identity, and for memory studies more broadly. The "multi-shaping contin-gency view of the technology-culture relationship" (Lievrouw, p. 41) is well suited to memory studies of advertis-ing, which although driven by profit motive, is "a cultural site that high-lights the abstract-concrete paradox, which is embedded within the process of collective recollecting" (Meyers, p. 735).

The analysis in this chapter is ori-ented by cultural and narrative dis-course theory (Genette, 1980; Williams, 1973) and the social memory position that the media facilitates the social con-struction of technology through media (Zelizer, 1995). Social memories that shape contemporary understandings are co-produced (Jasanoff, 2004) by individ-uals and groups who diffuse understand-ings that are adopted through networks of interaction (Latour, 2005). The adver-tising discourse of media corporations serves to educate the public on the use and understanding of new technologies and media practices while simultane-ously branding them for profit (March-and, 1985).

A core contention of collective mem-ory theory is that social ideas of the past can be exploited by contempo-rary stakeholders for economic gain. If the press serves as the public's senses (Park, 1940), collective memory serves as a sense-making function for those who are seeking "resources for mak-ing sense of the past" (Zelizer, 1995,

p. 214). Socially constructed memo-ries provide a "body of beliefs and ideas about the past" (Bodnar, p. 15) that can locate and unify groups around a shared past. The establishment of such an identity can be exploited to shape the present in contrast to past under-standings of objects such as technol-ogy and experiences such as watching TV. Marvin (1997) argues that "media are not fixed natural objects. They have no natural edges. They are constructed complexes of habits, beliefs, and proce-dures embedded in elaborate cultural codes of communication. The history of media is never more or less than the history of their uses" (p. 8). But how is that history recreated and negotiated through the media?

Journalism may be the first draft of history, but advertising has long exploited nostalgia to appeal to view-ers (Grainge, 2000): "Personal and his-torical nostalgia advertisements are linked to the consumer effects of, respec-tively, empathy and idealization of the self" (Stern, 1992, p. 11). In advertis-ing, though, "the past that is vivified is one that never existed, for it is so ideal-ized that any negative traces are screened out" (p. 11). At the same time, Braun et al. (2002) demonstrated that evocations of the past "could change what consumers remember about their childhood memo-ries" through nostalgia (p. 2).

Grainge (2000) argues that nostal-gia is more complex than commodifi-cation, but "a new kind of engagement with the past ... based fundamentally on its cultural mediation and textual reconfiguration of the present" (p. 33). As Lizardi (2015) points out, nostalgia "can function in a comparative sense, revealing the odd difference between then and now" (p. 15). Following this logic, personal habits like TV watching may be capable of being reconstructed as "branded space" (Banet-Weiser, p. 14) in the personal and shared nos-talgia of the binge-viewer, whose own identity is a co-mediated construction through advertising. My examination of binge-watching commercial rhetoric addresses the uses of social memory and nostalgia in contemporary construc-tions of media user identity.

For information on methods return to "Informational Television" on 106.

To learn about my methodology for this analysis of binge-viewer commercials, continue to the next note.

3. Here's an exhaustive breakdown of my methodological choices, including sampling and coding, for my analysis of binge-viewer depictions in commercials.

Methodology

The selection process of video advertising texts was considerably less straightforward than what I used in chapters 2 and 3 to gather journalism texts. Few libraries organize new TV commercials as systematically, which privileges the word over the moving image. While a number of ad archives do exist, none hold a comprehensive, contemporary catalog of commercials produced from 2012 to 2016, when binge-watching surged into the American zeitgeist. Therefore, I was forced to use public search engines and my intuition as a student of television, to select my texts. While I tried to be thorough and systematic, I acknowledge that this selection process may have omitted binge-watching commercials that, for whatever reason, I simply couldn't access or was unaware of. Furthermore, my subjectivity about what counts as a commercial worth examining is a reflection of my own position and values in relation to this research, and my contention that collective memory and nostalgia are a part of the binge-branding process. Since I intended to examine mediated constructions of binge-viewers, I gave weight to commercials that were instructional and didactic, particularly those featuring binge-viewers as the protagonists or central to the narrative.

I began with Google Video searches for each of the following keywords or strings: "binge-watch" OR "binge-view" OR "binge-view" OR "binge-watch" OR "binge-viewing" OR "binge-watching" OR "binge-viewing" OR "binge-watching" or "binge-viewer" OR "binge- viewer" OR "binge-watcher" OR "binge-watcher" OR "binge" AND "TV"

OR "streaming" OR "Netflix" OR "Hulu" OR "Amazon" OR "Roku" OR "television." Of the "about 2,310,000 results (0.47 seconds)" (Google), I filtered these first by whether they were commercials using the keyword "ad" OR "commercial" to reduce the search to "about 328,000 results (0.40 seconds)." From there I filtered by producers and content. Since I was interested in ads from media companies, I excised any ads that were merely using binge-watching to sell products. While it is fascinating that the term binge has now seeped into so many more activities, I determined that non-media company advertising was outside the scope of this project. I culled this list down to 25 technology company ads about binge-viewers, based on the number of views and the overlap in other searches I have done, through the online databases iSpot.tv, splendAd.com, InternetArchive, Coloribus, and Creativity (from *Ad Age*), as well as with commercials about binge-watching that I have personally encountered during my own copious TV and media consumption.

I then conducted a close reading of these 25 online video ads (they also aired on television or were streamed in between Netflix episodes). These promotional videos ranged from 30 to 206 seconds. I chose them because they were among the most viewed and shared industry commercials based on a Google Video search of "binge -watching." Beyond their popularity, the videos also represent a selection of the major streaming video, cable, internet, and television content providers (Hulu, Netflix, Comcast, Cox Cable, Disney, and T-Mobile). I made this choice because the size and reach of these companies gave them greater influence in the construction process, and because they stood to gain directly by cultivating binge-viewers to subscribe and use their services. Additionally, they shared the strategy of positioning binge-watching as distinct from old TV to sell their content, technology, and/or media services through the collective memory of PSAs.

Adapting Stern's (1992) critical methodology, I employed textual and narrative analysis "to locate manifestations of nostalgia in advertising text" (p. 12). Since nostalgia in advertising can be a construction of multiple cues (Whalen, 1983), I noted structural, linguistic, musical, cinematic, verbal, and thematic indicators during the analysis process (Chou & Lien, 2010). I repeatedly viewed the videos, taking notes, coding, and memoing until I reached a point of redundancy. I then organized the codes and categorized the data into three overlapping types: "Deviant Addict"; "Celebrity Public Service Announcements"; and "Addiction and Salvation." I then used these categories and these codes to analyze how the commercials exploit social memory of 20th-century TV to construct the binge-viewer. These were contrasted against the Dr. Jekyll examples of celebrity endorsements of binge-watching.

Return to "Informational Television" on 106.

4. PSAs have been studied by political and health communication scholars, as well as social psychologists interested in the effects of mass media messaging on audiences. Most commonly, PSAs are used to promote health campaigns (Fuhrel-Forbis, Nadorff & Snyder, 2009). Rice and Atkin (2009) define public communication campaigns thus:

(1) purposive attempts (2) to inform, persuade, or motivate behavior changes (3) in a relatively well-defined and large audience (4) generally for noncommercial benefits to the individuals and/or society at large (5) typically within a given time period (6) by means of organized communication activities involving mass media, and (7) often complimented by interpersonal support [p. 436].

Return to "Filmstrips to PSAs: A Dose of Dull History" on 106.

5. Twenty-first-century media scholars have found preachy, foreboding ads to be ineffective. Sly, Heald, and Ray (2001) argue that fear appeals in persuasion campaigns are less likely to motivate change than other tactics. This is particularly the case when the credibility and intent of the messenger are in question. Obvious overgeneralizations undermine credibility. Iles, Seate, & Waks (2016) argue that negative stereotyping of groups can also decrease audience sympathy for those groups along with messenger credibility. PSAs tend to be more effective when they account for diversity and individuality. As television shifted from mass to niche during the 2000s, public messaging campaigns have been forced to become self-aware, while acknowledging that the audience is comprised of diffuse and skeptical viewers: "The straightforward PSA—in which an earnest boldfaced name stares into the camera and urges action—gets little play in an environment cluttered with acrobatic messaging" (Johnson, 2010, p. 3).

Paul Rutherford (2000) argues that as the public sphere has transformed into a semiotic marketplace, public service campaigns are shifting into complicated art that plays with the economics of morality through consumption. Some media scholars are suggesting that satire can be effective in PSAs: Rather than preach, satirical campaigns can entertain first, and, by gathering an audience and establishing rapport, they can then impart wisdom (Johnson, 2010, p. 3). Acknowledgment of the PSAs' paternalistic past, which is easily found through video-sharing sites and blogs such as psa80s.com, has become essential for establishing the credibility of public messaging campaigns.

Return to Nostalgia 2.0 on 113.

6. The idealized past of nostalgia, then, has been perverted to promote present technology and culture. This problematizes conventional understandings of nostalgia in advertising, which Stern (1992) argued create a "desire to retreat from contemporary life by returning to a time in the distant past viewed as superior to the present" (p. 13). Rather than creating a yearning for the 20th century, these commercials serve

to distinguish contemporary streaming video behavior from the close-minded memory of broadcast television. The nostalgia is instead a shared reference point from which we can locate our contemporary progress.

This use of memory perverts nostalgia. It is a subversive reclamation of the present Golden Age against the pyrite past. It also complicates Marvin's (1997) depictions of the fears and fantasies that often accompany new technology. In the case of these binge-watching promos, the fears of the past are lampooned in present technology to promote the fantasies of consumption, agency, and the loss of control. The fears are employed not to stabilize present understandings, but to renegotiate them as more complicated. Despite that and because of it, neoliberal consumerism does remain the stabilizing force behind these inscriptions. However critically this aspect can be challenged as part of the ideological apparatus of late capitalism, there is an ambivalence and agency enmeshed through the co-construction of television's contemporary social identity. Are these media companies exploiting fears of broadcast TV paternalism to exert authority over contemporary TV consumption? Are they assuming that the constructed binge-viewer has so much information that we are "reduced to passivity and egoism" and that "the truth would be drowned in a sea of irrelevance" (Postman, 1985, p. xix)? Perhaps, but it's complicated. As with binge-watching, the process can appear hegemonic and empowering, industrially structured and user-generated, addicting and liberating. The two-pronged Jekyll and Hyde campaign, satirically positioned binge-viewers as agentic, while "idealizing" traditional broadcast TV and its couch potatoes as "completely lacking in freedom" (p. 220) both actively and linguistically. While potentially accurate, this binge-viewer construction was the campaign of powerful (new) media companies who stood to profit from the "freedom" and "evolution" of binge-viewers. We should not forget that it was an exploitation of the past by contemporary actors for economic gain.

To learn how viewers defined and practiced binge-watching from 2014 to 2018, return to Chapter 5 on 137.

Chapter 5

1.

Rationale for Interviews

Binge-watching is a hybrid of technology and culture that challenges unidirectional communication models of mass communication. It also complicates receiver-broadcaster power dynamics. To reflect this methodologically, I chose qualitative interviews with open-ended questions that attempt to put the viewer, as interviewee, on a more equal footing with the researcher (Lotz, 2000). In-depth conversations also allow for substantive and personal responses to "how" and "why" questions (Weiss, 1994) that provide more robust descriptions of media rituals than surveys or user data analysis. My perspective acknowledges that the viewer's position and control (Ang, 1991) are primary to the media behavior and, therefore, active in the content creation. My approach favors reflexive subjectivity over objectivity (Charmaz, 2014). I acknowledge that my position as researcher is in discourse with the interviewees and this project holistically (Torfing, 1999). My goal was for that openness to be reflected by the interviewees so that the conversations became dialogues of more equal positioning.

Participants and Procedures

During 2016 and 2017, I conducted 23 semi-structured interviews each lasting between 35 and 78 minutes. The questions I used grew from my earlier interviews and informal discussions (Steiner, 2017; Steiner & Xu 2020), as well as focus groups, viewer diaries and methodological course work during my graduate studies. Twelve women and 11 men participated. The interviewees were of diverse educational backgrounds and levels ranging from high school graduates to holders of professional degrees. They all lived in or around Philadelphia, though only five were area natives, and four were born outside of the United States. They were between 19 and 69 years old; nine identified as white, four as black, three as Asian, and one as Latino. Six did not indicate any racial identity in their self-descriptions. All of the interviews were conducted in person. During the later stages of information gathering (2017–2018), I also engaged in 14 informal conversations about TV-watching with people from interviewees' and my own social networks, which aided the iterative process of coding and analysis. These informal conversations ranging from 20 to 50 minutes were used to clarify themes.

I used open-ended questions and a semi-structured format that allowed the conversations and interviews to flow organically (Weiss, 1994). Semi-structured interviews were used because they provide researchers with the flexibility to ask both pre-established and improvised questions. Although most of the interviewees addressed (directly or indirectly) all 10 questions on the protocol, the order of the questions was adjusted according to the flow of the conversations (Brennen, 2013). Again, my goal was to loosen the interview structure in order to gather rich, personal insights from my interviewees.

Data Analysis

I employed qualitative and inductive methods (Emerson, Fretz, & Shaw, 1995) to memo and code the content (Charmaz, 2014). I followed Hesse-Biber and Leavy's (2010) four-step data analysis strategy: data preparation, data exploration, data reduction, and interpretation. As the interview process evolved, some repetitive keywords and themes arose, and I began to look for them in other interviews and conversations. I reviewed and coded the data descriptively while continuing to review earlier interviews and current literature on binge-watching, television, and viewers. Noticing patterns around immersion, genre/attentiveness, and motive, I turned, after a discussion with Lisa Perks, to the literature on presence and ludic media as theoretical perspectives for my data analysis. My incorporation of those lenses focused

the analysis on viewer descriptions of immersiveness, content selection, and perceived interruptions to TV flow. From there, I developed theoretical connections between binge-watching motives and attentiveness in relation to the rituals of time management and content control. By 2018 I had reached a point of saturation in the analysis that allowed me to address my research objectives for this area of the project: to understand how viewers defined and practiced binge-watching and how their rituals, motives and feelings shape our understanding of television in contrast to the mediated constructions of the earlier chapters. I stayed in touch with interviewees and periodically followed up with them between 2018 and 2021. Additionally, I have worked on several projects since 2018 which influenced my writing and updated this chapter during the COVID-19 pandemic.

To return to "Binge-Watching Research Arc," turn to 138.

2. Even in 2018, the subset of literature that focused primarily on viewers, rather than texts, paratexts, and industry (Jenner, 2021), was dominated by quantitative methods to measure the effects of binge-watching (Riddle et al., 2017; Shim & Kim, 2018; Walton-Pattison, Dombrowski, & Presseau, 2018.). As in television studies of the 20th century, large-scale surveys were administered, and audience responses were controlled and aggregated, thereby treating individual viewers as a homogenized mass of passive TV receivers rather than unique, active agents of cultural exchange. Because these articles built on the literature of 20th-century TV studies, the authors often approached binge-watching with an implicit bias that TV-watching may be harmful and addictive, and that binging may exacerbate those risks (Orosz et al., 2016).

The siloing of academic research creates echo chambers of ignorance. Scholars in behavioral health interrogate viewer experiences with little attention paid to their media and communication colleagues and vice versa. For example,

Walton-Pattison, Dombrowski, and Presseau (2016) claimed that their study "was the first to estimate binge watching frequency, [and] to propose a formal definition" (p. 6). Despite calling it media marathoning, Perks offered a definition in 2014, and Pittman and Sheehan did so in 2015. As I described in Chapter 2, the mainstream media has offered numerous definitions and estimates of frequency since 2012. Social health researchers Flayelle, Maurage, and Billieux (2017) claimed that their focus-group project was "a first step toward a genuine understanding of binge-watching behaviors through a qualitative analysis of the phenomenological characteristics of TV series watching" (p. 457). This ignores the developing body of media and communication literature that has since 2014 (Jenner) sought to assess binge-watching phenomenologically through qualitative methods (Steiner, 2017).

Petersen's (2016) interview-based analysis framed college students' binge-watching as habitual and pathological. While he uses in-depth interviews, he extrapolates the potential effects of binging on his interviewees' social and academic lives (Petersen et al., 2016). Such a framing, I believe, indicates a latent orientation toward 20th-century narratives of TV-watching that colors a study intended to "examine exactly how and why college students binge-watch" (p. 78). That orientation manifests in findings such as this: "while students easily recognize the benefits they get from binge-watching, they fail to see the ways their habit might hurt them" (p. 77). While Flayelle, Maurage, and Billieux (2017) recognize that much of the literature applies the "classic criteria used for other addictive disorders without exploring the uniqueness of binge-watching," they go on to state that their goal for using qualitative methods was to "generate the first steps toward an adequate theoretical rationale for these emerging problematic behaviors" (p. 457). This is a problematic assumption. Pittman and Sheehan (2015) provide a useful framework for analyzing emerging uses and gratifications of binge-viewers, but their quantitative surveys lack the personal descriptions that might address "the

relationship between binging, pleasure, and guilt."

Despite changes to viewer experience, quantitative media scholars continued through 2018 to study audiences and flows with 20th-century instruments designed for the broadcast television ecosystem, even when analyzing viewer uses of streaming technology. Schweidel and Moe (2016), for instance, first model binge-watching "viewing behavior" in a manner "consistent with prior research on live viewing" (p. 3). Their work on Hulu viewers' responses to advertising, shows that commercials may shorten binges and that genre plays a role in viewer responsiveness to advertising as a function of continued viewing and ad click-through (pp. 11–12). They also find that "users are more responsive to advertising earlier in their viewing sessions" (p.16). Because their study examines user data patterns only, it elides individual motives and feelings. Furthermore, using 2009 Hulu (which is largely subscription-based today) user data from computer viewers only, and basing "responsiveness" on clicks, confines these findings to a subset of viewers who may react differently to different kinds of intrusions on different kinds of platforms.

See why with "And Now a Word from Our Sponsors" on 140.

Logan (2013) found that viewers perceived online TV (OTV) advertising as more intrusive than traditional TV (p. 271). Her findings were based on survey results comparing intrusiveness and favorability for viewers who were watching TV websites and could not skip the commercials. She usefully points out that since "viewers of OTV are more hostile to the presence of advertising, advertisers should consider options that provide viewers with greater control over the advertising such as the choice of product categories that will be advertised within a program" (p. 272). Hulu attempted this before moving to a subscription model in 2016. YouTube is also moving to subscription models, with limited success. While Logan's quantitative methodology allowed for a large sample size, her surveys, by their nature, lack the descriptions of an individual viewer's feelings and experiences with interruptions, and their relation to viewer motivations and to genre selection. Logan also acknowledged that viewing duration and attentiveness were not examined (p. 272), and she suggested they should be in future research.

If you haven't already, consider returning to "Ad Reception and Interaction," on 159.

3. See also Pittman and Steiner (2019, 2021).

4. During these moments people feel, to varying degrees and across various dimensions, that what they are experiencing is "real" rather than a perception mediated by some kind of technology. This feeling is immersive (Biocca & Delaney, 1995), and the degree of intensity can vary based on a number of factors that affect the immersion. Reduction of media fidelity, outside distractions, as well as the insertion of unrelated or unrealistic content can degrade the intensity of presence. Feelings of presence are "maximized when a technology user's perceptions fail to accurately acknowledge any role of the technology in the experience" (ISPR, 2000, p. 5). Although this maximum presence seems more likely (if ever) to occur in a fully immersive virtual environment, when all senses are being engaged, it has been demonstrated that feelings of presence occur through less fully immersive media such as television (Bracken, et al., 2010; Lombard, et al., 2000).

Lombard and Ditton (1997) identified six measurable dimensions of presence, which, while distinctly defined, may be functionally symbiotic during an experience of presence. The dimensions closest to binge-watching's EVE and SOC motives include transportation, in the sense of viewers "being there"; social/perceptual realism in the sense that the events being viewed "could [or once did] exist in the physical world" (ISPR, 2000, p. 7C); and engagement in the sense of psychological immersion (p. 7D). The similarity of these dimensions to the descriptions of the EVE motive, indicates that presence may help explain why some people are motivated to binge-watch higher attentiveness shows such as complex dramas with winding plots that evolve slowly over multiple episodes.

Return to "Losing Yourself in a Story" on 142.

Chapter 6

1. Television's prewar years of experimentation and optimism could be imagined as an "agrarian period." However, in the 19th century, the vast majority of Americans lived in rural, farming communities. Before 1945 only a tiny fraction of Americans owned a television.

2.

Justifying Reflexivity

While I have provided a variety of evidence for my contention that binge-watching killed the idiot box, I have largely omitted myself from this story. That choice was based on the traditions and forms of this kind of academic endeavor. As a matter of formal integrity, social science literature has traditionally eschewed discussions of its authors. The subjectivity of a researcher, as with their subjects, is supposed to be controlled for by detached, objective methods. Since experimental replicability is valued, individual experience is seen as a hindrance to a project's validity and is best omitted. But doing so, also creates a wall that keeps readers from the stories behind the story. Not only can this make the reading experience rather dry, but it also omits details that may enhance the understanding of the project. Cultural and critical studies scholars argue that reflexivity is a crucial part of qualitative methodologies. This speaks to the lingering transmission/ritual dialectic in media and communication studies—a hybrid field with roots both in the sciences and the humanities (see Chapter 1). But exploratory research about "new" media topics can be an opportunity to apply newer methods.

In *The Makeover*, Sender (2012) considers the rise of makeover reality television from the viewers' and producers' perspectives through in-depth interviews in conjunction with textual analyses of the shows. She explores how audience research enriches our understanding of reflexivity, and how thinking through reflexivity challenges audience research. Like Ang (1991), Sender challenges those who position reality TV as lowbrow and those who assume its audience is simply being manipulated by profit-driven sensationalism that normalizes and evangelizes consumption. Her in-depth interviews are not only used to gather data about the viewers, but to reflect back on herself as a researcher within the meaning-making process. This is a great advantage of blending textual analysis with in-depth interviewing. It can illuminate and reflect, through language, the process of culture as meaning-making without flattening or diminishing the voices of those who are making meaning within it. Simultaneously it can serve to refine the culture of media studies. As Heath and Street (2008) advise, "think of culture as a verb rather than as a noun—a fixed thing" (p. 7). The power is in the movement. As Uotinen (2010) explains, "the concepts and tools of cultural studies shift the emphasis of technology studies from deterministic cause-and-effect relations and the research of technologies themselves towards researching people's experiences, understandings and agency" (p. 162). I believe it is impossible for a researcher to ignore the manifold political, social, economic, and professional motives at play in any decision to use qualitative methods, and so I must address them directly. Transparent reflexivity that reveals the researcher's positions and place within any work not only serves to acknowledge their role in affecting participants and interpreting texts, but also enhances the verisimilitude of the project itself (Freeman, 2015, p. 919). Reflexivity is not a panacea for the ethical challenges of social scientists. However, by weaving their "reflexive experience into the research process," researchers are empowered "to engage in a dialogue with their own ethical standpoint and ultimately to confront their own personal biases as researchers" (Hesse-Biber & Leavy, 2011, p. 84). Doing so helps protect the project's integrity.

As I have argued, binge-watching is a hybrid of technology and culture that has worked to change television's identity from an industry of transmission to an experience of identity. I believe this should be reflected in the study of TV. While quantitative methods remain the norm of binge-watching scholarship, I hope that this project can encourage other scholars to challenge assumptions that position researchers as neutral interpreters of phenomena. Interpretation requires perspective, and no two are identical. To understand my interpretations, I need to be introspective and ask who I am, and why I interpreted the way I did. May and Perry (2017) argue that contemporary social scientists must work to transform their identities as "legislators of knowledge." Doing so, they argue, "requires recasting the role of social scientists to focus on active intermediation as a set of reflexive practices concerning the boundaries of research and to produce a more mature and open social science" (p. 174). If television has evolved, perhaps the methods of those studying it should evolve too.

"Reflexive Narrative: My Backstory" on 181.

3. Throughout this project, I have struggled to find a way to bring the reader into the story in a fashion that reflects the immersion of attentive binge-watching. At the same time, showing how a muffin is made, may only be appealing if the performance contributes to other bakers' methods. I began thinking about how issues of believability, in terms of the Aristotelian "ethos," contribute to the rhetorical move of incorporating reflexive narrative in a qualitative, social science project on binge-watching. How does my identity as a binge-viewer empower and dis-empower my research methods and my selection and analyses of journalism, advertising, and interviews? How do I conceive of my own creditability of being a native user of the technology, and how would a non-native interpret the data differently? Knowledge of the TV content, the shared emotional responses, and the vernacular of binge-watching discourse, played into my selection of news

articles, commercials, and interviewing style. This knowledge also helped me ask relevant questions and find more relevant patterns. But the knowledge played both ways. Being a binge-viewer may have caused me to overlook, under-emphasize, or take for granted details that an outsider might notice.

I believe this can be remedied through reflexivity to give a richer sense of what I, as a researcher and a binge-viewer, am experiencing in this project. Articulating my identity at this moment, may allow readers to discover aspects of this research that I had not. In this way it reflects the shifting identity of TV-viewers as producers in contemporary media. Additionally, it can illuminate why I am choosing to study binge-watching, a nascent media behavior that enjoys lower cultural status within the academy. Where do I position myself in terms of its cultural value and what does that say about me as a researcher? Why do I think binge-watching is worth studying at all? What is the real story of my interest?

To find out, return to "Reflexive Binge" on 184.

To chart a new path, return to the start of the book.

If you are done, close the book and find something good to binge-watch.

References

Adalian, J. (2013, April 12). House of Cards' showrunner answers vulture readers' questions. *Vulture.* https://www.vulture.com/2013/04/your-house-of-cards-questions-have-been-answered.html.

Adalian, J. (2020, September 30). The first 2020 presidential debate scored massive ratings. *Vulture.* https://www.vulture.com/2020/09/tv-ratings-for-the-first-2020-presidential-debate-score-big.html.

Adorno, T. (2001). How to look at television. In J.M. Bernstein (Ed.), *Adorno: The Culture Industry* (pp. 158–178). New York: Routledge.

Agostino, D. (1980). New technologies: Problem or solution? *Journal of Communication, 30*(3), 198–206.

Allan, P. (2015, December 1). How to break your Netflix binge-watching habit. *Life Hacker.* https://lifehacker.com/how-to-break-your-netflix-binge-watching-habit-1745394858.

Althusser, L. (1989). Ideology and ideological state apparatuses. In D. Latimer (Ed.), *Contemporary Critical Theory* (pp. 61–102). San Diego: Harcourt Brace Jovanovich.

Amazon Fire TV. (2015). Show hole. Amazon. http://www.ispot.tv/ad/Aw_U/amazon-fire-tv-show-hole.

Ammer, C. (2013). *The American Heritage Dictionary of Idioms.* Boston: Houghton Mifflin.

Anderson, A. (2016). 'Heroes' showrunner Tim Kring on why TV should be more like Netflix. *The Hollywood Reporter.* https://www.hollywoodreporter.com/news/heroes-showrunner-tim-kring-why-tv-should-be-more-like-netflix-941027.

Anderson, D.R., & Kirkorian, H.L. (2006). Attention and television. In Jennings Bryant and Peter Vorderer (Eds.), *Psychology of Entertainment* (pp. 35–54). New York: Routledge.

Andrejevic, M. (2008). Watching television without pity: The productivity of online fans. *Television & New Media, 9*(1), 24–46.

Ang, I. (1985). *Watching Dallas.* London: Methuen.

_____. (1991). *Desperately Seeking the Audience.* New York: Routledge.

Artemas, K., Vos, T.P., & Duffy, M. (2018). Journalism hits a wall: Rhetorical construction of newspapers' editorial and advertising relationship. *Journalism Studies, 19*(7), 1004–1020. https://doi.org/10.1080/1461670X.2016.1249006.

Bandura, A., Ross, D., & Ross S. (1963). Imitation of film-mediated aggressive models. *Journal of Abnormal and Social Psychology 66:* 3–11.

Banet-Weiser, S. (2012). *Authentic™: The Politics of Ambivalence in a Brand Culture.* New York: New York University Press.

Barney, C. (2013a, February 26). Binge TV: 9 great shows to gorge on. *San Jose Mercury News.* https://www.mercurynews.com/2013/02/26/binge-tv-9-great-shows-to-gorge-on/.

_____. (2013b, February 27). Binge watching is catching on with avid TV fans. *San Jose Mercury News.* https://www.mercurynews.com/2013/02/27/binge-watching-is-catching-on-with-avid-tv-fans/.

Barrett, C. (2004, May 30). My 47hr TV

Binge. *The People* (London, England), p. 34.

Baughman, J. (2007). Same time, same station: Creating American television, 1948–1961. In *Same Time, Same Station*. Baltimore: Johns Hopkins University Press.

Bazilian, E. (2015, August 31). Orange Is the New Black star Pablo Schreiber on the perils of live-tweeting. *AdWeek.* https://www.adweek.com/convergent-tv/orange-new-black-star-pablo-schreiber-perils-live-tweeting-166607/.

Beal, G.M., & Bohlen, J.M. (1956). *The diffusion process.* Ames: Iowa Cooperative Extension Service Report 18. http://ageconsearch.umn.edu/record/17351/files/ar560111.pdf.

Bearden, M. (2008, August 30). Religion rocks. *Tampa Tribune.*

Belcher C. (2016). There is no such thing as a post-racial prison: Neoliberal multiculturalism and the white savior complex on *Orange Is the New Black. Television & New Media.* doi: 1527476416647498.

Bennett, T. (2009). Popular culture and the 'Turn to Gramsci.' In J. Storey (Ed.), *Cultural Theory and Popular Culture: A Reader* (pp. 81–87). Harlow, UK: Pearson Education.

Berger, M. (1956, January 13). About New York: YUkon 5, a dream exchange, will handle 30,000 calls for arthritis TV show. *New York Times.*

Berkowitz, D. (2010). The ironic hero of Virginia Tech: Healing trauma through mythical narrative and collective memory. *Journalism, 11*(6), 643–659.

Besco, G.S. (1952). Television and its effects. *English Journal, 41*(3), 151.

Beshaj, L. (2015). Figurative transformation of free compound words into adjectival phraseological units in the Albanian and English language to be acquired from the students. *European Journal of Language and Literature, 2*(1), 70–77.

Bianculli, D. (1984, January 18). VCR decision is victory for users. *Philadelphia Inquirer,* 6F.

_____. (2016). *The Platinum Age of Television.* New York: Doubleday.

Biderman, D. (2016, January 15). 11 minutes of action. *Wall Street Journal.* https://www.wsj.com/articles/SB10001424052748704281204575002852055561406.

Bilyk, K. (2016, March 28). 5 ways to stop binge-watching Netflix and actually get sh*t done. *Elite Daily.* https://www.elitedaily.com/life/binge-watch-netflix-get-sht-done/1341656.

Binge Becomes (2014, December 18–24). Binge watching becomes a new holiday tradition. *The Home News.* https://issuu.com/idpcreative/docs/the_home_news_december_18.

Biocca, F., & Delaney, B. (1995). Immersive virtual reality technology. In F. Biocca & M.R. Levy (Eds.), *Communication in the Age of Virtual Reality* (pp. 57–124). Hillsdale, NJ: Lawrence Erlbaum.

Blazer, J.A. (1964). Fantasy and its effects. *The Journal of General Psychology, 70*(1), 163–182.

Blumler, J.G., & Katz, E. (1974). *The Uses of Mass Communications: Current Perspectives on Gratifications Research.* Beverly Hills: Sage Publications.

Bobo, J. (1995). *Black Women as Cultural Readers.* New York: Columbia University Press.

Bodnar, J. (1992). *Remaking America: Public Memory, Commemoration, and Patriotism in the Twentieth Century.* Princeton: Princeton University Press.

Bourdaa, M., Chin, B., & Lamerichs, N. (2016). The transmedia practices of Battlestar Galactica: Studying the industry, stars, and fans. In N. Tindall & A. Hutchins (Eds.), *Public Relations and Participatory Culture* (pp. 215–225). New York: Routledge.

Boym, S. (2007). Nostalgia and its discontents. *Hedgehog Review, 9*(2), 7–18.

Bradbury, R. (1953). *The Golden Apples of the Sun.* New York: Doubleday.

Bradshaw, P. (2021, May 25). Kevin Spacey and the rise of uncancel culture. *The Guardian.* https://www.theguardian.com/film/2021/may/25/kevin-spacey-problem-uncancel-culture.

Braun, J. (2015). *This Program Is Brought to You By...: Distributing Television News Online.* New Haven: Yale University Press.

Braun, K.A., Ellis, R., & Loftus, E.F. (2002).

Make my memory: How advertising can change our memories of the past. *Psychology and Marketing, 19*(1), 1–23.

Brennen, B. (2013). *Qualitative Research Methods for Media Studies*. New York: Routledge.

Brohm, J.M. (1978). *Sports—A Prison of Measured Time: Essays*. Ink Links.

Brown, W.J. (2015). Examining four processes of audience involvement with media personae: transportation, parasocial interaction, identification, and worship. *Communication Theory, 25*(3), 259–283. https://doi.org/10.1111/comt.12053.

Bundy, B. (2003, AprIL 18). Family Guy finds a new home on DVD: Fans drawn to witty, twisted humour. *Edmonton Journal*, p. E10.

Burber, M. (1937). *I and Thou*. New York: Charles Scribner's Sons.

Burke, K. (1945). *A Grammar of Motives*. New York: Prentice-Hall. http://www.communicationcache.com/uploads/1/0/8/8/10887248/kenneth_burke_-_a_grammar_of_motives_1945.pdf.

———. (1966). *Language as Symbolic Action: Essays on Life, Literature, and Method*. Berkeley: University of California Press

Burke, P. (2005). *History and Social Theory 2nd Edition*. Ithaca: Cornell University Press.

Camp, D. (1993). NAFTA on my mind after long TV binge: SU2 edition. *Toronto Star.*

Cancer. (1951, June 11). Cancer fund nets $1,127,211. *The Sun.*

Carey, J.W. (1989). A cultural approach to communication. In *Communication as Culture: Essays on Media and Society* (pp. 11–28). New York: Routledge.

——— (2008). *Communication as Culture, Revised Edition*. New York: Routledge.

Carpenter, C.R. (1955). Psychological research using television. *American Psychologist, 10*(10), 606–610.

Cassidy, C. (1962). On the aisle: Lyric lists 'nabucco' among eleven possibilities for 1963 season. *Chicago Daily Tribune.*

Castro, D., Rigby, J.M., Cabral, D., & Nisi, V. (2021). The binge-watcher's journey: Investigating motivations, contexts, and affective states surrounding Netflix viewing. *Convergence, 27*(1), 3–20. https://doi.org/10.1177/1354856519890856.

CDC. (2006). Overweight & obesity statistics. *National Institute of Diabetes and Digestive and Kidney Diseases.* https://www.niddk.nih.gov/health-information/health-statistics/overweight-obesity.

Chang, H. (2008). *Autoethnography as Method*. Walnut Creek, CA: Left Coast Press.

Charmaz, K. (2014). *Constructing Grounded Theory* (2nd Edition). Thousand Oaks: Sage.

Chen, A.H. (2016). Group takes another crack at 'your brain on drugs' ad. CNN. http://www.cnn.com/2016/08/30/health/new-brain-on-drugs-fried-egg-psa/index.html.

Cheng, C., Wang, M., & Perfetti, C.A. (2011). Acquisition of compound words in Chinese–English bilingual children: Decomposition and cross-language activation. *Applied Psycholinguistics, 32*(3), 583–600.

Chmielewski, D.C. (2013, February 1). Binge-viewing transforms TV; services like Netflix are letting fans watch multiple episodes or even entire seasons of shows all at once. *Los Angeles Times*. https://www.latimes.com/entertainment/envelope/la-xpm-2013-feb-01-la-et-ct-binge-viewing-20130201-story.html.

Choi, M. (2012). Can't stop, won't stop: In praise of binge TV consumption. *Wired, 20*(1). https://www.wired.com/2011/12/pl_column_tvseries/.

Chou, H., & Lien, N. (2010). Advertising effects of songs' nostalgia and lyrics' relevance. *Asia Pacific Journal of Marketing and Logistics, 22*(3), 314–329.

Chow, A. (2021, October 1). How Seinfeld became one of TV's great moneymakers. *Time*. https://time.com/6103335/seinfeld-netflix-business/.

Christine, Q. (2012). Television goes online: Myths and realities in the contemporary context. *Global Media Journal, 12*(20), 1.

Coffin, T.E. (1955). Television's impact on society. *American Psychologist, 10*(10), 630–641.

Colbert. (2015). Hilary Clinton binge-watches The Good Wife. *The Late Show with Stephen Colbert.* https://www.youtube.com/watch?v=_by4NUtNARY.

Coleman, M., & Augustine, C.Y. (2014). Blogging as religious feminist activism: Ministry to, through, with, and from. In G. Messina-Dysert, & R.R. Ruether (Eds.), *Feminism and Religion in the 21st Century: Technology, Dialogue, and Expanding Borders.* New York: Routledge.

Collier, R. (2011, December 4). Farewell, my friend sleep. *Ottawa Citizen*, p. A11.

Collins, K. (2012). Murrow and Friendly's *Small World*: Television conversation at the crossroads. *Journal of Popular Film and Television, 40*(1), 4–13, https://doi.org/10.1080/01956051.2011.602919.

Collins Language. (2015). 'Binge-watch'—Collins word of the year 2015. *Collins Dictionary.* https://www.collinsdictionary.com/word-lovers-blog/new/binge-watch-collins-word-of-the-year-2015,251,HCB.html.

Conklin, W.R. (1950, November 7). Questions swamp Dewey marathon. *New York Times.*

Conlin, L., Billings, A., & Averset, L. (2016). Time-shifting vs. appointment viewing: The role of fear of missing out within TV consumption behaviors. *Comunicación y Sociedad, 29*(4), 151–164.

Consumer. (2013, May 10–16). Consumers love on-demand video and binge viewing. *The Online Reporter.* http://www.onlinereporter.com/2015/08/01/the-online-reporter-829-may-10-16-2013/.

Cooke, A. (1959, July 20). Dr. Castro strengthens his hold on Cuba. *Manchester Guardian.*

Cornell, C. (1993, January 7). Father gets a lock on children's TV watching. *Philadelphia Inquirer.*

couch potato. (2011). In M.H. Manser (Ed.), *Good Word Guide* (7th ed.). London: Bloomsbury. http://search.credoreference.com/content/entry/acbgwg/couch_potato/0.

Courtois, C., Verdegem, P., & De Marez, L. (2013). The triple articulation of media technologies in audiovisual media consumption. *Television & New Media, 14*(5), 421–439.

Coward, R. (1990). Literature, television, and cultural values. *The Yearbook of English Studies, 20,* 82–91.

Cowley, G. (1985, October 6). Care scare—working parents, provides face concerns about abuse. *Seattle Times,* p. K1.

Cox. (2013, September 13). Cox's fall FreeView offers more than 500 free episodes. *PRNewswire.*

Cox Communication. (2015). Delivery guy. http://adland.tv/commercials/coxcommunications-pizza-delivery-guy-2015-30-usa.

Crankshaw, E. (1960, November 20). Chance to curb Mr. K. *The Observer.*

Curran, H.V., & Monaghan, L. (2001). In and out of the K-hole: A comparison of the acute and residual effects of ketamine in frequent and infrequent ketamine users. *Addiction, 96*(5): 749–60.

Da Costa, J.C.R. (2021). Binge-watching: Self-care or self-harm? Understanding the health subjectivities of binge-watchers. *Journal of Health Psychology, 26*(9), 1420–1432. https://doi.org/10.1177/1359105319877231.

Daily Defender. (1956, September 25). The importance of registration. *Chicago Daily Defender.*

Dalley, J. (2004, August 20). Love and horror go hand in hand. *Financial Times.*

Danforth, E. (1952, July 27). The man worries about 100 badge men on expenses in our Olympic army. *The Atlanta Journal and the Atlanta Constitution (1950–1968).*

Davies, P. (2003, January 31). Telewest plans PVR, but not until 2004. (Cable UK). *New Media Markets,* p. 6.

Dayan, D., & Katz, E. (1992). *Media Events: The Live Broadcasting of History.* Cambridge: Harvard University Press.

DeCarvalho, L.J., & Cox, N.B. (2016). Extended "visiting hours": Deconstructing identity in Netflix's promotional campaigns for Orange Is the New Black. *Television & New Media.* doi:10.1177/1527476416647495.

De Keere, K., Thunnissen, E., & Kuipers, G. (2021). Defusing moral panic: Legitimizing binge-watching as manageable, high-quality, middle-class hedonism. *Media, Culture & Society, 43*(4), 629–647. https://doi.org/10.1177/0163443720972315.

Deloitte. (2015). Digital democracy survey: A multi-generational view of consumer technology, media and telecom trends. *Digital Democracy Survey 9th Edition.* http://www2.deloitte.com/content/dam/Deloitte/us/Documents/technology-media-telecommunications/us-tmt-DDS_Executive_Summary_Report_Final_2015-04-20.pdf.

Derrida, J. (1994). *Specters of Marx: The State of the Debt, the Work of Mourning, and the New International.* New York: Routledge.

Diamant, L. (1971). *Television's Classic Commercials: The Golden Years 1948–1958.* New York: Hastings House Publishers.

DiMaggio, P., & Cohen, J.N. (2003). Information inequality and network externalities: A comparative study of the diffusion of television and the Internet. https://www.russellsage.org/sites/all/files/u4/DiMaggio%20%26%20Cohen.pdf.

Draper, J.V., Kaber, D.B., & Usher, J.M. (1998). Telepresence. Human factors. *The Journal of the Human Factors and Ergonomics Society, 40*(3), 354–354.

D'Souza, D. (2020). Netflix doesn't want to talk about binge-watching. *Investopedia.* https://www.investopedia.com/tech/netflix-obsessed-binge-watching-and-its-problem/.

Dulles, F.R. (1940). *America Learns to Play: A History of Popular Recreation, 1607–1940.* New York: D. Appleton-Century.

Dwyer, E. (2016). Netflix & binge: New binge scale reveals TV series we devour and those we savor. *Netflix Media Center.* https://media.netflix.com/en/press-releases/netflix-binge-new-binge-scale-reveals-tv-series-we-devour-and-those-we-savor-1.

Ellingsen, S. (2014). Seismic shifts: Platforms, content creators and spreadable media. *Media International Australia, Incorporating Culture & Policy* (150), 106–113.

Ellis, C., Adams, T.E., & Bochner, A.P. (2011). Autoethnography: An overview.

Forum: Qualitative Social Research, 12(1).

Emerson, R.M., Fretz, R.I., & Shaw, L.L. (1995). *Writing Ethnographic Field Notes.* Chicago: University of Chicago Press.

Epstein, A. (2020, January 10). Thanks to streaming, we may never reach the peak of "peak TV." *Quartz.* https://qz.com/1783165/thanks-to-streaming-we-may-never-reach-the-peak-of-peak-tv/.

Epstein, J.E. (2010, October 15). Role reversal: Why TV is replacing movies as elite entertainment. *Melville House.* http://www.mhpbooks.com/role-reversal-why-tv-is-replacing-movies-as-elite-entertainment/.

Feeney, N. (2013, September 30). Netflix and on-demand aren't killing 'Water-Cooler TV'—they're saving it. *The Atlantic.* https://www.theatlantic.com/entertainment/archive/2013/09/netflix-and-on-demand-arent-killing-water-cooler-tv-theyre-saving-it/280113/.

_____. (2014, February 18). When, exactly, does watching a lot of Netflix become a 'binge'? https://www.theatlantic.com/entertainment/archive/2014/02/when-exactly-does-watching-a-lot-of-netflix-become-a-binge/283844/.

Felix, E.H. (1931). *Television, Its Methods and Uses.* New York: McGraw-Hill.

Fernández-Morales, M., & Menéndez-Menéndez, M.I. (2016). "When in Rome, Use What You've Got": A discussion of female agency through *Orange Is the New Black. Television & New Media.* doi: 1527476416647493.

Fields, R.D. (2016). Does TV rot your brain? *Scientific American.* http://www.scientificamerican.com/article/does-tv-rot-your-brain/.

Fisher, N. (2014, January 30). Confessions of a college TV binge-watcher. *Whitman Wire.* https://whitmanwire.com/arts/2014/01/30/confessions-of-a-college-tv-binge-watcher/.

Fiske, J. (1987). *Television Culture.* New York: Methuen.

_____. (1989). *Understanding Popular Culture.* Boston: Unwin Hyman.

Flayelle, M., Maurage, P., & Billieux, J. (2017). Toward an in-depth understanding of binge-watching behavior: A qualitative approach with focus group. *Journal of Behavioral Addictions 6*, 15–15.

Foucault, M. (1990). *The History of Sexuality*. New York: Vintage.

4 games kick off TV binge: Gator, sun bowls, blue-gray, east-west tilts open marathon. (1967, December 30). *Boston Globe*, p. 13.

Fox, S. & Rainie, L. (2014). Part 1: How the internet has woven itself into American life. *The Web at 25 in the U.S.* Pew Research. https://www.pewresearch.org/internet/2014/02/27/part-1-how-the-internet-has-woven-itself-into-american-life/.

Freeborn, D. (1990, April 19). Group plugs family unity with unplugged TV. *Star Tribune: Newspaper of the Twin Cities*.

Freeman, H. (2013, August 8). Arrested Development creator Mitch Hurwitz: 'I'm really, really happy with it, for the dumbest reasons.' *The Guardian*. https://www.theguardian.com/tv-and-radio/tvandradioblog/2013/aug/08/arrested-development-creator-mitch-hurwitz.

Freeman, J. (2015). Trying not to lie ... and failing: Autoethnography, memory, malleability. *The Qualitative Report, 20*(6), 918.

Fretts, B. (2003, July 25). "The Hollywood Squares." *Entertainment Weekly*. https://ew.com/article/2003/07/25/hollywood-squares/.

Fuhrel-Forbis, A., Nadorff, P., & Snyder, L. (2009). Analysis of public service announcements on national television, 2001–2006. *Social Marketing Quarterly, 15*(1), 49–69.

Gaines, E. (2007). The narrative semiotics of The Daily Show. *Semiotica* (166), pp. 81–96.

Gamson, W.A., & Modigliani, A. (1987). The changing culture of affirmative action. In P. Burstein (Ed.), *Equal Employment Opportunity: Labor Market Discrimination and Public Policy* (p. 373). New York: Aldine de Gruyter.

Gans, H. (1999). Deciding what's news. In H. Tumbler (Ed.), *News: A Reader* (pp. 235–248). New York: Oxford University Press.

Gaver, W.W. (1991, April). Technology affordances. In *Proceedings of the SIGCHI Conference on Human Factors in Computing Systems* (pp. 79–84). ACM.

Gay, V. (1993). Tv spots: All editions 1. *Newsday*.

———. (2013, July 13). How will binge watching change television? The effect, even the number of binge TV watchers, is uncertain. *Guelph Mercury*.

Geertz, C. (1973). *The Interpretation of Cultures: Selected Essays*. New York: Basic Books.

Genette, G. (1980). *Narrative Discourse: An Essay in Method*. Ithaca: Cornell University Press.

Geraghty, C. (1991). *Women and Soap Operas*. Cambridge: Polity Press.

Gerbner, G. (1976). Living with television: The violence profile. *Journal of Communication, 26*(2), 172–194.

Gibbs, A. (2016, April 13). New TV binge-watching world record set at 94 hours. *CNBC*. https://www.cnbc.com/2016/04/13/new-tv-binge-watching-world-record-set-at-94-hours.html.

Gieber, W.J. (1964). News is what newspapermen make it. In L.A. Dexter and D.M. White (Eds.), *People, Society, and Mass Communication* (pp. 171–180). New York: Free Press.

Gladstone, B. (2017). *The Trouble with Reality*. New York: Workman.

Goel, Saurabh. (2013). Cloud-based mobile video streaming techniques. *International Journal of Wireless & Mobile Networks, 5*(1), 85–93.

Goff, P.A. (2014, August 25). America's lack of a police behavior database is a disgrace. That's why I'm leading a team to build one. *The New Republic*. https://newrepublic.com/article/119207/police-behavior-database-why-one-doesnt-exist-and-why-one-soon-will.

Golda, E. (1975). How I stopped smoking: TV public service announcements provided impetus. *American Journal of Public Health, 65*(7), 752.

Goldberg, C. (1999, July 23). The Kennedy burial: The public; feelings of deep grief, even when their cause surpasses understanding. *Te New York Times.*

Goldfein, J. (2002, May 14). Always in the dark. *The Village Voice, 47*(19), 142.

Goldstein, J. (2013, June 6). Television

binge watching: If it sounds so bad why does it feel so good? *Washington Post.*

Gould, J. (1948, August 1). Family Life, 1948 A.T. (After Television). *New York Times (1923-Current File)*, p. SM12.

Grainge, P. (2000). Nostalgia and style in retro America: Moods, modes, and media recycling. *Journal of American and Comparative Cultures, 23*(1): 27–34.

Grandinetti, J. (2017). From primetime to anytime. In M. Wiatrowski & C. Barker (Eds.), *A Netflix Reader: Critical Essays on Streaming Media, Digital Delivery, and Instant Access* (pp. 11–30). Jefferson, NC: McFarland.

Greenwald, A. (2013, March 6). Isolated power. *Grantland.* http://grantland.com/features/netflix-housecards-gamble/.

Gregory, D. (2004). *Change Your Underwear Twice a Week: Lessons from the Golden Age of the Classroom Filmstrips.* New York: Artisan.

GregSerl. (1998, December 20). "Binge Watch." https://groups.google.com/g/alt.tv.x-files.analysis/c/st0q1e2jarQ/m/QHksrhRqk2QJ. From: Pagano, S. (1998, December 14). *Some HTGSC thoughts.* https://groups.google.com/g/alt.tv.x-files.analysis/c/st0q1e2jarQ/m/2OjGU3PUEugJ.

Griffin, J. (2010, March 13). An art education on film; festival starts Thursday, offers screenings of 230 works from 23 countries. *The Gazette.*

Griffin, M. (2006, October 22). Turn on, tune in, pig out. *Sunday Age.*

Grindrod, J. (2013, July 9). My current dance with binge viewing. *Lima News.*

Guinness. (2015). http://www.guinnessworldrecords.com/world-records/longest-marathon-watching-films/.

———— (2016). http://www.guinnessworldrecords.com/world-records/longest-marathon-watching-television/.

Haag, E.V.D. (1957). *The Menace of Mass Media.* New York: New Leader Publishing Association.

Hall, S. (1980). Cultural studies: Two paradigms. *Media, Culture and Society (2)* 57–71.

———. (1990). Encoding, decoding. In S. During (Ed.), *The Cultural Studies Reader* (pp. 90–102).

Hall, S., Critcher, C., Jefferson, T., Clarke, J., & Roberts, B. (1978). *Policing the Crisis.* London: Macmillan.

Hall, V. (1991, May 31). Diversion overkill what big brother is watching isn't the problem. *Kansas City Star,* p. C9.

Halliburton, C. (1954, July 27). South of the Mason-Dixon. *Philadelphia Tribune*

Halpern, W.I. (1975). The effects of television on children and adolescents: Turned-on toddlers. *The Journal of Communication, 25*(4), 66.

Hamilton, R.V., & Lawless, R.H. (1956). Television within the social matrix. *The Public Opinion Quarterly, 20*(2), 393–403.

Harlow, J. (2007, May 27). The way we watch now. *Sunday Times.*

Harper, P.C., Jr. (1971, July 11). Executives held shunning public eye. *New York Times,* p. F13.

Harris, G. (2011). Inward, outward, onward: Autoethnography of a dissertation in (qualitative) transitional space. *Qualitative Inquiry, 17*(8), 725–731.

Hartmann, M. 2006. The triple articulation of ICTs. Media as technological objects, symbolic environments and individual texts. T. Berker, M. Hartmann, Y. Punie, and K. Ward (Eds.), *Domestication of Media and Technology* (pp. 80–102). Berkshire: Open University Press.

Hay, J. (2001). Locating the televisual. *Television & New Media, 2*(3): 205–34

Healy, Jane M. (2004). Early television exposure and subsequent attention problems in children. (Commentaries). *Pediatrics, 113*(4), 708–13.

Heath, S.B., & Street, S.V. (2008). *On Ethnography.* New York: Teachers College Press.

Hesse-Biber, S.N., & Leavy, P. (2011). *The Practice of Qualitative Research* (2nd Ed.). Thousand Oaks: CA Sage.

Hewitt, M. (2013). Binge TV viewing: What to watch for your next... *The Ocean Country Register.* https://www.ocregister.com/2013/07/30/binge-tv-viewing-what-to-watch-for-your-next-session/.

Hibberd, J. (2013, September 30). 'Breaking Bad' series finale ratings smash all records. *Entertainment*

Weekly. https://ew.com/article/2013/09/30/breaking-bad-series-finale-ratings/.

Hill, A. (2005). *Reality TV: Audience and Popular Factual Television.* New York: Routledge.

Hill, G. (1954, March 30). Los Angeles gets a telethon curb. *New York Times.*

Hills, M. (2018). Traversing the "Whoniverse." M. Boni (Ed.), *World Building. Transmedia, Fans, Industries* (pp. 343–361). Amsterdam: Amsterdam University Press. https://doi.org/10.1515/9789048525317-019.

Himmelweit, H.T., Oppenheim, A.N., & Vince, P. (1958). *Television and the Child: An Empirical Study of the Effect of Television on the Young.* New York: Published for the Nuffield Foundation by the Oxford University Press.

Hofstadter, R. (1966). *Anti-Intellectualism in American Life.* New York: Knopf.

Holloway, I., Wheeler, S., & Allen, D. (2002). *Qualitative Research in Nursing.* Malden, MA: Blackwell.

Hollywood & Swine. (2013, June 3). Binge TV watching now leading cause of death among students. *Variety, 320,* 114. https://variety.com/2013/tv/news/humor-binge-tv-watching-now-leading-cause-of-death-among-students-1200493369/.

Holmes, L. (2015). Television 2015: Is there really too much TV? *NPR.* http://www.npr.org/sections/monkeysee/2015/08/16/432458841/television-2015-is-there-really-too-much-tv.

Honey, C. (1993, July 15). Unplugged in a land of couch potatoes, a few bravely disconnect and declare, out, darn set. *Grand Rapids Press,* p. D1.

Hong, H., & Kierkegaard, S. (2013). *The Essential Kierkegaard.* Princeton: Princeton University Press.

Horkheimer, M., & Adorno, T. (1977). The culture industry: Enlightenment as mass deception. J. Curran, M. Gurevitch, and J. Woollacott (Eds.), *Mass Communication and Society* (pp. 349–83). Beverly Hills: Sage.

Huffpost TV. (2013, December 30). Which TV shows does Obama watch? *The Huffington Post.* http://huff.to/1ka6IBz.

Hulu. (2015). No commercials plan. http://www.ispot.tv/ad/AV_b/hulu-nocommercials-plan-weepy-song-by-tobias-jesso-jr.

Hussain, S., & Lapinski, M. (2017). Nostalgic emotional appeals for smoking prevention. *Communication Research Reports, 34*(1), 48–57.

Huyssen, A. (2003). Present pasts: Media, politics, amnesia. *Present Pasts: Urban Palimpsests and the Politics of Memory.* Stanford: Stanford University Press.

Hyphens (n.d.). Free grammar help hyphens. H.G. Publishing. https://www.hgpublishing.com/Grammar/Hyphens.html.

Iles, I.A., Seate, A.A., & Waks, L. (2016). Eating disorder public service announcements. *Health Education, 116*(5), 476–488.

Ingraham, J. (1952, November 3). Television marathon tonight. *New York Times,* L11.

Isaacs, S. (1984). Cheers and jeers for images, lines: TV sports. *Newsday.*

ISPR. (2000). International Society for Presence Research: The Concept of Presence: Explication Statement. Retrieved 4/20/2015 from http://ispr.info/.

Itzkoff, D. (2015, April 6). With Marvel's 'Daredevil,' Netflix looks to build its own superteam. *New York Times.* http://www.nytimes.com/2015/04/07/arts/television/with-marvels-daredevil-netflix-looks-to-build-its-own-superteam.html.

Ives, H.E. (1927). Television. *Transactions of the American Institute of Electrical Engineers, XIX,* 913–917.

Iyengar, S., & Kinder, D.R. (1987). *News That Matters: Television and American Opinion.* Chicago: University of Chicago Press.

Jackson, M.E. (1952). Sports of the world. *Atlanta Daily World.*

_____. (1959, September 17). Sports of the world. *Atlanta Daily World,* p. 5.

Jarvis, S. (n.d.). Presidential nominating conventions and television. *Museum of TV.* http://www.museum.tv/eotv/presidential.htm.

Jasanoff, S. (2004). *States of Knowledge: The Co-Production of Science and Social Order.* London: Routledge.

Jeffries, D. (2018). The worlds align: Media convergence and complementary storyworlds in Marvel's Thor: The Dark World. In *World Building. Transmedia, Fans, Industries* (pp. 288–303). Amsterdam: Amsterdam University Press. https://doi.org/10.1515/9789048525317-019.

Jenkins, H. (2006). *Convergence Culture: Where Old and New Media Collide.* New York: New York University Press.

Jenner, M. (2014). Is this TVIV? On Netflix, TVIII and binge-watching. *New Media & Society.* 10.1177/1461444814541523.

———. (2015). Binge-watching: Video-on-demand, quality TV and mainstreaming fandom. *International Journal of Cultural Studies, 20*(3). 10.1177/1367877915606485.

———. (2018). *Netflix and the Re-Invention of Television.* Cham: Palgrave Macmillian.

———. (2019). Control issues: Binge-watching, channel-surfing and cultural value. *Participations, (16)*2.

Johnson, C. (2012). *Branding Television.* London: Routledge.

Johnson, G. (2011). Psychedelic universe. *New York Times Book Review,* 14.

Johnson, T. (2010, August 21). Humor sells orgs' environmental causes. *Variety.* http://variety.com/2010/biz/news/humor-sells-orgs-environmental-causes-1118023164/.

Jurgensen, J. (2012, July 13). Binge viewing: TV's lost weekends. *Wall Street Journal.* https://www.wsj.com/articles/SB10001424052702303740704577521300806686174.

———. (2013, December 13). Netflix says binge viewing is no 'House of Cards.' *Wall Street Journal.* https://www.wsj.com/articles/SB10001424052702303932504579254031017586624.

Kamenetz, R. (1979, August 2). To TV or not TV. *The Sun,* A19.

Kane, C. (2015, March 21). White sox pitcher Chris Sale has had enough of binge-watching TV. *TCA Regional News.*

Karmakar, M. (2015). Viewing patterns and addiction to television among adults who self-identify as binge-watchers. 143rd APHA Annual Meeting and Exposition (October 31–November 4, 2015). *APHA.* https://apha.confex.com/apha/143am/webprogram/Paper335049.html.

Katz, E. (2009). The end of television? *The Annals of the American Academy of Political and Social Science, 625*(1): 6–18.

Kellner, D. (2001). Cultural studies and social theory: A critical intervention. In B. Smart & G. Ritzer (Eds.), *Handbook of Social Theory* (pp. 395–409). Thousand Oaks: Sage.

Kelly, G.A. (1955). Television and the teacher. *American Psychologist, 10*(10), 590–592.

Kelly, L. (2010). Message in a bottle. *Washington Post.* http://www.washingtonpost.com/wp-srv/artsandliving/entertainmentnews/lost-message-in-a-bottle/

Kelty, C., & Landecker, H. (2009). Ten thousand journal articles later: Ethnography of "the literature" in science. *Empiria, 18,* 173–191.

Kennedy, L. (1962, September 21). Them and us and the liberals. *The Spectator.*

King, H., & Goldman, D. (2016, April 21). Comcast will let you replace your cable box with an app. http://money.cnn.com/2016/04/21/technology/comcast-xfinity-cable-app/index.html.

Kirk, C. (1978). Music records: California clips. *Variety, 291*(5), 68.

Kisselhoff, J. (1995). *The Box: An Oral History of Television, 1929–1961.* New York: Viking.

Klein, F.C. (1984, March 29). Basketball binge: Watching the NCAAs. *Wall Street Journal,* p. 1.

Knifton, S. (1992, May 31). Tower of babble: Bill McKibben's trip through a 24-hour TV day shows what it does to us—and how it fails us. *Daily News,* p. 42.

Kompare, D. (2006). Publishing flow: DVD box sets and the reconception of television. *Television, 7,* 335. doi/10.1177/1527476404270609.

Kooser, A. (2012, June 6). Man attempts eye-busting 250 Netflix movies in one month. CNET. https://www.cnet.com/news/man-attempts-eye-busting-250-netflix-movies-in-one-month/.

Krey, Z. (2016, March 2). Binge-watching: To stream or not to stream. *University Wire.*

Kruger, J.S., et al. (2015). Looking into screen time: Mental health and binge watching 143rd APHA Annual Meeting and Exposition (October 31–November 4, 2015). *APHA.* https://apha.confex.com/apha/143am/webprogram/Paper335164.htm.

Kuperinsky, A. (2014, May 25). Binge-watching: How the hungry habit is transforming TV. *NJ.com.* https://www.nj.com/entertainment/2014/05/beau_willimon_house_of_cards_binge_watching.html.

Lacob, J. (2013, February 5). "House of Cards": Should you binge-watch Netflix's political drama? *The Daily Beast.* https://www.thedailybeast.com/house-of-cards-should-you-binge-watch-netflixs-political-drama.

Lahut, J. (2020, April 24). Trump reportedly watches up to 7 hours of cable news every morning before getting to the oval office as late as noon. *Business Insider.* https://www.businessinsider.com/trump-is-watching-7-hours-of-tv-and-getting-to-the-oval-office-at-noon-report-2020-4.

Latour, B. (2005). *Reassembling the Social: An Introduction to Actor-Network Theory.* Oxford: Oxford University Press.

Laurent, L. (1957, July 12). Child's TV addiction follows adult pattern. *Washington Post and Times Herald*, p. B10.

———. (1960, September 22). Morning, noon or night TV reflects our times. *Washington Post*, D6.

Lazarsfeld, P., Berelson, B., & Gaudet, H. (1944). *The People's Choice.* New York: Columbia University Press.

Leverette, M., Ott, B.L., Buckley, C.L. (2008). *It's Not TV: Watching HBO in the Post-Television Era.* New York: Routledge.

Lev-Ram, M. (2016, June 7). How Netflix became Hollywood's frenemy. *Fortune.* http://fortune.com/netflix-versus-hollywood/.

Levy, M. (1987). Some problems of VCR research. *The American Behavioral Scientist*, 30(5), 461.

Li, H., & Edwards, S.M. (2002). Measuring the intrusiveness of advertisements: Scale development and validation. *Journal of Advertising*, 31(2), 37–47.

Liebers, N., & Schramm, H. (2019). Parasocial interactions and relationships with media characters—an inventory of 60 years of research. *Communication Research Trends*, 38(2), 4–31.

Lindley, C. (2005). The semiotics of time structure in Ludic space as a foundation for analysis and design. *Game Studies*, 5(1). http://www.gamestudies.org/0501/lindley/.

Littlejohn, S.W., & Foss, K.A. (2009). *Encyclopedia of Communication Theory.* Los Angeles: Sage.

Littleton, C. (2016, November 1). Viacom's Chris McCarthy: Millennial mindset sees multiculturalism as new normal. *Variety.* http://variety.com/2016/tv/news/chris-mccarthy-vh1-martha-and-snoop-inclusion-summit-1201906511/.

Lizardi, R., & Jordan, M.F. (2012). *Playlist Pasts: New Media, Constructed Nostalgic Subjectivity and the Disappearance of Shared History.* ProQuest Dissertations and Theses.

Lloyd-Kolkin, D., and Tyner, K.R. (1991). *Media & You.* Englewood Cliffs, N.J.: Educational Technology Publications.

Logan, K. (2013). And now a word from our sponsor: Do consumers perceive advertising on traditional television and online streaming video differently? *Journal of Marketing Communications*, 19(4), 258.

Lombard, M., & Ditton, T.B. (1997). At the heart of it all: The concept of presence. *Journal of Computer-Mediated Communication*, 13.

Lombard, M., & Ditton, T.B., Crane, D., Davis, B., Gil-Egui, G., Horvath, K., Rossman, J., & Park, S. (2000). Measuring presence: A literature-based approach to the development of a standardized paper-and-pencil instrument. Presented at the Third International Workshop on Presence, Delft, The Netherlands.

Lorando, M. (1999, December 1). It's a wonderful month holiday specials fill the air with tidings of comfort and joy. *Times-Picayune*, p. E1.

Los Angeles Times. (1950, November 7). New idea in politics. *Los Angeles Times.*

———. (1954, February 25). Chef Milani in TV marathon today. *Los Angeles Times.*

_____. (2006, September 6). Binge TV: New breed of couch potato gets fix from hot DVD releases. *Los Angeles Times*, p. 52.

Lotz, A. (2000). Assessing qualitative television audience research: Incorporating feminist and anthropological theoretical innovation. *Communication Theory, 10*, 447–467.

_____. (2014). *The Television Will Be Revolutionized* (2nd ed.). New York: New York University Press.

_____. (2017). *Portals: A Treatise on Internet-Distributed Television*. Ann Arbor: Michigan Publishing.

Lynch, K. (2014). Video: TV watching marathon world record set on TiVo stand at CES 2014. *Guinness World Records*. http://www.guinness worldrecords.com/news/2014/1/video-tv-watching-marathon-world-record-set-on-tivo-stand-at-ces-2014-54560.

MacDonald, G. (2005, June 4). Bring on the Ted Knight marathon. TV is now the fastest-growing segment of the DVD market. *The Globe and Mail*, p. R9.

Maisel, B. (1982, June 10). Soccer big here? no way. *Baltimore Sun*, p. C1.

Manjoo, F. (2013, May 27). Arrested development was the ultimate DVR show. *Slate*. https://slate.com/tech nology/2013/05/arrested-develop ment-easter-eggs-it-was-the-ultimate-dvr-show-too-bad-almost-no-one-had-a-dvr-when-it-aired.html.

Manly, L. (2013, August 9). Post-Water-Cooler TV. *New York Times*. https://www.nytimes.com/2013/08/11/arts/television/how-to-make-a-tv-drama-in-the-twitter-age.html.

Mann, J. (1984, January 18). Home TV taping legal, Supreme Court decides. *Los Angeles Times*, p. 1.

Marchand, R. (1985). *Advertising the American Dream: Making Way for Modernity, 1920–1940*. Berkeley: University of California Press.

Marchegiani, C., & Phau, I. (2010). Away from "unified nostalgia": Conceptual differences of personal and historical nostalgia appeals in advertising. *Journal of Promotion Management, 16*(1), 80–95.

Marcuse, H. (1968). *One-Dimensional Man*. London: Sphere.

Marechal, A.J. (2013). Next level for Netflix: Netcaster aims to be considered a serious player with original programming, but on its own terms. *Daily Variety, 318*(4), 1.

Marvin, C. (1997). *When Old Technologies Were New*. Oxford: Oxford University Press.

Mason, H. (2015, June 10). Breaking down the differences between procedural and serialized television. *Geek & Sundry*. https://geekandsundry. com/procedural-versus-serialized-television/.

Masters, J. (1988, August 28). Time again for the great pulp write-off. *Toronto Star*, p. D4.

Matier, P., & Ross, A. (1998, April 22). Governor race ads sop up TV availability / little air time left for other elections. *San Francisco Chronicle*.

Matthew, A. (2014, November 16). Binge watching: where immersion, indulgence and escapism meet. *Associated Press*. http://newsok.com/article/feed/760542.

May, T., & Perry, B. (2017). *Reflexivity: A Critical Guide*. Los Angeles: Sage.

McClintock, P. (2012, August 8). Aurora shooting: 20 percent of moviegoers still skittish. *The Hollywood Reporter*. https://www.hollywoodreporter.com/news/dark-knight-rises-aurora-colo rado-shooting-total-recall-357891.

McCombs, M. (2005). The agenda setting function of the press. In G. Overhol ser & K.H. Jamieson (Eds.), *The Press* (pp 156–168). Oxford: Oxford University Press.

McCombs, M. & Reynolds, A. (2009). How news shapes our civic agenda. In Bryant, J., & Oliver, M.B. (Eds.). *Media Effects: Advances in Theory and Research* (pp. 1–16). New York: Routledge.

McCombs, M., & Shaw, D. (1972). The agenda-setting function of mass media. *Public Opinion Quarterly, 36*(2): 176–187.

McCracken, G. (2013, May 24). From *Arrested Development* to *Dr. Who*, binge watching is changing our culture. *Wired*. https://www.wired.com/2013/05/beyond-arrested-develop ment-how-binge-watching-is-changing-our-narrative-culture/.

McCullough, J.M. (1953, January 17). Leaders use radio and TV in pleas to approve pact. *Philadelphia Inquirer*, A1.

McDonald, E.F. (1958). *Television's New Dimension: Subscription TV*. Elsevier.

McDowell, E. (1978, March 21). Home video systems still seek success on market. *New York Times*, p. 71.

McLuhan, M. (1964). *Understanding the Media*. New York: McGraw-Hill.

McNamara, M. (2012, January 15). Critic's notebook: The side effects of binge television. *Los Angeles Times*.

Meerloo, J.A. (1954). Television addiction and reactive apathy. *The Journal of Nervous and Mental Disease, 120*(3–4), 290–291.

Mendelsohn, H. (1989). Socio-psychological construction and the mass communication effects dialectic. *Communication Research, 16*, 813–823.

Meyer, C. (2013, February 26). Go on a binge. *Honolulu Star-Advertiser*. https://www.pressreader.com/usa/honolulu-star-advertiser/20130207/282544425692544.

Meyers, O. (2009). The engine's in the front, but its heart's in the same place: Advertising, nostalgia, and the construction of commodities as realms of memory. *Journal of Popular Culture, 42*(4): 733–755.

Meyrowitz, J. (2009). We liked to watch: Television as progenitor of the surveillance society. *Annals of the American Academy of Political and Social Science, 625*(1), 32–48.

Miller, J. (1951, November 6). Dilworth Hits Gang. *Philadelphia Inquirer, 2*.

Mills, C.W. (1999). The sociological imagination. In C. Lemert (Ed.), *Social Theory: The Multicultural and Classic Readings* (pp. 351–352). Boulder: Westview.

Minow, N. (1961, May 9). Television and the public interest. *National broadcast association*. Retrieved from: http://www.americanrhetoric.com/speeches/newtonminow.htm

Mittell, J. (2000). The cultural power of an anti-television metaphor: Questioning the "plug-in drug" and a TV-free America. *Television & New Media, 1*(2), 215–238.

Moore, K. (2020, March 31). How long would it take to watch all of Netflix? *What's on Netflix*. https://www.whats-on-netflix.com/news/how-long-would-it-take-to-watch-all-of-netflix/.

Morley, D. (2003). *Television, Audiences, and Cultural Studies*. New York: Taylor and Francis.

Mullen, M.G. (2003). *The Rise of Cable Programming in the United States: Revolution or Evolution?* Austin: University of Texas Press.

Murphy, J., & Gross, R. (1966). *Learning by Television*. New York: Fund for the Advancement of Education.

Nelson, J.R. (2013, June 21). John on demand: The idea of binge-watching TV programs is hard to digest. *Poughkeepsie Journal*.

Netflix. (2015). Binge responsibly. https://www.youtube.com/watch?v=HSVjIU6fzeE.

New York Times. (1953, December 12). Face on TV set goes, mystery lingers on. *New York Times*.

Newman, M.Z., & Levine, E. (2012). *Legitimating Television: Media Convergence and Cultural Status*. New York: Routledge.

Newport. (1953, December 12). Ghost face finally leaves TV screen. *Newport Daily News*, 7.

Norman, D.A. (1988). *The Psychology of Everyday Things*. New York: Basic Books.

Northover, K. (2009, July 7). Damned if you don't dig footy, Foxtel or a 25-year loan. *The Age* (Melbourne, Australia), p. 18.

Nussbaum, E. (2003, August 17). Taking back television, one disc at a time. *New York Times*.

———. (2011, August 1). My 'Breaking Bad' bender. *New York Times*.

O'Brien, B. (2015, December 9). Binge-watching: To stream or not to stream. *University Wire*.

O'Connor, J.J. (1976, July 6). TV: Networks' 4th of July coverage is impressive. *New York Times*, p. 44.

O'Keefe, D. (2005). *The Real Festivus*. London: Penguin.

Oliveira, M. (2013a, March 8). Study uses "House of Cards" to see if Canadian Netflix users like binge viewing. *The Canadian Press*.

_____. (2013b, March 11). Binge viewing in Canada. *Telegraph-Journal*.

Orosz, G., Bothe, B., & Toth-Kiraly, I. (2016). The development of the problematic series watching scale (PSWS). *Journal of Behavioral Addictions, 5*(1), 144. 10.1556/2006.5.2016.011.

Ostrow, J. (2012, April 29). No more waiting: Movies, TV shows are available early and everywhere. *Denver Post*.

Ouellette, L., & Lewis, J. (2000). Moving beyond the "vast wasteland": Cultural policy and television in the United States. *Television & New Media, 1*(1), 95–115.

Oxford. (2013, November 19). "Word of the Year 2013." *Oxford Words Blog.* http://blog.oxforddictionaries.com/2013/11/word-of-the-year-runners-up/.

Pagels, J. (2012, July 9). Stop binge-watching TV. *Slate.* http://www.slate.com/blogs/browbeat/2012/07/09/binge_watching_tv_why_you_need_to_stop_.html.

Pamer, M. (2006, August 27). The Emmys, TV, straight up: Some DVD fans live for the binge, and the industry seems to like their choices. *Los Angeles Times*, p. E1.

Pang, A.S. (2014, February 13). In defense of binge-watching. *Slate.* https://slate.com/technology/2014/02/is-binge-watching-the-new-season-of-house-of-cards-bad-for-you.html.

Parham, C.P. (2014). Beyond the interview: A historian's journey into community storytelling. *Storytelling, Self, Society, 10*(2), 194.

Park, R.E. (1940). News as a form of knowledge: A chapter in the sociology of knowledge. *American Journal of Sociology, 45*(5), 669–686. http://www.jstor.org/stable/2770043.

Parker, E., & Dunn, D. (1972). Information technology: Its social potential. *Science, 176*(4042), 1392–1399.

Paskin, W. (2015, December 23). What does "peak TV" really mean? *Slate.* https://slate.com/culture/2015/12/what-does-peak-tv-really-mean.html.

Patel, S. (2017, February 22). Inside Disney's troubled $675 mil. Maker Studios acquisition. *Digiday.* https://digiday.com/future-of-tv/disney-maker-studios/.

Patterson, T., & Seib, P. (2005). Informing the public. In G. Overholser & K.H. Jamieson (Eds.), *The Press* (pp. 189–202). Oxford: Oxford University Press.

Pearson, R. (2011). Cult television as digital television's cutting edge. J. Bennett and N. Strange (Eds.), *Console-Ing Passions: Television as Digital Media.* Durham: Duke University Press.

Pena, L.L. (2015). Breaking binge: Exploring the effects of binge watching on television viewer reception. *Dissertations—ALL Paper 283.* http://surface.syr.edu/cgi/viewcontent.cgi?article=1283&context=etd.

Pendennis. (1955, May 29). Table talk. *The Observer*.

Perks, L.G. (2015). *Media Marathoning: Immersions in Morality.* New York: Lexington Boks.

Perks, L.G., Steiner, E., Pierce-Grove, R., Mikos, L. (2021). Binge-watching audience typologies. In M. Jenner (Ed.), *Binge-Watching and Contemporary Television Research* (pp. 131–142). Edinburgh: Edinburgh University Press.

Perren, A. (2010). Business as unusual: Conglomerate-sized challenges for film and television in the digital arena. *Journal of Popular Film and Television, 38*(2), 72–78.

Petersen, T.G., Boyd, A., Clark, K., & Castor, E.J. (2016). To binge or not to binge: A qualitative analysis of binge watching habits of college students. *Florida Communication Journal, 44*(1): 77–88.

Pew. (2018). Internet/Broadband Fact Sheet. *Pew Research Center.* http://www.pewinternet.org/fact-sheet/internet-broadband/.

Phalen, P.F., & Ducey, R.V. (2012). Audience behavior in the multi-screen "video-verse." *International Journal on Media Management, 14*(2), 141–156. DOI: 10.1080/14241277.2012.657811.

Pierce-Grove, R. (2017). Just one more: How journalists frame binge watching. *First Monday.* DOI: http://dx.doi.org/10.5210/fm.v22i1.7269.

Pinch, T.J., & Bijker, W.E. (1987). The social construction of facts and artifacts: Or how the sociology of science and the sociology of technology might benefit each other. *The Social*

Construction of Technological Systems: New Directions in the Sociology and History of Technology, 17.

Pine, B. J., & Gilmore, J.H. (1998). Welcome to the experience economy. *Harvard Business Review.* https://hbr.org/1998/07/welcome-to-the-experience-economy.

———. (1999). *The Experience Cconomy.* Cambridge: Harvard Business Review Press.

Pittman, M., & Sheehan, K. (2015). Sprinting a media marathon: Uses and gratifications of binge-watching television through Netflix. *First Monday, 20*(10).

Pittman, M., & Steiner, E. (2019). Narrative transportation or narrative completion? Attentiveness during binge-watching moderates regret. *Social Sciences, 8*(99).

———. (2021). Distinguishing feast-watching from cringe-watching: Planned, social, and attentive binge-watching predicts increased well-being and decreased regret. *Convergence: The International Journal of Research into New Media Technologies.* https://doi.org/10.1177/1354856521999183.

Plaugic, L. & Miller, R. (2015, December 30). How Netflix and Amazon have changed the rules of TV. *The Verge.* https://www.theverge.com/2015/12/30/10647736/netflix-hulu-amazon-original-shows-streaming-tv-2015.

Podeschi, R. (1987). Purpose, pluralism, and public teacher education. *Journal of Thought, 22*(2), 8.

Porter, C. (2016, March 24). A guide to binge watching. *The Orion.* https://theorion.com/54635/arts/a-guide-to-binge-watching/.

Postman, N. (1982). The Las Vegasizing of America (The humanities and electronic entertainment). *ETC: A Review of General Semantics, 39*(3), 263–272.

———. (1985). *Amusing Ourselves to Death: Public Discourse in the Age of Show Business.* London: Methuen.

Pothier, D. (1981, February 15). And now comes a revolution in entertainment. *Philadelphia Inquirer,* L1.

Price, V., & Tewksbury, D. (1997). News values and public opinion: A theoretical account of media priming and framing. In G.A. Barett & F.J. Boster (Eds.), *Progress in Communication Sciences: Advances in Persuasion* (Vol. 13, pp. 173–212). Greenwich, CT: Ablex.

PRNewswire. (2013). Netflix declares binge watching is the new normal. *CISION.* https://www.prnewswire.com/news-releases/netflix-declares-binge-watching-is-the-new-normal-235713431.html.

Radway, J. (2009). Reading the romance. In J. Storey (Ed.), *Cultural Theory and Popular Culture: A Reader 4th Edition* (pp. 199–215). Harlow, UK: Pearson Education Limited.

Rainey, S. (2015, January 22). The days of talking TV at the water cooler are over. *The Telegraph.* http://www.businessinsider.com/the-days-of-talking-tv-at-the-water-cooler-are-over-2015-1.

Ramble, C. (2002). Temporal disjunction and collectivity in Mustang, Nepal. *Current Anthropology, 43*(S4), S75–S84.

Reeves, J.L., et al. (2002). The *Sopranos* as HBO brand equity: The art of commerce in the age of digital reproduction. In D. Lavery (Ed.), *This Thing of Ours: Investigating the Sopranos* (pp. 42–57). New York: Columbia University Press.

Riccio, A. (2013, February, 6). Binge-watching makes TV better. https://www.cnn.com/2013/02/06/opinion/riccio-binge-tv-watching/index.html.

Rice, R., & Atkin, C. (2009). *Public Communication Campaigns* (3rd ed.). Thousand Oaks: Sage.

Richardson, M. (1962, December 2). The endless street. *The Observer.*

Ricklefs, R. (1976, October 12). The television era: Three families show how generation of TV has altered lifestyles. *Wall Street Journal,* p. 1.

Riddle, K. (2010). Always on my mind: Exploring how frequent, recent, and vivid television portrayals are used in the formation of social reality judgments. *Media Psychology, 13*(2), 155–179. 10.1080/15213261003800140.

Riddle, K., Peebles, A., Davis, C., Xu, F., & Schroeder, E. (2017). The addictive potential of television binge watching: Comparing intentional and unintentional binges. *Psychology of Popular Media Culture, 7*(4): 589–604.

Rizzo-Young, K. (2002, April 22). Family life turns on when the television's turned off. *Buffalo News*, p. A6.

Roberts, K. (2010). *Cyber Junkie.* Center City, MN: Hazelden Publishing.

Robertson, V.L.D. (2014). Of ponies and men: My Little Pony: Friendship is Magic and the Brony fandom. *International Journal of Cultural Studies, 17*(1), 21–37. https://doi.org/10.1177/1367877912464368.

Rochlin, M. (2003, January 26). Always the odd man in; John C. Reilly is following in the footsteps of borgnine, hackman and malden—but could they carry a tune as well as a film? *Los Angeles Times*, p. E6.

Rogan, J. (2016, August 17). Episode 684 with Brian Redban. *The Joe Rogan Experience.* http://jrefan.com/the-joe-rogan-experience-episode-684-with-brian-redban/.

Rogers, N. (2012, March 21). Channel 77: Just one more episode. and another. and another. *Madison Capital Times.*

Rosen, G. (1948, December 22). New Orleans on a video binge as WDSU-TV unveils operation. *Variety*, 24.

———. (1955, February 16). Coke's king-size. *Variety*, 21.

Rosenbloom, S. (2005, October 27). All you can repeat: Binge viewing of TV series on DVD is creating a new breed of aficionados. *National Post*, p. AL5.

Rovere, R., Lawrenson, H., & Smith, R.P. (1960, October 1). "A last look at television." *Esquire.*

Rowan, C. (1984, November 4). TV and teen-age suicides. *The San Diego Union*, p. C3.

Rubin, A., & Perse, E. (1987). Audience activity and soap opera involvement: A uses and effects investigation. *Human Communication Research, 14*(2), 246–268.

Ryan, M. (2015). Entertaining fantasies: Lifestyle and social life in 1980s America. *Journal of Communication Inquiry, 39*(1), 82–101.

Saboo, A. (2013). Netflix report details binge viewing habits. *Fiercecable.*

Salvation by television (education). (1962). *Time, 79*(21), 62.

Sarnoff, D. (1941). Possible social effects of television. *Annals of the American Academy of Political and Social Science, 213*, 145–152.

Saunders, D. (2001, December 19). Reality-TV binge gives rise to Gi Geraldo. *Rocky Mountain News* (CO), p. 2D.

Schickel, R. (1962). *The Television Problem.* New York: American Jewish Committee.

Schierl, T. (2007). Ökonomie der Prominenz: Celebrity sells: Zur medialen Produktion und Reproduktion von Prominenz. In T. Schierl (Ed.), *Prominenz in den Medien. Zur Genese und Verwertung von Prominenten in Sport, Wirtschaft, und Kultur* (pp. 98–121). Koeln, Germany: Halem Verlag.

Schlesinger, P. (1972). The sociology of knowledge. Presented at the 1972 meeting of British Sociology Association, p. 4.

Schleuder, J.F., White, A.V., & Cameron, G.T. (1993). Priming effects of television news bumpers and teasers on attention and memory. *Journal of Broadcasting & Electronic Media, 37*(4), 437–452.

Schneier, M. (2015, December 6). The post-binge-watching blues. *New York Times.*

Schrag, O.C. (1997). *The Self After Postmodernity.* New Haven: Yale University Press.

Schütz, A. (1967). *The Phenomenology of the Social World.* Evanston, IL: Northwestern University Press. (Original work published 1932.)

Schwartz, B. (1998). Frame images: Towards a semiotics of collective memory. *Semiotica, 121*(1–2), 1–40.

Schweidel, D., & Moe, W. (2016). Binge watching and advertising. *Journal of Marketing, 80*(5), 1–19.

Scieretta, P. (2013, February Retrieved from: https://www.slashfilm.com/is-netflixs-full-season-release-strategy-a-smart-business-model/.

Seggel, H. (2000, May 31). TV Jones diary: One week as a tube boob. *Bitch, 11*, 66.

Seigel, A.M. & O'Connolly, W.G. (1999). *The New York Times Manual of Style.* New York: Three Rivers Press.

Seitz, M.Z. (2016, June 13). How comedy usurped drama as the TV genre of our time. *Vulture.* https://www.vulture.com/2016/06/comedy-tv-genre-of-our-time.html.

Seitz, P. (2013, December 20). Netflix binge viewing leads to comedian purge spewing. *Investor's Business Daily.*

Seldes, G. (1950). *The Great Audience.* New York: Viking.

Sender, K. (2012). *The Makeover: Reality Television and Reflexive Audiences.* New York: New York University Press.

Senter, J. (2001, September 18). Media unable to deal with Tuesday's attack. *Badger Herald* (University of Wisconsin).

Serazio, M. (2015). Selling (digital) millennials: The social construction and technological bias of a consumer generation. *Television & New Media, 16*(7), 599–615.

_____. (2019). *The Power of Sports.* New York: New York University Press.

Serjeant, J. (2008, August 28). David Duchovny's sex disorder likened to alcoholism. *Reuters.* https://www.reuters.com/article/us-duchovny-idUSN2835847820080829.

Setoodeh, R. (2006, October 23). Technology: Kickin' and streaming. *Newsweek, 148,* 75–76.

Shaumyan, S. (1987). *A Semiotic Theory of Language (Advances in Semiotics).* Bloomington: Indiana University Press.

Shihadah, M. (2017, March, 10). AI and computer vision are coming—what marketers need to know. Martech Advisor. https://www.martechadvisor.com/articles/cloudiaaspaas/ai-and-computer-vision-arecoming-what-marketers-need-to-know/.

Shiller, R. (2019). *Narrative Economics: How Stories Go Viral & Drive Major Economic Events.* Princeton: Princeton University Press.

Shim, H., & Kim, K. (2018). An exploration of the motivations for binge-watching and the role of individual differences. *Computers in Human Behavior, 82,* 94–100.

Shuit, D.P. (1992, May 20). Gray Davis is banking on a 'hail mary' upset powered by TV binge. *Los Angeles Times,* p. A3.

Sigal, L.V. (1999). Reporters and officials: The organization and politics of newsmaking. In H. Tumbler (Ed.), *News: A Reader* (pp. 224–234). New York: Oxford University Press.

Simons, T. (2011, October). Binge TV. *Mpls.St.Paul Magazine, 39,* 136.

Sims, D. (2015, June 24). Hannibal is dead, long live Hannibal? *The Atlantic.* https://www.theatlantic.com/entertainment/archive/2015/06/nbc-hannibal-canceled-netflix/396671/.

Sling TV (2014). Dangers of binge watching: A PSA. https://www.youtube.com/watch?v=ybt-6MNFj7Q.

Sly, D.F., Heald, G.R., & Ray, S. (2001). The Florida "truth" anti-tobacco media evaluation: Design, first year results, and implications for planning future state media evaluations. *Tobacco Control, 10*(1), 9–15.

Smith, A. (2001). TV / RADIO—Sundays on HBO are an oasis in TV's strange summer meltdown. *Providence Journal.*

Smith, C. (2014, January 16). The Netflix effect: how binge watching is changing television. *Tech Radar.* https://www.techradar.com/news/internet/the-netflix-effect-how-binge-watching-is-changing-television-1215808.

Snyder, M. (2015, August 16). Cutting the cord: We like binge-watching solo. *USA Today.* https://www.usatoday.com/story/tech/2015/08/16/cutting-cord-we-like-binge-watching-solo/31446403/.

Sopkin, C. (1968). *Seven Glorious Days, Seven Fun-Filled Nights: One Man's Struggle to Survive a Week Watching Commercial Television in America.* New York: Simon & Schuster.

Spacey, K. (2013, August 22). The MacTaggart Lecture: How Netflix killed the watercooler moment—and breathed new life into TV. *The Guardian.* https://www.theguardian.com/commentisfree/2013/aug/22/netflix-model-watercooler-moment-stories.

Spangler, T. (2014, June 25). 'Breaking Bad,' 'House of Cards,' 'Game of Thrones' Top List of Binge-Watched Shows. *Variety.* https://variety.com/2014/digital/news/breaking-bad-house-of-cards-game-of-thrones-top-list-of-binge-watched-shows-1201247099/.

_____. (2016, April 12). TV binge-watching world record set. *Variety.* http://variety.com/2016/digital/news/tv-binge-watching-world-record-set-94-hours-1201751436/.

Spigel, L. (1992). *Make Room for TV: Television and the Family Ideal in Postwar America.* Chicago: University of Chicago Press.

Spitzberg, B.H., & Cupach, W.R. (2008). Fanning the flames of fandom: Celebrity worship, parasocial interaction, and stalking. In J.R. Meloy, L. Sheridan, & J. Hoffmann (Eds.), *Stalking, Threatening and Attacking Public Figures: A Psychological and Behavioral Analysis* (pp. 287–321). New York: Oxford University Press.

Stacey, J. (1994). *Star Gazing: Hollywood Cinema and Female Spectatorship.* London: Routledge.

Steiner, E. (2017). Binge-watching in practice: The rituals, motives, and feelings of Netflix streaming video viewers In M. Wiatrowski & C. Barker (Eds.), *A Netflix Reader: Critical Essays on Streaming Media, Digital Delivery, and Instant Access* (pp. 141–161). Jefferson, NC: McFarland.

———. (2021). Commercial constructions of binge-viewers: A typology of the new and improved couch potato as seen on TV. In M. Jenner (Ed.), *Binge-Watching and Contemporary Television Research* (pp. 65–81). Edinburgh: Edinburgh University Press.

Steiner, E., & Xu, K. (2020). Binge-watching motivates change: How the uses and gratifications of streaming video viewers are challenging traditional audience research. *Convergence: The International Journal of Research into New Media Technologies, 26*(1), 82–101.

Stelter, B. (2013, February 1). New way to deliver a drama: All 13 episodes in one sitting. *New York Times.*

Stern, B.B. (1992). Historical and personal nostalgia in advertising text: The fin de siècle effect. *Journal of Advertising, 21*(4), 11–22.

Stevens, C.E. (2021). Historical binge-watching: Marathon viewing on videotape. In M. Jenner (Ed.), *Binge-Watching and Contemporary Television Research* (pp. 23–39). Edinburgh: Edinburgh University Press.

Stever, G.S. (2009). Parasocial and social interaction with celebrities: Classification of media fans. *Journal of Media Psychology, 14*, 1–39.

Storey, J. (1996). *What Is Cultural Studies? A Reader.* New York,: Arnold.

———. (2012). *Cultural Theory and Popular Culture: An Introduction* (6th ed.). Harlow, UK: Pearson Education Limited.

Study. (2013, March 8). MarketCast study finds TV "binge viewing" creates engaged viewer. *CISION.* http://www.prweb.com/releases/2013/3/prweb10513066.htm.

Sun. (1956, December 28). British paper sets TV drive. *Baltimore Sun.*

Sung, Y.H., Kang, E.Y., & Wee, L. (2015). A bad habit for your health? An exploration of psychological factors for binge-watching behavior. In 65th ICA Annual Conference (Anonymous) Puerto Rico.

Swisher, K. (2016, July 5). Comcast will let customers get Netflix on their set-top box. *Vox.* https://www.vox.com/2016/7/5/12096380/comcast-to-let-netflix-onto-its-x1-platform-which-is-a-very-big-deal.

Szklarski, C. (2013, December 19). TV binge-watchers tune out of regularly scheduled programming. *The Canadian Press.*

T-Mobile. (2015). Binge watchers anonymous with Aaron Paul. https://www.youtube.com/watch?v=nkci1kQQwgA.

Taber, N. (2010). Institutional ethnography, autoethnography, and narrative: An argument for incorporating multiple methodologies. *Qualitative Research, 10*(1), 5–25.

Taylor, A. (2009). The "phantasmodesty" of Henry Adams. *Common Knowledge, 15*(3), 373–394. https://doi.org/10.1215/0961754X-2009-019.

Thompson, A. (1988, January 6). Boy finds life after TV during year's boycott. *Toronto Star.*

Thompson, E., & Mittell, J. (2013). *How to Watch Television.* New York: New York University.

Thompson, R.J. (1996). *Television's Second Golden Age: From Hill Street Blues to ER: Hill Street Blues, St. Elsewhere, Cagney & Lacey, Moonlighting, L.A.*

Law, Thirtysomething, China Beach, Twin Peaks, Northern Exposure, Picket Fences, with Brief Reflections on Homicide, NYPD Blue, Chicago Hope, and Other Quality Dramas. New York: Continuum.

TiVo. (2014). TiVo sets Guinness world record at 2014 international CES. *YouTube*. http://www.youtube.com/watch?v=h0Ty1hC2gFc

Torfing, J. (1999). *New Theories of Discourse: Laclau, Mouffe and Zizek*. Malden, MA: Blackwell.

Tribbey, C. (2014). Cable show analyzes binge-viewing. *Home Media Magazine, 36*(14), 7.

Tryon, C. (2013). *On-Demand Culture: Digital Delivery and the Future of Movies*. New Brunswick: Rutgers University Press.

Turnstall, T. (1988, July 6). In France the pleasures of eating are more in talking. *New York Times*. https://www.nytimes.com/1988/07/06/style/in-france-the-pleasures-of-eating-are-more-in-the-talking.html.

Turow, J. (2017). *The Aisles Have Eyes: How Retailers Track Your Shopping, Strip Your Privacy, and Define Your Power*. New Haven: Yale University Press.

TVHistory. Television history—the first 75 years. http://www.tvhistory.tv/pre-1935.htm.

Uotinen, J. (2010). Digital television and the machine that goes "PING!": Autoethnography as a method for cultural studies of technology. *Journal for Cultural Research, 14*(2), 161–175.

Variety. (1948a, December 1). CBS switch in its show technique. *Variety*, 23.

_____ (1948b, December 1). WCAU-TV's daytime binge. *Variety*, 31.

_____ (1948c, December 8). Yuletide binge. *Variety*, 31.

Verini, B. (2014, JunE 17). The revolution will be televised and binge watched. *Variety, 324*, 49–50.

Vogue. (1970). People are talking about: Jeremy Clyde and Paul Jones. *Vogue, 156*(7), 66.

Voice, of the people. (1950, June 9). *Chicago Daily Tribune*.

Vološinov, V. (1973). *Marxism and the Philosophy of Language*. New York: Seminar Press.

Wagner, G. (1978). The end of the humanities. *Modern Age, 22*(2), 187–190.

Wall Street Journal Staff Reporter. (1961, October 10). Toy makers see 12%–13% sales gain in '61; retail volume may advance to $2 billion. *Wall Street Journal*.

Walter L.R. (1961, September 27). Letters to the editor. *Washington Post and Times Herald*.

Walton-Pattison, E., Dombrowski, S.U., & Presseau, J. (2016). 'Just one more episode': Frequency and theoretical correlates of television binge watching. *Journal of Health Psychology*. DOI:10.1177/1359105316643379.

Ward, B. (2014, January 6). The lost weekends: binge viewing our favorite TV shows makes us feel good, but is it good for us? *Minneapolis Star Tribune*. https://www.startribune.com/binge-tv-viewing-is-a-popular-indulgence-for-better-or-worse/238655421/.

Ward, D., & Wackman, S.W. (1971). Family and media influences on adolescent consumer learning. *The American Behavioral Scientist, 14*(3), 415.

Warner, T. (2002, January 29). Addicts, stuck to their couches. *The Wenatchee World* (WA), p. A7.

Washington Post. (1956, August 8). And now, a word... *Washington Post and Times Herald*.

Watson, A. (2020, July 17). Number of Netflix paying streaming subscribers worldwide from 3rd quarter 2011 to 2nd quarter 2020. *Statista*. https://www.statista.com/statistics/250934/quarterly-number-of-netflix-streaming-subscribers-worldwide/.

Weaver, W. (1968). The mathematics of communication. *Mathematics in the Modern World: Readings from Scientific American* (pp. 313–317). San Francisco: W.H. Freeman and Company.

Weedon, C. (2009). Feminism and the principles of poststructuralism. In J. Storey (Ed.), *Cultural Theory and Popular Culture: A Reader 4th Edition* (pp. 320–331). Harlow, UK: Pearson Education Limited.

Weisman, J. (2013, September 22). Emmys: Vince Gilligan Credits Netflix. *Variety*. http://variety.com/2013/tv/awards/breaking-bad-amc-vince-gilligan-credits-netflix-1200660762/.

Weiss, R. (1994). *Learning from Strangers: The Art and Method of Qualitative Interview Studies.* New York: Free Press.

Werts, D. (2004, January 15). Binge viewing. *Milwaukee Journal Sentinel.*

_____. (2006, April 30). TV or more TV? That is the question now that you can watch your favorite shows on your computer, cell phone or iPod. *Knight Ridder Tribune Business News.*

Whalen, B. (1983). Semiotics: An art or powerful research tool? *Marketing News* (17), 8.

Wheeler, K.S. (2015). The relationships between television viewing behaviors, attachment, loneliness, depression, and psychological well-being. Georgia Southern University. http://digitalcommons.georgiasouthern.edu/honors-theses/98/

Wickstrom, A. (1983, October 30). The VCR: How it can benefit the TV viewer and movie lover. *Philadelphia Inquirer.*

_____. (1986, December 21). For late shoppers, a cache of creative gifts. *Philadelphia Inquirer,* p. S11.

Williams, R. (1973). *The Country and the City.* New York: Oxford University Press.

_____. (1989). *Resources of Hope: Culture, Democracy, Socialism.* New York: Verso.

_____. (1990). *Television: Technology and Cultural Form* (2nd ed.). New York: Routledge.

Williams, R., & O'Connor, A. (1989b). *Raymond Williams on television: Selected writings.* New York: Routledge.

Winter, J.P. & Eyal, C.H. (1981). Agenda-setting for the civil rights issue. *Public Opinion Quarterly,* 45, 376–383.

Withdrawal pangs. (1973, August 10). *New York Times,* p. 30.

Wohlsen, M. (2014, May 15). When TV is obsolete, TV shows will enter their real golden era. *Wired.*

Wolcott, J. (2016). There's too much television. *Vanity Fair.* Retrieved from: http://www.vanityfair.com/culture/2015/12/james-wolcott-too-much-television

Wolf, J. (2005). TV talent eyes DVD as gift to posterity. *Home Media Retailing,* 27(46), 13.

Wolters, L. (1953, October 14). Television news and views. *Chicago Daily Tribune* B7.

_____. (1955, December 11). Program boss takes a look into future. *Chicago Daily Tribune.*

Wong, T. (2013, December 28). Netflix, binge watching and the changing landscape of television. *Toronto Star.*

Wood, S. (2013, December 26). To binge watch your favorite shows. *Courier Post.*

Woodruff, M. (2012, June 6). Here's what happened when this guy tried to watch 400 hours of Netflix films in 30 days. *Business Insider.* http://www.businessinsider.com/mark-malkoffs-30-day-netflix-challenge-2012-6.

Wortham, J. (2007, December 17). After 10 years of blogs, the future's brighter than ever. *Wired.* http://archive.wired.com/entertainment/theweb/news/2007/12/blog_anniversary

Xfinity. (2015). Cold. XFINITY Watchathon Week. Retrieved from: http://www.ispot.tv/ad/7iLX/xfinity-watchathon-week-cold

Yang, X., & Smith, R.E. (2009). Beyond attention effects: Modeling the persuasive and emotional effects of advertising creativity. *Marketing Science,* 28(5), 935–949.

Zelizer, B. (1995). Reading the past against the grain: The shape of memory studies. *Critical Studies in Mass Communication,* 12(2), 214–239.

_____. (2005). Definitions of journalism. In G. Overholser & K.H. Jamieson (Eds.), *The Press* (pp. 66–82). New York: Oxford University Press.

Zerubavel, E. (1996). Social memories: Steps to a sociology of the past. *Qualitative Sociology,* 19(3), 283.

Zolotow, S. (1955, July 6). Power may star for playwrights. *New York Times.*

Index